D1737320

THE REAL WORLD OF
CHILD INTERROGATIONS

THE REAL WORLD OF
CHILD INTERROGATIONS

By

RALPH UNDERWAGER

and

HOLLIDA WAKEFIELD

With
Ross Legrand
Christine Samples Bartz

C H A R L E S   C   T H O M A S   •   P U B L I S H E R
Springfield • Illinois • U.S.A.

Published and Distributed Throughout the World by

CHARLES C THOMAS • PUBLISHER
2600 South First Street
Springfield, Illinois 62794-9265

With **THOMAS BOOKS** *careful attention is given to all details of manufacturing
and design. It is the Publisher's desire to present books that are satisfactory as to their
physical qualities and artistic possibilities and appropriate for their particular use.*
THOMAS BOOKS *will be true to those laws of quality that assure a good name
and good will.*

Printed in the United States of America
SC-R-3

Library of Congress Cataloging-in-Publication Data

Underwager, Ralph.
   The real world of child interrogations / by Ralph Underwager and
Hollida Wakefield with Ross Legrand, Christine Samples Bartz.
     p. cm.
   Includes bibliographical references.
   ISBN 0-398-05620-X
   1. Child molesting—United States—Investigation. 2. Interviewing
in child abuse. I. Underwager, Ralph C. II. Title.
   [DNLM: 1. Child Abuse, Sexual. 2. Interview, Psychological—in
infancy & childhood. 3. Interview, Psychological—methods.
   4. Persuasive Communication. WA 320 W147r]
HV8079.C48W356   1989
363.2′595554—dc20
DNLM/DLC
for Library of Congress   89-5224
                                   CIP

To Paul E. Meehl, Ph.D.
Regents Professor, University of Minnesota

Who taught us respect for the real world,
the value of faith and reason,
and to aim at straight thinking

INTRODUCTION

Throughout our careers as psychologists, we have provided therapy to sex offenders, victims, families, and adults who were victimized as children. In the beginning, although we occasionally saw a case involving false allegations, most of our sexual abuse cases were actual abuse which we discovered, reported, and treated. For the most part, we worked with the justice system to respond to abuse with treatment and rehabilitation of the offender, the family, and the victim. Prosecution of the offender was not a primary nor superordinate goal. We also provided treatment for sexual offenders throughout this period.

But five years ago we started seeing a change in the cases we encountered. A South Dakota woman was accused of sexually abusing two teenage retarded sons and a normal son, age ten. The allegation was that she had repeated intercourse with them. The woman steadfastly denied abusing her three boys. The public defender had contacted dozens of psychologists before she found anyone who was willing to look at the case. We agreed to evaluate the documents and the attorney retained us as experts. We suggested that the sheriff and social worker had pressured and influenced the boys to produce the statements about abuse through numerous coercive interviews with them. Ralph testified in April, 1984, and the result was a hung jury. The state did not try her again.

Following this, in August, 1984, we became involved in the notorious Scott County cases. The county attorney, Ms. Kathleen Morris, charged 25 adults in the small town of Jordan with sexually abusing 40 children in what she believed to be two interlocking sex rings. Initially there were allegations of child pornography production and connections with organized crime. Ms. Morris directed and controlled the investigation by the law enforcement and human services agencies of Scott County, Minnesota that produced the charges. The investigation had begun in late September, 1983 and by the spring of 1984, the parents had been arrested and charged, and the children had been placed in foster homes where they remained for over a year and a half.

Mr. Barry Voss, attorney for Mrs. Bentz, asked us to examine the documents and perhaps testify in the trial of Robert and Lois Bentz, the first of the adults to be tried. The Bentzes were charged with sexually abusing at least nine children, including their three sons. We studied police reports, case worker reports, psychological evaluations, videotaped interviews of children, charges, and statements supposedly made by the children. What we saw convinced us that the statements about sexual abuse being made by the children were the result of regular, repeated interviews and intense pressure to describe abuse. Also, the bizarre and improbable nature of the accusations increased the likelihood that they were not true. At the trial Ralph testified as to the likely effects of the process these children had been put through by the county.

On September 19th the jury returned a not guilty verdict. The next month, after the jury had been impaneled but before testimony was to begin in the trial of Don and Cindy Buchan, the prosecutor, Ms. Morris, dropped all charges against all the adults except one who had already pled guilty. Ms. Morris stated that she dropped the charges because the judge had ruled that she had to give the defense all police notes and that to do so would endanger an ongoing major investigation. As the interviews progressed, the stories had grown to include accounts of ritual murders and religious rites along with the deviant sexual orgies and this was now touted as a major ongoing investigation.

The Attorney General of Minnesota, Hubert Humphrey III, took over the investigation of these charges after Ms. Morris dropped them. In February of 1985, the Attorney General issued a report of the five-month investigation by the FBI, Minnesota's BCA, and the Attorney General's office. The report concluded that the statements made by the children were not credible, because the procedures followed in the investigation exerted undue and coercive influence upon them. They determined that the children had been questioned repeatedly, over an extended period of time, by the prosecutor, police, therapists, social workers, and foster parents, all who believed that the abuse was real. For some children, the allegations of sexual abuse evolved into stories of mutilations and homicides. However, the report says the children stated they lied about the murders, because they were afraid of the interrogators and wanted to please them. One lad said he got the idea for his story of ritualistic torturing from a TV show he had watched (Humphrey, 1985; Erickson, 1985).

The national publicity given to the Scott County cases led to calls to us from all over the United States. Five years later we have consulted or testified in cases of sexual abuse throughout the United States, the military justice system, Canada, New Zealand, England, and Australia.

Over the past five years, we have now been actively involved in over three hundred cases of child sexual abuse accusations and have consulted in many others. This active involvement has included reviewing documents and audio- and videotapes, testifying in court, interviewing and/or testing alleged victims, evaluating alleged perpetrators, and evaluating and/or providing therapy to victims, families, and perpetrators. We have conducted research projects in six areas related to child sexual abuse. They are: (1) the interrogation of children as it is done in the real world; (2) therapy given to children when there is an accusation of sexual abuse; (3) judicial assessment of competence; (4) use of anatomically detailed dolls; (5) MMPI profiles of persons falsely accused; and (6) consequences to mental health professionals who aid in the defense of a person accused of sexual abuse. These research efforts are described in our book, *Accusations of Child Sexual Abuse.* The seventh area of research is the systematic analysis of cases where we have been consultants and expert witnesses. This is the beginning of that analysis.

Table 1 gives a summary of the 330 cases in which we have been involved in the last five years and the outcomes for those which have been adjudicated. We classified the cases as divorce and custody, day care, teacher or other professional (coach, priest, doctor, counselor, etc.), friend or neighbor, stepfather or other relative, stranger, and own child (not in a divorce and custody situation) in order to compare the outcomes in different types of cases.

The outcomes of the 291 adjudicated cases were classified in three categories. Acquittal/no abuse includes the following: the charges were dropped, the case was dismissed by the judge, the individual was acquitted in criminal court, and the family or civil court determined that no abuse had occurred. The category, guilty/abuse, includes the following: the individual pled guilty, the individual was found guilty in a criminal trial, and the court determined that abuse had occurred in family or civil court. The third category is a plea bargain or stipulation. In a fourth group are cases where there has been no adjudication to date.

Of the 330 cases, 191 (58%) involved criminal charges, 119 (36%) were in family court, 9 (3%) were military court-martials, and 26 (8%) were civil suits for damages. (Because several cases involved more than one type of court, the totals add up to more than 330 and 100%.)

Table 1

Adjudication of Different Types of Cases

Type of Case	*Adjudicated Cases*									*No Adjudi-cation*
	Acquittal/ No Abuse		Guilty/ Abuse		Plea Bargain/ Stipulation		Total Adjudicated			
	N	%	N	%	N	%	N	%		
Divorce/Custody N= 130	89	78%	20	18%	5	4%	114	100%		16
Day Care N=34	13	48%	11	41%	3	11%	27	100%		7
Teacher N=20	13	81%	1	6%	2	13%	16	100%		4
Friend/Neighbor N=50	19	40%	21	45%	7	15%	47	100%		3
Stepfather/Relative N=54	22	45%	20	41%	7	14%	49	100%		5
Own Child N=41	22	60%	12	32%	3	8%	37	100%		4
Stranger N=1	0	0%	1	100%	0	0%	1	100%		0
Total N=330	178	61%	86	30%	27	9%	291	100%		39

Based upon our experience, research, and review of the literature, we believe there are serious problems in the procedures followed when there is an accusation of child sexual abuse. The system of laws, policies, and procedures determining the way accusations of child sexual abuse are handled has developed in the absence of empirical data (American Psychological Association, 1987; Finkelhor, 1984; Finkelhor, 1986; Furby, Weinrott & Blackshaw, 1989; Lusk & Waterman, 1986; Sgroi, 1982). It is not unusual for social change to occur without factual support for the changes. Child sexual abuse is what political scientists term a *valence issue,* that is, an issue that has a strong symbolic character and elicits a uniform emotional response so that there is little disagreement (Nelson, 1984).

Facts are not required to unleash passion or guide new policies. What is supposed to be the most restrained and rational deliberative body in our nation, the U.S. Supreme Court, has frequently based decisions on psychological assumptions not supported by any data (Melton, 1987a). Psychology, too, has often confused assumptions with fact and anointed error with the benison of science (Scarr, 1985). When false myths are claimed to be true, science has failed its function to describe reality (Melton, 1987b). When myth and reality are confused, the greatest danger is the emergence of mistaken policies and procedures sure to produce the unintended consequences effect. Another consequence of erroneous myths is that real problems and needs are ignored and not understood. The end result may be that the cure is worse than the disease.

A second problem we see with the child sexual abuse system is the rapid extension of criminal sanctions in two directions. High frequency behaviors that heretofore have been understood to be within a normal range, such as bathing with children, tickling, affectionate pats, touching genitals (Rosenfeld, Bailey, Siegel & Bailey, 1986; Rosenfeld, Siegel & Bailey, 1987) are now behaviors for which people may be accused of sexual abuse. On the other hand, very low frequency behaviors which clearly are criminal, such as ritual satanic murders, torture, coprophilia, urophilia, and cannibalism are given credence and raised to the level of commonplace occurrence. People are sent to prison with no consideration of antecedent probabilities, that is, the inherent incredibility of bizarre and highly improbable accounts.

A third problem is the abdication of the justice system's responsibility for fact finding to law enforcement and mental health professionals who are empowered to make decisions that dramatically and permanently affect people's lives. Judges, prosecutors, and juries often rubber stamp the opinions and decisions of such experts, who have no accountability for their decisions. We have seen courts approve as experts persons with only undergraduate degrees or less, one or two weekend seminars or workshops, and maybe a four-hour inservice training program. Conferring great power on persons with little knowledge, no sophistication or depth, and limited abilities can only increase the risk of error and fail to protect children.

A major problem is the way children are interviewed. The typical investigative procedures involve repeated interrogations by police, social workers, and/or mental health professionals. This experience may result in adults inadvertently molding and developing an account of sexual abuse in a nonabused child. It may create confusion of fact and fantasy and teach the child to please adults by giving them what they want. It is through this process that a false accusation may be developed.

We have observed in the system a complete lack of attention to the consequences of embroiling a child in a false accusation. We have seen little awareness of what it does to a child if a mistake is made and nonabused children are treated as if they had been abused. This experience is neither innocuous, benign, nor inconsequential. It is harmful and may be permanently damaging and destructive. It is both puzzling and ironic that those most vociferous in championing the welfare of children and the need to protect them remain oblivious to the possible harm of a mistaken adult belief that a child has been abused.

The total number of reported cases of child sexual abuse has increased markedly in the past decade. Although the number of false allegations included in these reports is indeterminate, there are estimates of the number of false allegations of child abuse and neglect in general. Douglas Besharov, the former director of the National Center on Child Abuse and Neglect, reports that 65 percent of all reports of suspected child abuse turn out to be unfounded. This determination, involving about 750,000 children each year, is made after abuse has been reported and a child protection agency does an investigation. In contrast, in 1976 only 35% of all reports of suspected child abuse were unfounded (Besharov, 1985a, 1985b, 1985c, 1986).

Even following this extensive screening of reports, at any one time around 400,000 families across the country are under the supervision of child protection. However, a study conducted for the U.S. National Center of Child Abuse and Neglect found that in about half of these cases, the parents never actually maltreated their children (Besharov, 1985c). This figure is for child maltreatment in general. But there is no reason to assume that it is any different with reports of child sexual abuse. In fact, the ten-fold increase in reported cases of child sexual abuse in the past decade makes it likely that many of these cases involve people who have not abused their children. (See Wakefield & Underwager, 1988 for a discussion of false accusations.)

When suggestive and coercive interviews result in false allegations of sexual abuse, the entire system is weakened. Besharov points out that the dramatic increase in unfounded reports prevents help from reaching children who need it. The great number of junk cases weakens the system and we are now facing " . . . an imminent social tragedy; the nationwide collapse of child protective efforts caused by a flood of unfounded reports" (Besharov, 1986, p. 22). The protective service agencies are making mistakes on both sides. Because the system is so overloaded, children who actually are abused are not properly protected. Studies indicate that 25 to 50 percent of the children who die under circumstances suspicious of abuse or neglect have been reported to child protection (Besharov, 1988).

We believe that false allegations of sexual abuse have become a serious problem. Out of over three hundred cases in which we have been involved over the past five years, in three-fifths of those adjudicated there was a determination of no abuse. The percentage of false allegations is particularly high in certain types of situations, such as acrimonious custody and visitation disputes.

The people who are the target of a false report of child abuse are subjected to enormous stress and trauma. The investigation is difficult and invades the privacy of the family. If the report is founded, it can cost thousands of dollars to fight the charges. Our therapy caseload now includes people recovering from the effects of a false accusation along with people who are victims or perpetrators of actual abuse.

In the past, most child sex abuse cases were discovered when a child spontaneously told someone about it. But now the abuse is often alleged only after an adult began questioning a child. The proliferation of prevention programs in the schools and the media attention to sexual abuse has resulted in parents, doctors, teachers, and others becoming hypersensitive to the possibility that a child may be sexually abused. Any suspicious circumstances may result in misinterpretation and questioning of a young child who then becomes vulnerable to all of the effects of influence and selective reinforcement. When a story about abuse develops in this fashion, it is not a deliberate fabrication. In most cases of false accusations, the adults are caught up in the account and believe it is true.

With the increase in reported child sexual abuse, and the number of cases which depend upon the uncorroborated testimony of a young child, there has been controversy about the susceptibility of children's memory to suggestion and the reliability of their testimony. This has resulted in a number of research studies addressing this issue. What we have found, and report on in Chapters 1 and 2, is that no one has come close in duplicating in laboratory research what takes place when children are interviewed in the real world. Neither professional nor lay people have any idea of what actually happens when children are interrogated by adults who are trying to substantiate abuse. None of the research studies contain the level of suggestions, pressure, and coercion frequently exerted on children in real life situations. To treat children in an experiment in the way they are treated in the real world would be grossly unethical behavior for a psychologist.

The purpose of this book is to show what really happens in child interrogations. Many researchers have acknowledged the difference between what they do and the real world. They have called for more ecologically valid studies, that is, information about what the real world is like when children are interrogated (Ceci, Toglia, & Ross, 1987). This book is built around interviews in real cases and we have selected actual interviews as the central part of the chapters. These are interviews that we reviewed and analyzed as part of our services in consulting on a case. The interviews we have included in the book are not the worst examples of those we have reviewed but are typical of those we have seen. Over the past four years we have developed a rating system for analyzing the tapes. This is described in Chapter 2 and the ratings are also included in the transcripts in the book.

The case histories that accompany the interviews in the chapters are based on actual cases on which we have consulted, although we have changed names and other identifying details. In some of the chapters we have combined several cases in order to completely disguise the history, but there is nothing described that we haven't encountered in one of our cases. At the same time, the central focus of each chapter, the actual interview, is left unchanged. Each chapter illustrates a specific problem area we have observed in our experience. The cases from which the interviews are taken come from all over the United States.

Our purpose in publishing these interviews is to demonstrate what really happens in many cases of alleged child sexual abuse. Our hope is that by recognizing the problems, the process can be improved. It is not necessary to subject children to the type of interviews seen here.

We know enough to do it better.

CONTENTS

THE REAL WORLD OF
CHILD INTERROGATIONS

Chapter 1

INTERROGATION OF CHILDREN

HOLLIDA WAKEFIELD, RALPH UNDERWAGER AND ROSS LEGRAND

How can children say sexual things happened to them that didn't happen?

This is the fundamental question when we must decide whether an accusation of child sexual abuse is true or false. The question is most pointed when there is an uncorroborated statement by a child about sexual abuse which the accused perpetrator denies. If the sexual abuse is not real, then how and why is the child telling about sexual behaviors and describing abusive acts? How can children talk about sexual acts if they haven't experienced them?

When there is an accusation of child sexual abuse, children often are the only witnesses offered. Frequently, no corroborating or supporting evidence is found in spite of extensive effort. Then the accusation rests solely upon a child's alleged words. Increasingly, adults report a statement, claim the child said it, and, under new legislation establishing exceptions to the hearsay rule, the adult report is admissible as evidence. The person accused is saying, "No! I didn't do that!," but adults can't believe that a young child would make up an account of sexual abuse so the story is often unconditionally accepted. Adults may believe the simplistic maxim, "Children never lie about sexual abuse." Therefore, whenever a child supposedly makes a disclosure about sexual abuse, those adults immediately believe that the abuse is real.

But it is mistake to pose the question in the form of whether the child has lied. To lie assumes a conscious, willful, and deliberate purpose and intent to deceive. Young children are unlikely to have the cognitive capacity or the maliciousness to lie in this way, although some older children and adolescents may. Children don't know what they don't know. Their experience is limited and their store of available knowledge is small. When asked questions they don't understand or to which they have no answer, they can blithely give an answer without knowing it is

3

mistaken. Adults who lack knowledge about children's developing capacities may not see how the child has responded without knowledge and take the answer literally, especially if it suits their purposes. Unless there is strong evidence of deliberate, intentional dissembling, it is foolish to spend much time or energy on the question of children lying. It is almost always the wrong question.

THE FIRST SOURCE OF ANSWERS

When trying to understand a child's behavior, the first place to look is in the environment of the child and observable behaviors, not to inferred internal states or dispositions. The farther away an interpretation is from observable events, the greater the probability of error. The more complex the inferred causal chain and the more speculative the inferred internal events, the more likelihood there is to introduce error. Therefore, before speculating about processes going on inside a child, which can only be guesses, it is best to get as much data and clarity as possible about the environment and the child's actual observed behavior. Reports of children's behavior made by adults with either a bias or a benefit to be gained should not be immediately accepted as accurate. Retrospective accounts and parental descriptions of children's behavior have been shown by years of research to be unreliable.

It is surprising that so many mental health professionals apparently think first of dynamic, internal, private events (i.e., intervening variables such as shame, fear, anxiety, guilt, embarrassment, etc.) when interpreting the behavior of a child rather than considering environmental variables. We have seen this exclusive focus on inferred private, subjective events in almost every case where mental health professionals believe the abuse was real but the allegations turn out to be false. When behaviors are explained and interpreted by inferring unobservable internal events inside a young child, the alternative interpretation of causal environmental influences outside the child is seldom considered.

An example we have seen many times is that a child's lack of response to questions is interpreted to mean the child is ashamed. The adult assumes children are ashamed of sex and of being sexually abused. Therefore, the child's nonresponse is seen as consistent with sexual abuse. The child's silence then is transformed into denial of the sexual abuse. Because denial is bad for the child and disclosure is good for the child, the adult coerces the child to produce affirmations of abuse.

Under this pressure the child may say something interpreted as support for abuse. This interpretation is then offered in testimony as evidence for abuse. What began as observed behavior of silence or nonresponsiveness by the child has been changed by an intellectual alchemy into evidence of abuse.

When an adult believes there was abuse and a child says there was no abuse, the adult may assume that the child has a secret about abuse. Therefore the child is believed to have been threatened by the perpetrator to keep the hideous secret. To tell the secret is good because then the child can be saved. The adult must press the child to reveal the secret in order to protect the child from the violent and abusive perpetrator. A line of questions about secrets begins. If a child answers questions with a "No," the questions are repeated. Denials are ignored. Adult pressure continues until some response affirming a secret about abuse is obtained. The adult is reinforced by the role of the virtuous and noble protector and saviour of children.

But it is more parsimonious to ask if the child's nonresponse may be caused by strangeness of the environment, an unfamiliar adult, or other external factors. Or it may simply be that nothing happened and the child can't say anything about a nonevent. It takes less of a leap of faith to understand nonresponse or denial to be caused by environmental variables or the absence of any abuse than to infer the chain of speculative intervening variables required to say nonresponse and initial denial supports a hypothesis of abuse. In a curious turnabout, those who claim most strongly that children must be believed don't believe the child when the child says no abuse occurred. What is believed is limited to statements supporting the accusation of abuse.

Environmental cues and constraints are powerful determinants of behavior for both adults and children. Children are more susceptible to environmental influences than are adults. Therefore, the place to begin understanding a child's behavior is in the environment. This does not exclude later consideration of internal, private events but rather is likely to sharpen and focus any discussion of internal events, reducing speculative invention of nonempirical intervening variables.

When a mental health professional fails to consider environmental factors when dealing with an accusation of sexual abuse, there are three possible causes: (1) the professional may be ignorant, ill-trained and unaware of the scientific facts about environmental influence; (2) the professional may be committed to a theoretical position (i.e., Freudianism, ego-psychology) that minimizes or denies the influence of the environment and emphasizes internal subjective processes; (3) the professional unwittingly may be projecting onto the child an adult subjective experience of adult internal motivations and intents. An adult cannot know what it is like to be a child. The adult mind cannot function without adult capacities. Therefore an adult may project onto the child an adult perception of what it is like to be abused. Whatever the cause, failure to consider environmental influences when evaluating an allegation of child sexual abuse based solely upon statements of a young child shows a flawed, mistaken, and biased approach.

ADULT SOCIAL INFLUENCE

When examining the environment of a child the first question to ask is what degree, level, and type of adult social influence is exerted upon the child in that specific environment. The power and centrality of social influence is one of the best established facts in psychology. To ignore the impact of social influence upon any human interactive behavior reduces the credibility of any explanation offered. How adults behave toward children during the course of a developing sexual abuse accusation must be considered a possible causal factor in producing statements by a child. Before assuming that an accusation is true in the absence of independent, corroborating data, adult social influence as a cause of children's statements must be ruled out.

Physics, the paradigm of hard science, is forced by experiment to continue to embrace quantum mechanics and the basic concept of the Heisenberg Uncertainty Principle that any measurement or observation changes and interferes with what is being measured. Physicists have no convincing reason to believe that the objects of which the world is made exist independently of their somewhat puzzled observers (Economist, 1989). When the best knowledge and understanding of the world we live in cannot prove that reality is beyond the mind of the observer, surely psychologists should attend to the process of observation and assessment in human interactions.

We have seen again and again, in sexual abuse cases throughout this and other countries the massive imposition of adult social influence on suggestible children. Children are interrogated repeatedly by adults who believe that the abuse is real. The adult behaviors toward the children are frequently coercive, leading, suggestive, and punitive. Under such pressure, children may produce statements which adults then believe prove sexual abuse. Through this environment of powerful adult influence the child may be taught an account of sexual abuse that is false.

By the time this process of adult social influence has been repeated, sometimes over a number of months or even years, a nonabused child may come to believe the story. When a child has been taught inadvertently a fabricated story, repeated it enough to produce subjective certainty, for that child a nonevent has become reality. This is not a benign or innocuous experience. It may result in long-term damage to a child. This also means that the child may appear truthful, credible, and reliable, because for the child it is a real story. Reliance by a fact-finder upon the demeanor of a witness to assess credibility is then an error. Christiansen (1987) points out that cross-examination, which is supposed to give the trier of fact a basis for evaluating the credibility of the witness, will probably fail with a child witness whose memory has been falsified by being taught a story.

VICTIMS OF GOOD INTENTIONS

An adult is seldom deliberately trying to brainwash the child or develop a fabricated account of sexual abuse, although this may happen occasionally in divorce and custody situations. Thoennes and Pearson (1988) state that court counselors in their study saw deliberate false reporting in 13 percent of the accusations arising in contested custody cases. However, deliberate fabrications probably account for a small minority of the total cases of false accusations. Instead, an interviewer is likely to have a preconceived idea about abuse along with a lack of awareness of suggestibility of children and environmental factors, including the stimulus value of adults.

In the cases we have examined which turn out to involve false accusations, the interviewers show little understanding of the impact their procedures have on the children being assessed. This is true of mental health and law enforcement professionals as well as lay people. Much of the literature on child sexual abuse does not deal forthrightly with this issue but rather proceeds on the assumption that whatever a child says must be believed. This literature does not discuss the impact of the interrogation process upon statements used to establish that abuse occurred. This is surprising and distressing in that any knowledgeable and competent mental health professional knows that in any human interaction involving two or more people, factors of social influence are at work.

BELIEF IN THE FACE OF UNPOPULAR FACTS

Many professionals are convinced that any alleged disclosures from a child must be unconditionally believed. Yuille (undated) points out that children's disclosures of abuse are now given so much credibility that it is often sufficient for the child to show sexual symbolism in play for a social agency to remove the child from home. If interrogators assume that abuse occurred, they will perceive their role as substantiating the abuse so that appropriate action can be taken to protect the child and punish the perpetrator. Raskin and Yuille (in press) state, "It is common practice for interviewers to assume that the allegations are true and that the purpose of the assessment is to obtain information that can be used to arrive at that conclusion."

An adult who believes the accusation will question the child in a way that shapes, molds, and creates statements about abuse. The attempt to get statements about abuse may result in incredible pressure and coercion. DeLipsey and James state regarding their review of videotaped interviews that " . . . the most distressing problems were the use of leading and suggestive questions and coercion to make the child confirm certain information" (p. 238).

Years of research in social psychology demonstrate the principles of behavior that are involved in adult social influence on children (see Wakefield & Underwager, 1988). Together with the evidence for suggestibility, these unpopular facts may disconfirm or falsify many allegations of child sexual abuse. But what happens when there is scientific evidence contrary to strongly held beliefs?

What should happen is described by Skinner (Mahoney, 1976), "Science is a willingness to accept facts even when they are opposed to our wishes." Hardly anyone would say that we should deliberately ignore facts. Scientists agree that a good theory is one that can be tested and proven false. When a theory or concept is falsified, it is reasonable to expect that some attitudes and beliefs will change in accordance with the facts.

What does happen is demonstrated by a large body of research. People don't like to see or hear anything that conflicts with deeply held beliefs or wishes. Some time ago the response to bad news was to kill the messenger — literally. Today, it is more likely that the source of facts contrary to firmly held dogmas is demeaned and belittled. When those who ignore the scientific facts disconfirming their beliefs are confronted with those facts, the best prediction is that they will demean the source and refuse to change their beliefs or behaviors (Aronson, 1988; Festinger, Riecken, & Schachter, 1958; Lord, Ross, & Lepper, 1979; Ross & Lepper, 1980; Ross, Lepper & Hubbard, 1976).

What are these facts from social psychology? There are several areas of the science of psychology that appear in every introductory psychology textbook, including expectancy effects and experimenter bias, conformity and compliance, and reinforcement theory. These are firmly grounded in theory and the research literature. Every psychologist ought to be familiar with them and understand their basic principles. They cannot be gainsaid or ignored without truncating the body of scientific fact psychology has built. These are the unpopular facts that must be acknowledged.

The research on the expectancy effect and experimenter bias demonstrates that expectancies about an outcome of an experiment or interaction can influence the outcome itself. Biased investigators will err in the direction of their expectancies when they summarize, analyze, and interpret their data, and their own attitudes and expectancies will influence the actual behavior of their subjects. The expectancy and bias of interrogators has like effects.

In interviews, the bias of the interviewer can affect both the selection of the information to be recorded and the substance of the information itself. Subjects respond the way they feel to be most proper in light of the interviewer's verbally and nonverbally communicated expectancies. Garbarino and Scott (1988) state that in interviews with children, expectations of the professional, unfounded in empirical data, in which the professional strongly believes, can influence what information is given by the children. If the professional believes that all or most allegations of abuse are real, he or she will produce information to validate abuse.

The research on conformity and compliance demonstrates how the desire to get approval from others exerts a powerful influence upon behavior. In interviews with children there is pressure to conform to the perceived expectations of the adults. This can only be avoided by a careful effort by interviewers who recognize their own stimulus value and minimize cues on how to respond.

Reinforcement theory describes how behavior is controlled by the consequences that follow the behavior. Theories on parenting techniques recognize that the best way to change the behavior of a child is to use attention, praise, approval, and other social reinforcement. Children are sensitive to approval from adults and will learn quickly to behave in the way that gets rewarded. They are reinforced for making certain statements simply by a smile, a nod, an approving tone of voice, or saying "What else?" If interviewers are not aware of this, they will inadvertently reinforce responses of the child that confirm their prior biases.

In many cases the reinforcement given to children is obvious. A child may be told that she is brave and that "Mommy will be proud of you for telling the scary secret," or a child is told that he can go for a treat after he tells about the abuse. Slicner and Hanson (1989) describe interviews where children were promised or given candy, food, beverages, and toys, including one interviewer who presented a child with five lollipops in the course of one interview, while keeping one in her own mouth throughout the session. They describe another where the child, exhausted after a two-and-one-half hour interview with five adults pleading for details, was told that as soon as she complied, she would be taken to lunch at McDonalds. DeLipsey and James (1988) noted frequent instances of bribery and coercion in their review of videotaped interviews. They report that uncooperative children were often offered candy and food or denied access to the lavatory until they finished the interview.

It is also reinforcing to remove an aversive stimulus. When an adult stops asking repeated questions when the child produces the desired answer after several repetitions, the cessation reinforces a specific answer and may also reinforce giving an answer approved by the interrogator. Slicner and Hanson (1989) state that "both the proximity of concluding a lengthy and excruciating interview, as well as the promise of food in exchange for providing a statement serve as powerful reinforcers" (p. 69).

Where adult reinforcement of a child is not obvious, it still must be considered as a potential factor in the production of statements. Study of the process of psychotherapy shows there is a strong effect of subtle verbal and nonverbal behaviors by therapists to produce conformity by the client to the values and attitudes of the therapist (Garfield & Bergin, 1978; Tjeltveit, 1983). The same process is present in the interaction between an interrogator and a child and should be acknowledged.

THE CHILD IS AN OBJECT, NOT A PERSON

When an adult relates to a child by ignoring the interactive nature of the relationship, denying any impact of the adult's behavior, intents, and purposes, and refusing to consider environmental variables, that adult has objectified the child. The child is not treated as a person, is not understood to be a child, but is only an object for the adult's agenda.

This is the same basic problem feminists have objected to in their discussion of male-female relationships. When a man approaches a woman with nothing in his mind but his own agenda—sexual satisfaction—and shows no awareness of the other person's value, needs, desires, capacities, or personhood, the woman is turned into an object. This demeans, diminishes, and renders powerless the person objectified. Feminists have shown that this is a form of oppression and victimization. In this instance the rhetoric matches the reality. Male dominance over and control of women has generated deep, enduring, and often devastating pain. It has produced costs to individuals, society, the economy, culture, and nation.

If children are to be treated as persons in their own right, adults must be aware of their own position of power and ability to dominate a child. Adults must control their own purposes, assumptions, and behavior toward a child and acknowledge the potential for their behavior to influence the child. If this is not done, there is no way the adult can avoid objectifying the child. It is tragic that an attempt to ensure that children are treated as persons winds up not treating them as persons. We can and must do better in discovering ways to relate to children that foster their individuality and their personhood.

HOW DOES IT GET STARTED?

The development of the system we now have for responding to allegations of child sexual abuse is a social process. The main players are medicine, politics, the judicial system, including social workers and law enforcement, and psychology. The relationships among the persons who are in these institutions, guided by shared norms, beliefs, and values, are the social characteristics of the child abuse system. A model that explains how this started is the "invisible college" concept (Crane, 1972) which shows the powerful informal communication networks linking the judicial system, the media, and groups of researchers and political figures.

Studies of bibliographic citations analyzing the communications patterns empirically demonstrate the reality of the invisible college (Dunn, 1981; Lipton & Hershaft, 1985; Price, 1965; Price & Beaver, 1966; Yokote & Utterbach, 1974).

The invisible college connected with sexual abuse is readily evident in the interlocking system of a small number of researchers, prosecutors, mental health professionals, and politicians who revolve through seminars, workshops, lectures, training sessions, media presentations, and literature. There is a common set of beliefs and values, a common set of attitudes, and a common set of behaviors characterizing this group both in this country and abroad. The result is the rapid dissemination of views, research findings, and assessment methodologies through this network and their use in the real world. Examples are rapid proliferation of the use of dolls, coloring books, prevention programs, and unsupported maxims such as children are traumatized by testifying in the presence of the accused. All of these became standard operating procedure in accusations of child abuse in the absence of credible evidence to support their use.

An example of how such a system can function to produce policies and behaviors based upon dubious theories and research is the medical research on herpes. Lipton and Hershaft (1985) describe how an article published in a prestigious American Medical Association journal was widely accepted, touted as fact, and advanced as a basis for treatment, though highly vulnerable to scientific criticism and of doubtful value. The few attempts to analyze systematically the problem of unsound or fake research have raised great anxiety about the quality of scientific research. Even more fearsome is professional readiness to accept research without exercising critical acumen. Some professionals do not read research literature but rely upon casual word of mouth or informal discussions. Many professionals who read research literature never read the methodology section but skip to the results and discussion sections. The result may be that flawed findings are given credence and limited results are overgeneralized.

A COMMON PATTERN

We have examined transcripts, audio- and videotapes, charges, psychological evaluations, and testimony from hundreds of cases (Wakefield & Underwager, 1988) and have found that the way children are interrogated when sexual abuse is suspected shows a common pattern across this and other countries. The system of reporting laws, child protection agencies, law enforcement officials, prosecutors, and the laws and regulatory codes governing these agencies shape the common pattern.

An adult usually first suspects possible sexual abuse of a child. (Although an older child may spontaneously say something to an adult, with younger children the process most often begins not with the child but with an adult.) The most frequent trigger for the suspicion is some sort of change in the child's behavior such as bed wetting or nightmares or physical conditions such as a redness or soreness in the genital area.

The adult then questions the child and calls the authorities. If the adult is not a parent, the parents are also informed, although in some instances the first the parent learns of the accusation is when the authorities arrive and begin an investigation. An initial report is made either to the child protection agency or to the police. If the first report is made to the police, the police will then inform child protection. The first person who has contact with the child or the child's family is usually a social worker.

Sometimes the child is first taken to the family physician or to a hospital emergency room where the adult tells the doctor that abuse is suspected. The doctor may question the child and then make a report to child protection. Although there are seldom clear physical signs of sexual abuse, the notes of the physician frequently state "suspected sexual abuse" based on the history given by the adult.

The parent or other reporting adult has probably questioned the child before the police department or child protection agency gets involved. The strong emotion triggered by a suspicion of sexual abuse may result in intense, repeated, and suggestive questioning. Then when the official talks to the adult, the adult will give his or her recollection of whatever the child said in response to this questioning along whatever suspicions led to the original report of abuse. If the investigating official believes that children must always be believed and false allegations are rare, this account will be accepted as factual. The initial official contact with the child will therefore be based upon the assumption that the abuse really happened. This bias affects the way the official questions the child and the subsequent outcome of the investigation.

What happens in this first official interrogation is important in assessing the weight to be given to any statements a child makes. The younger and more suggestible the child is, the greater the significance and effect of this first interrogation. It will set the direction and the scope for all future contacts with the child. But it is probably the least documented and most likely distorted of the succession of interrogations.

The first official interrogation of a child may range from a single social worker interviewing the child to several people, including police, social workers and prosecutors, coming unexpectedly to the home and taking the child to the police station, as happened in one of the cases in Jordan, Minnesota. There is often a social worker and a police officer, or two or more officials. Particularly in divorce and custody cases, the accusing parent may take the child to a child protection worker, physician, or mental health professional for the first official interview, be present for the interview, and even participate in it.

The initial interrogation by officials is usually not recorded. There may or may not be notes or reports and the amount of information available about this first interview is generally minimal. Most often, the only information is a report summarizing what the child supposedly said during the interview. However, if the interview is not recorded, there is no way to know what actually went on. We have found that reports of what supposedly transpired in an interview are often markedly different from what actually took place, which we later discover when we are able to view the videotape of the actual interview.

Often interviewers ask a question or make a statement to which the child gives little response. After the question is repeated several times, the child may finally nod or answer yes. But in the written report, the child is presented as making the statement rather than only agreeing with the interviewer's statement. There is seldom mention of any denials which may have preceded the eventual affirmation. This is probably not a deliberate misrepresentation; instead, the prior beliefs and bias of the interrogator lead to an erroneous recollection of what actually happened. Herbert, Grams, and Goranson (1987) state that tape recordings are essential for accurate knowledge of what went on in an interview. Without them, the conclusions drawn about the interview by the interviewer are likely to contain significant factual distortions. They found that without taping, interviewers reflected their bias by giving inaccurate and mistaken reports about the interview.

Following the first official interrogation, there is a wide variation in what happens next. Sometimes there is only the initial interview. There may be an additional interrogation which is tape recorded. But the child may be questioned repeatedly by social workers, prosecutors, therapists, parents, siblings, or others. Sometimes the child is taken from the parents and placed in foster care where the foster parents ask questions and encourage talk about the abuse. The child may be placed in sexual abuse therapy where he or she talks regularly to a therapist about the abuse. If the issue is brought to adjudication, either in criminal, civil, family, or juvenile court, the child may be questioned frequently by the prosecutor or attorney and brought into the courtroom to be familiarized with the environment. Through this the account of the abuse is further rehearsed. It is often months, or even years, before the judicial system makes a determination about the abuse.

This pattern is not limited to the United States. We are familiar with similar techniques and problems from cases in Canada, New Zealand, Australia, The United Kingdom, and the Netherlands. Hayes (1987) describes interviews in England in which great pressure is put on the child to disclose the abuse, including the use of directed play with dolls and leading and coercive questions. Interviews of this sort were used in Cleveland, England, with the result that dozens of children were falsely identified as having been sexually abused by their parents. As in the United States, the problem was with interviewers "who commence an interview with a preconception that abuse has taken place" (Enright, 1987, p. 672).

INTERROGATION AS A LEARNING EXPERIENCE

Children may be interviewed dozens of times before a legal determination is made about abuse. In every interview the child learns more about what the interrogator expects and learns what to say or do that will get a positive response from the interrogator. The child learns the language of the sexual abuse literature, such as the distinction between "good touch" and "bad touch." The child learns about sexual behavior, including deviant behavior, and learns to equate sexual touch with touch that hurts. The child learns the victim role and learns to express anger towards the alleged abuser. The child learns the story and may come to believe it happened, even if the allegations are false.

The interviewer must know something about the allegations in order to ask any questions. The interviewer's own assumptions determine the questions asked and the direction of the interview is determined by these questions. This results in a bias in the interview procedures of even the most skillful investigators. If the interrogator is unaware of this and has strong and certain beliefs, this bias will be very powerful, resulting in an interview directed not towards determining the truth but towards substantiating abuse.

The bias results in the interviewer attending to information that supports presupposed beliefs and ignoring details which don't support these personal assumptions or which suggest a different direction. Statements from the child that do not fit into the interviewer's beliefs are seen as evasions or confusions. When a child says that nothing happened the interrogator keeps repeating the question and asking other questions until the child finally affirms the abuse. If the interrogator is sure that he or she is right, the theory is apt to be falsely confirmed.

In a study about the interrogation of children, it was found that the belief of the interrogator about the truth of the allegations was predictive of the outcomes of the interrogation (Dent, 1982). If the initial first interrogation involves an adult who has the belief that abuse occurred and who the abuser is, that prior belief will affect the outcomes of the interrogation.

The child tries to figure out and produce what the adult wants to hear. The desired responses are cued to the child by tone of voice, inflections, small body movements, and postures, as well as by suggestive and repeated questions. This is particularly true when the child has an inadequate memory of what is being asked. Children are apt to add material when they do not remember and the practice of asking children, "What else," is likely to increase the number of errors by adding extraneous and contradictory information (Saywitz, 1987).

The variables of power, authority, status, and credibility of the adult interrogator interact with the limited capacity and competencies of the child to produce a powerful confounding of this interrogation process. This entire process contaminates, confuses, and lowers the reliability of statements made by children.

There is no evidence that this is a reliable process for assessing possible sexual abuse in children. The overlooked reality is that each of these interrogation experiences is a learning experience for the child. The younger the child, the more powerful the teaching and learning experience. But people interrogating children seldom show any awareness of their own stimulus value or of the impact of their procedures as a learning experience upon the children and the reliability of statements made by them.

TYPES OF QUESTIONS

Different kinds of questions will elicit different responses. An open-ended question calls for spontaneous, free recall. For example, a parent might ask a weeping child, "What happened?" If open-ended questioning does not produce sufficient information, the interviewer may turn to more specific questions, such as, "Did he hit you?" At this point, the questioner has taken a more active role and the witness a more passive one. Research has shown that while specific questions result in an overall increase in the number of statements a witness makes in comparison to free recall, the increase is due to a rise in both accurate and inaccurate statements (Dent & Stephenson, 1979; Lipton, 1977). Thus the memory for an event can be made more elaborate, but the greater detail will include more false memories as well as more truth. Child witnesses are more subject to this error than adults because they give fewer answers in free recall (Kobasigawa, 1974; Mandler & Johnson, 1977; Perlmutter & Ricks, 1979) and therefore may cause interviewers to turn sooner to specific, closed questions and to use proportionately more of them.

Turtle and Wells (1987), commenting on the recent research on children as witnesses, observe that the paucity of children's recall:

> ... can lead to an inordinate amount of subsequent questioning from various agents throughout the legal proceeding and hence to a greater exposure to possible misleading information. Unfortunately for the system ... children suffer from a greater susceptibility to having their testimony distorted by such misleading information (p. 240).

Although young children may say little in response to open questions, they will answer leading and closed questions. Hughes and Grieve (1983) point out that when adults ask young children questions, they assume that if children don't know the answer, they will decline to answer the question ("I don't know") or else give an answer whose incorrect nature reveals their lack of knowledge. However, their study indicates that when children are presented with bizarre questions intended to be unanswerable, they almost always give answers. The authors conclude that children are well practiced at trying to make sense of situations and that we must reexamine what we assume to be happening when we ask children questions. Adults interviewing children about possible sexual abuse must realize that children may attempt to answer whatever question is asked, even if they don't have any knowledge of the events being asked about. Also, the question asked may not be the question the child is answering—the child may have a completely different sense of what the question is about.

Adults are more suggestible when an authoritative rather than a nonauthoritative person asks leading questions (Eagly, 1983; Loftus, 1979). Ceci, Ross, and Toglia (1987) state that the young children's suggestibility could be partially accounted for, because they are likely to conform to what they believe to be the expectations of the adult. It may well be that young children are especially affected by suggestion and leading questions simply because so many people are generally authoritative in relation to them. This would be particularly pronounced if the child is being interrogated by someone identified as a doctor, a therapist, or a police officer. Parents are also authority figures to their children.

In a more active line of questioning, the interrogator is supplying information to the witness. "Did Allen hit you on the arm?" and similar questions can give shape and content to the recall of a memory that is, in fact, vague. There have been many studies that demonstrate how the memories of both children and adults can be distorted by the introduction of false information into questions (see Loftus & Davies, 1984). When an unsure or reluctant witness causes the questioner to guess at what might have occurred and thereby provide information for the witness to affirm or deny, the resultant testimony may be the truth or it may be a fabrication that is mutually agreed upon and believed to be true by both parties.

BEHAVIORAL INDICATORS OF SEXUAL ABUSE

A frequent trigger for suspicion of possible sexual abuse is one of the so-called behavioral indicators. Many lists of behaviors believed to be caused by sexual abuse have been widely publicized with the instruction to look for sexual abuse when a behavior on the list is observed. These behavioral indicators may be observed by a teacher at a preschool, a neighbor, a parent, or by a spouse in the midst of a bitter custody battle. A single behavior, i.e., aggression toward another child, may result in an adult questioning a child in a way that inadvertently elicits statements confirming abuse. Also, once the process has begun, the the presence of one of the behavioral indicators may be used as evidence to validate the abuse.

As concern about child sexual abuse mounted in the United States, more and more people have been asked to help detect and prevent it.

Intervention is particularly demanded in the case of very young children, who are not only unable to defend themselves but are also less able to give voice to their problems. Television programs, workshops, newspapers, pamphlets, and magazines are asking parents, relatives, teachers, physicians, clergy, day care workers, and neighbors to be alert to the physical and behavioral signs of sexual abuse in children and to report their suspicions to medical or legal authorities.

One list of behavioral symptoms was published by the prestigious *Journal of the American Medical Association* (AMA, 1985) and has been widely reprinted. We are advised to look for children who have one or more of the following behaviors:

1. Become withdrawn and daydream excessively
2. Evidence poor peer relationships
3. Experience poor self-esteem
4. Seem frightened or phobic, especially of adults
5. Experience deterioration of body image
6. Express general feelings of shame or guilt
7. Exhibit a sudden deterioration in academic performance
8. Show pseudomature personality development
9. Attempt suicide
10. Exhibit a positive relationship toward the offender
11. Display regressive behavior
12. Display enuresis and/or encopresis
13. Engage in excessive masturbation
14. Engage in highly sexualized play
15. Become sexually promiscuous

Such a list is less than helpful. How does a deterioration in body image manifest itself? If a neighbor is unsure whether sexual abuse has occurred next door and who the offender might be, should any sign of a too positive relationship with an adult or its opposite, fear of an adult, be considered suspicious? Because acting too maturely or too immaturely are both symptoms, can a minister be expected to know the range of maturity a child of a given age should display?

Here is another list of symptoms. This list is offered by Sgroi (1982):

1. Overly compliant behavior
2. Acting-out aggressive behavior
3. Pseudomature behavior
4. Hints about sexual activity

5. Persistent and inappropriate sexual play with peers or toys or with themselves
6. Sexually aggressive behavior with others
7. Detailed and age-inappropriate understanding of sexual behavior
8. Arriving early at school or leaving late with few, if any, absences
9. Poor peer relationships or inability to make friends
10. Lack of trust, particularly with significant others
11. Nonparticipation in school and school activities
12. Inability to concentrate in school
13. Sudden drop in school performance
14. Extraordinary fear of males, of strangers, or of being left alone
15. Complaints of fatigue or physical illness, which could mask depression
16. Low self-esteem

There is some agreement between these two lists, such as problems with various fears, peer relationships, and sexual knowledge or activity that seem beyond a young child's years. There are also symptoms that appear on one list, but not the other, such as daydreaming, depression, and being too compliant. We might decide that behaviors found on both lists are better indicators of sexual abuse than those found on only one. Or, if a child shows many symptoms rather than only one, perhaps that fact should strengthen our faith in the diagnosis of abuse. Unfortunately there is no evidence that either of these strategies will be effective.

The task of detecting abuse is made more difficult because these two lists, long as they are, are not exhaustive. A survey of many such compilations proposed by various experts (Cohen, 1985) adds the following behavioral signs to those listed above:

1. Loss of appetite
2. Clinging to a parent
3. Tics
4. Hypervigilance
5. Running away
6. Irritability
7. Difficulty with eye contact
8. Hyperactivity
9. Extreme interest in fire
10. Unprovoked crying
11. Taking an excessive number of baths

12. Suspiciousness
13. Sleepwalking
14. Sudden massive weight gain or loss
15. Excessive urination
16. Medical conditions such as pneumonia or mononucleosis
17. Confusion
18. Nightmares
19. A poor mother-daughter relationship
20. Overdependency

At this point it seems that nearly every problem behavior ever detected in children has been offered by someone as a sign of child sexual abuse. The problem is the high probability that any normal child might at some point in childhood exhibit one or more of these behaviors and thereby risk being perceived as an abuse victim. To spread these lists of behavioral indicators without appropriate cautions and information about their limitations can generate mistakes, confusion, overreaction, and overinterpretation.

Note the following list of children's behaviors:

1. Depression
2. Overly dependent behavior
3. Aggression
4. Whining
5. Demanding
6. Lack of affectionate behaviors
7. Feminine (passive) aggressiveness
8. Encopresis
9. Anxiety
10. Neurotic problems
11. Anxiety about sexual matters
12. Problems of both over- and undercontrol

These symptoms, however, are not claimed as signs of child sexual abuse but as behaviors indicative of parental conflict in the home that may or may not lead to divorce (Emery, 1982). Many of these symptoms overlap with the suggested signs for sexual abuse. Neurotic problems could subsume a variety of fears, depression might manifest itself in withdrawal or other signs of sadness, and overcontrol could look a lot like pseudomaturity.

Moreover, the leading diagnostic manual for psychologists and psychiatrists, *Diagnostic and Statistical Manual of Mental Disorders,* Third Edition-Revised (American Psychiatric Association, 1987) describes clinical categories, such as childhood depression, separation anxiety, and disorders of adjustment that share many of the behaviors proposed as symptoms of sexual abuse. Suggested behavioral indicators from the various lists are found in many different situations, including conflict between parents, divorce, economic stress, wartime separations, absent father, natural disaster, and almost any stressful situation children experience (Emery, 1982; Hughes & Barad, 1983; Jaffe, Wolfe, Wilson, & Zak, 1986; Porter & O'Leary, 1980; Wallerstein & Kelly, 1980; Wolman, 1983). Possible consequences following an allegation of sexual abuse—a frightening or painful physical examination, separation from one or both parents, removal to a foster home, repeated interviews by different people—are themselves sources of significant stress.

Children who are distressed, whether by bitter arguing between parents, by physical or emotional but nonsexual abuse, or by any number of sad or frightening events, may reflect their distress in a wide variety of ways. Some will strike out while others will withdraw. Some will develop fears, others will report physical ailments. Which signs develop in a particular child under stress will be a complex function of the genetic predispositions and the learning environment of that child. The problem, therefore, is one of symptom specificity. There is no behavior or set of behaviors that are specific to victims of child sexual abuse or that can lead with reasonably high accuracy to that diagnosis. There simply is no empirical evidence supporting the suggestion that behaviors on the lists are causally linked to child sexual abuse.

There is one symptom that seems to stand out from the others on these lists as a more valid indicator of sexual abuse, and that is age-inappropriate sexual play or knowledge (although sexual anxieties are also listed as stemming from parental conflicts). In a society in which we think sexuality is only broached with young children in general and vague terms, if at all, detailed sex knowledge of a child is considered unusual. Unfortunately, we lack the necessary information to assess the predictive value of what may appear to be precocious sexuality. We don't think of the many ways we may expose children to sexuality. What children normally and naturally do sexually is likely to be much more frequent and involved than most people assume (Gundersen, Melas & Skar, 1981; Martinson, 1981). Without knowing what a normal level is, we cannot determine what is precocious, greater interest than normal, and what may indicate abuse.

Based on a four-year study of the behaviors of children in elementary school located in an affluent suburb, kindergarten through sixth grade, Best (1983) describes an informal curriculum of sex education.

> ...still another curriculum, this time a well hidden one that the children were working out for themselves. They knew it had to be kept sub rosa, because not only did adults not supply it for them: they actually seemed to avoid it. The children sensed and respected adult reticence in this matter and protected adults from the third curriculum. ...This curriculum had to do not with the way boys became boys or girls, girls, but with the way they related to one another. It was a do-it-yourself, self-taught education in sex relations. Unlike the first and second adult-imposed curricula, this one was organized and managed by the boys and girls themselves (p. 5)

> So, while the adults hemmed and hawed, the children went about learning and experimenting on their own, careful to protect the frightened adult world from the facts of life. They indulged the adult world's need for ignorance, all the while garnering what they could from whatever source they could to expand on their personal observations. They found ways to circumvent adult scrutiny and allay suspicion. They had learned very early, for example, that they would be rebuked if found playing "doctor," so rather than ceasing to engage in such activities, they found ways to hide them from surveillance. Under a multitude of pretexts they felt and touched one another without arousing the suspicion of watchful adults (p. 109).

Best describes a progression of a structured sequence of child game behaviors by which children explore and teach themselves about sex. They are: (1) House; (2) Look and See; (3) Show and Tell; (4) Chase, Catch, and Kiss; (5) Girlfriend-Boyfriend; and (6) Fucking. The Doctor game was not played in the school but appears to have been played in earlier years so that when children came to kindergarten they had already progressed to playing House. An entire first-grade class played house under the supervision of their teacher. When the "mother" had finished the role playing of getting all the "children" put to bed, she and the "father" disappeared behind the blackboard and they "kissed and kissed" (p. 110). Two third-grade girls were deeply upset and fearful of being pregnant because they had been "fucking" in the tool shed with second and third grade boys. This turned out to be rubbing genitals together rather than coitus. When reassured they could not be pregnant, the girls said " ... with considerable excitement that fucking was fun,

more fun than anything they had ever done. It made them feel 'good' "
(p. 122).

The lack of base rate data on what level of knowledge children actually
have, the demonstrated interest and sexual activities of children, and the
adult need to remain ignorant of children's sexuality make the potential
behavioral indicator of precocious sexual knowledge weaker and less
significant than it might appear at first impression. Due to restrictions
placed on the study of the sexual lives of children, we have not learned
what proportion of abused and nonabused children display sexual behaviors in spontaneous play. We do not know how many children imitate
sexual behaviors modeled by siblings, relatives, or playmates. We do not
know how many children have access to depictions of explicit sexual acts
in magazines or cable television or on X-rated video cassettes, and whether
exposure to these models leads to imitation. Therefore, while precocious
sexual activities of young children may seem more indicative of sexual
abuse than do other behavioral signs, there is too little known to form a
conclusion.

NONDISCRIMINATORY SIGNS

In assessing a behavioral indicator, we must take into account the
likelihood of whether a particular symptom or set of symptoms could be
the result of sexual abuse or some other cause. Estimates of the prevalence of child sexual abuse range widely. Taken as a whole, various
studies suggest that approximately 20 percent of women report having
had some type of sexual contact with an adult during childhood. Females
are believed to have had such sexual contact at twice the rate of males.
One problem with such estimates is that the type of sexual contact
reported may range from a single act of exhibitionism through subtle
fondling to repeated attempts at penetration. We do not know how severe
or how frequent such sexual contacts must be before they result in
emotional trauma and noticeable behavioral symptoms, nor do we know
how the nature of the contacts is related to the number and severity of
symptoms (Wakefield & Underwager, 1988).

Let us suppose that roughly 20 percent of females and 10 percent of
males in the United States have sexual contact with an adult sometime
before the age of 18. This averages to 15 percent of the total population.
We are particularly concerned here with children so young that they
have difficulty understanding and communicating the abuse to an adult.

About 80 percent of sexual abuse occurs with children over the age of eight, according to the National Center on Child Abuse and Neglect (NCCAN), (1981b) as they begin to develop more sexually mature features, and only 20 percent with children eight or under. If we use the 15 percent estimate of abuse for all children and limit our estimate to children age eight or younger, then in the general population of young children, perhaps 3 percent have been subjected to some type of sexual contact with an adult.

How does this estimate of the prevalence of sexual abuse compare with other childhood difficulties that might produce the same behavioral symptoms? Estimates of physical abuse and emotional abuse run several times that of sexual abuse (NCCAN, 1981a). Over 40 percent of all children in the United States will live in a one-parent household for at least part of their childhood, primarily due to divorce (Emery, 1982). Many more will endure parental conflict that does not lead to divorce. Add to this the relatively small number of children who will develop genuine childhood mental illnesses. In sum, the probability that a young child who is showing problem behaviors is the victim of sexual abuse is far less than the probability of some other cause. The teacher, minister, or other person, who, with all good intentions, jumps to the conclusion that a young child showing one or more of the long list of suggested behavioral indicators has been molested is likely to be making a grave mistake.

It is an error in diagnosis to use nondiscriminating signs to make a diagnosis. If a sign can be caused by different variables, it cannot to be used to select a single one. Most of the proposed behavioral indicators of abuse result from stress in general and are not specific to the stress of sexual abuse.

The base rates of the presence of many such behaviors in normal children, in troubled children, in nonabused children, and as part of the developmental process for all children, is so high that any attempt to use them as indicating abuse will result in a high rate of error and damage to children. Douglas Besharov, the first head of the NCCAN, states that the only time that behavioral indicators are useful is when there is an unexplained physical injury (1985b).

A HISTORY OF BEHAVIORAL INDICATORS

In the late 19th and early 20th centuries there was a great deal of public attention given to the pernicious and destructive habit of masturbation by children. This campaign to stamp out masturbation was part of a movement to increase healthy life styles in the populace. Masturbation was said to produce blindness, dementia, all manner of physical illness, and thus destroy children. The antimasturbation campaign caused some extreme responses. Female children had clitorectomies (surgical removal of the clitoris) performed. Male children were kept in hand restraints for years. Today there is general consensus that this antimasturbation campaign was built on foolishness and error.

Among others, J. Kellogg, M.D., originator of corn flakes, produced several manuals for parents to help them stamp out the evil of masturbation. In his books, he listed behavioral signs for parents to be alert for in order to determine whether their child was masturbating (Money, 1985). These behavioral signs for masturbation included the following (current suggested behavioral indicators for sexual abuse are in italics):

1. General debility, including exhaustion (*Complaints of fatigue or physical illness which could mask depression*)
2. Sudden change in disposition (*Display regressive behavior*)
3. Lassitude, dislike for play and lifelessness (*Become withdrawn and daydream excessively*)
4. Sleeplessness (*Nightmares; Sleepwalking*)
5. Failure of mental capacity (*Sudden deterioration in academic performance; Inability to concentrate in school; Sudden drop in school performance*)
6. Untrustworthiness (*Poor peer relationships or inability to make friends; Acting-out aggressive behavior; Lack of trust, particularly with significant others*)
7. Love of solitude (*Become withdrawn and daydream excessively*)
8. Bashfulness (*Seems frightened or phobic, especially of adults*)
9. Unnatural boldness (*Acting-out aggressive behavior; Persistent and inappropriate sexual play with peers or toys or with themselves; Become sexually promiscuous*)
10. Easily frightened (*Seems frightened or phobic, especially of adults*)
11. Confusion of ideas (including vulgar joking) (*Confusion; Hints about sexual activity*)
12. Capricious appetite (*Sudden massive weight gain or loss*)

13. Unnatural paleness (*Experience deterioration of body image; Complaints of fatigue or physical illness which could mask depression*)
14. Wetting the bed (*Display enuresis and/or encopresis; Excessive urination*)
15. Unchastity of speech, including fondness for obscene stories (*Hints about sexual activity; Engage in highly sexualized play*)
16. Early symptoms of consumption, or what are supposed to be such, including cough, short breathing, and soreness of the lungs (*Medical conditions such as pneumonia or mononucleosis*)

The behavioral indicators parents could use then to know if their children were masturbating are the same behavioral indicators now said to suggest that a child has been sexually abused. John Money (1985) states,

> Kellogg's listing of suspicious signs has been given a new lease on life currently by the professional detectives of sexual child-abuse. Here is an example of those who have not learned from history being condemned to repeat it, replete with all its dreadful consequences (p. 97).

The cautions about suggested behavioral signs do not mean that adults should not try to identify and aid children who show signs of distress. A sensitive and caring adult who notices problem behaviors by a child will want to try to find out what is wrong. But the adult must keep an open mind about what might be troubling the child and must be careful about the nature of the questions asked. A rush to judgment and premature closure on sexual abuse as a cause of the problems behaviors should be avoided. The odds are against this diagnosis.

RESEARCH ON MEMORY AND SUGGESTIBILITY IN CHILDREN

After the turn of the century there were many studies on children's memory and suggestibility. Many professionals concluded from this research that "children are the most dangerous of all witnesses," and demanded that children's testimony be excluded from the court record (Goodman, 1984). At the same time, the spontaneous account of an event by children was thought to be reliable. The overall picture from the early studies is of a potentially accurate witness, who can recount events and answer nonleading questions fairly accurately, but whose report can easily be contaminated by suggestion.

Later studies compared the memory and suggestibility of children to that of adults. Much research demonstrates that adults' memories are influenced by suggestion. Loftus (1979) and Loftus and Davies (1984) summarize the results of studies in which subjects are presented with a film of a complex event and afterwards asked a series of questions. Some of the questions are designed to present misleading information. The subjects presented with the misleading question are afterwards more likely to "recall" having seen something that was not present in the film. This false information will be integrated into the memory. Once the alteration occurs, it becomes entrenched and it is difficult to induce a witness to retrieve the original memory. The question that has been investigated in studies of children's memory and suggestibility is how suggestible they are in comparison to adults.

Children typically recall less than do adults (Johnson & Foley, 1984), but their free recall is generally accurate. However, since the typical interview with children contains a large proportion of leading questions, in evaluating their ability to serve as witnesses memory is only one consideration. What is their suggestibility compared to adults? It is well established that adults are influenced by leading questions. Are children influenced in the same way?

There has been a debate concerning whether children are more susceptible than adults to distortions of memory caused by leading questions. The older studies concluded that children were more suggestible. Newer studies found that both adults and children are influenced by leading questions but were inconsistent as to whether children were more suggestible. However, recent studies have found young children to be more suggestible than adults and younger children to be more suggestible than older children (Ceci, Ross, & Toglia, 1987; Goodman, Aman & Hirschman, 1987; Goodman, Hepps & Reed, 1986; Goodman & Reed, 1986; King & Yuille, 1987). Young children are particularly bad at making eyewitness identifications, especially when the target individual is not present in the lineup. In such cases, the child makes a very large number of false identifications (Peters, 1987, 1988).

Part of what happens with younger children is that the less a child remembers, the more he or she can be misled, and the younger the child is, the less he or she will remember. The less a child reports in free recall, the sooner the interviewer will turn to using leading questions. Also, children may have a different perception of tasks than do the adults. Children are likely to draw upon all available information in the interview situation to provide the interviewer what they believe the interviewer wishes to hear. Cole and Loftus (1987) state that " ... the demand characteristics of being given certain information by an adult, and even of being questioned by an adult are powerful components of suggestibility in young children" (p. 199) and Ceci et al. (1987) indicate that the young children's suggestibility could be partially accounted for because that they are especially likely to conform to what they believe to be the expectations of the adult. To avoid this, King and Yuille (1987) stress that the child be told that the interviewer is only interested in what the child remembers and that admissions of memory failure and memory gaps are expected.

A problem with all of this research in suggestibility is its ecological validity. Actual situations faced by a child witness cannot be reproduced in a laboratory study. For example, in a typical study, children are presented the misleading information once and may be given two or three leading questions and/or misleading information. Our research suggests that leading questions and other types of error-inducing questioning occurs from one-half to four-fifths of the time in the typical interview of a child witness in real life.

In the research studies, the children are tested immediately or after several days. But in the sex abuse cases in which children are required to testify as witnesses, the children are often interviewed many times by a variety of people over a long period of time. Ornstein and Gordon (1988) stress that we have no information in the literature on the ability of children to remember salient events over months or sometimes years. In situations where a child will eventually testify, the memory will consist of a combination of recall and reconstruction influenced by all of the interrogations, conversations, and sexual abuse therapy that have occurred during the delay. The longer the delay, the greater the possibility of social influence and the more the memory may consist of reconstruction rather than recall.

Most of the experiments are on children's recollections of events that they have observed. But when children are witnesses in sex abuse cases, they are believed to have been involved in a traumatic event. Although two recent studies have used actual events—a visit to the dentist (Peters, 1987) and a shot at the doctor's office (Goodman et al., 1986)—these events are likely to be less stress producing than sexual abuse. In addition, as Raskin and Yuille (in press) point out, providing testimony in a sexual abuse case may have profound effects on the child's life. A disclosure of sexual abuse may lead to the break-up of the home or placement in a foster home. In research studies, the children are unaffected by the events they are reporting and their testimony has no consequences. Raskin and Yuille state that "these differences . . . place severe limitations on the conclusions that may be drawn from the published literature" (p. 189).

In summary, children's memories in a free recall situation may be quite accurate. If the child is interviewed carefully and leading questions and suggestion avoided, a child witness can be competent to provide testimony. However, the suggestive and coercive nature of the interrogations commonly imposed upon children means that the weight accorded to what they say must be carefully assessed after making a determination of the nature and extent of adult social influence imposed upon the child.

FREQUENTLY USED INTERROGATION TECHNIQUES

There are several techniques that are commonly used in the interrogations. These include the use of anatomical dolls, books such as *Red Flag Green Flag People* (Rape and Crises Abuse Center, 1985), puppets, drawings, role play, establishing rapport with the child, establishing the credibility of the interrogator, and attempts to determine the competency of the child. But there is no evidence establishing that these procedures are reliable or valid techniques in assessing possible sexual abuse in children. Their use is likely to contaminate and influence the statements children may make and therefore raise serious questions about the reliability of the statements.

Drawings

Children's drawings are often used in assessing possible sexual abuse. The rationale for this is that the drawings of children with emotional problems are believed to differ from the drawings of normal children (DiLeo, 1973; Koppitz, 1968; Myers, 1978; Yates, Beutler & Crago, 1985). The assumption is that qualitative features of the drawings may be used as signs that indicate the child has been sexually abused.

However, the research does not support this assumption. In surveys of the DAP (Draw A Person), Harris (1963) and Roback (1968) both conclude that there is very little evidence to support the use of signs as valid indicators of personality characteristics. There is no research supporting the claim that qualitative signs such as elongated or squat figures, smoke or no smoke from chimneys, absence or presence of windows, or hands in front of the genital area have any relationship to sexual abuse.

There is so much variability in children's drawings that nothing reliable can be said about the particular features of one. Buros (1972) classifies children's drawings as projective tests and stresses that the examiner can project his interpretations on the drawings unless well-developed criteria for classifying and interpreting the drawings exist. There are no reliable or valid criteria for using the drawings to assess possible sexual abuse. There are major shortcomings in the few research studies which claim that the drawings of abused and nonabused children differ (Wakefield & Underwager, 1988). We know of no good research establishing that the drawings can be used diagnostically, especially to substantiate sexual abuse.

The only valid use of drawings is in opening up a line of communication between the evaluator and the child. But if they are used this way, the interviewer must remain objective and impartial avoiding cues and selective reinforcement of responses.

Books

There are a number of books that are used in assessing sexual abuse. A typical book is the coloring book, *Red Flag Green Flag People* (Rape and Crises Abuse Center, 1985). In this book, the child is led through a series of pages that present good touch and bad touch. After several pages, a child is asked to color portions of a figure that may have been touched. When the child colors a genital area this is regarded as evidence that the child has been abused.

When used in this way, a book becomes a programmed learning text. The progression of stimuli are arranged in the fashion of programmed texts used to teach students about biology, math, or geography. Children's responses in this situation do not represent a true account but rather the effectiveness of the book as a programmed text. None of these books have been validated for diagnosing child sexual abuse. They should not be used as diagnostic devised to conclude that a suspected case of sexual abuse is real.

Play Therapy

Although there is no evidence that play therapy has any efficacy or utility as a therapeutic procedure for sexual abuse (Wakefield & Underwager, 1988) children are frequently given therapy before there has been any determination by the judicial system that sexual abuse has occurred.

The play therapy sessions focus on reenactments and discussions of the abuse that can serve to model and encourage statements about abuse. Young children may be given dozens of sessions of play therapy over many months and may begin believing that they have been sexually abused even if there has been no abuse. The play therapy is often combined with interviews and questioning by the therapist about the abuse. The behavior of the child in the play therapy sessions is used to form conclusions about abuse and material from the play therapy sessions is often reported to the prosecution, child protection workers, and the courts as support for the accusation. This material is often given without any empirical basis.

What is now called play therapy during the handling of a sexual abuse allegation is not in any sense the play therapy as defined and described earlier in the professional literature. In traditional play therapy, the therapist maintained a completely accepting attitude and avoided directive suggestions or insinuations. The child was the active, initiating person in the interaction. No probing questions, no suggestions, no prearranged use of toys, no prompting, and no guiding was permitted (Axline, 1969). What is passed off as play therapy in a sexual abuse allegation has the adult as the active, initiating, probing, guiding, directing, and controlling person while the child is passive, conforming, and compliant. Analysis of actual play therapy sessions shows a consistent finding that the adults are actively talking and initiating behavior with the child from half to three-fourths of the time. (Wakefield & Underwager, 1988).

A major difficulty with the use of play therapy as an investigative tool is the unexamined assumption that play reflects reality. In one case, a child who probed toy animals with a toy stick was said to be reenacting the alleged insertion of objects into her vagina by another child while in her day care center (Hartman & Burgess, 1988). Children have been said to be showing signs of abuse when they play with certain figures at a sand table, when a girl avoids playing with boy dolls, when a doll the adult labels as "Daddy" is placed in a doll house the adult labels as "jail." But there is no evidence that behaviors occurring in play therapy can be used as signs to establish the truth of events that are believed to have happened in the past. Nevertheless, the behaviors of the child in play therapy together with the statements the child is said to have made are often used to prove that the child has been abused by the person accused.

Dolls

The anatomically correct dolls are widely used in the assessment of cases of child sexual abuse. They have been criticized and recently there have been several studies concerning their use. Some of the studies report differences between abused and nonabused children; others report no differences. However, the studies claiming to show differences between the responses of sexually abused and nonabused children have major methodological shortcomings which limit any conclusions that can be drawn from them. Taken as a whole, there is no evidence from the research on dolls supporting their use as valid methods for diagnosing sexual abuse.

A major difficulty in the unquestioned acceptance of these dolls is that until recently there has been little information about how normal children respond to the dolls. Baseline information about the antecedent probability of a child's response to the dolls is necessary in order to interpret what responses to such dolls mean.

Recent research indicates that the normal, nonabused children may respond to the dolls in a way that is likely to trigger suspicions of abuse in the investigator. Gabriel (1985) describes a study of 19 nonabused children who were observed with the dolls and other toys. These children showed several behaviors which could have been interpreted by other interviewers as indicating likely sexual abuse. Gabriel concludes that "On the evidence of the dolls alone, when used as part of a 'fishing expedition' exercise, the suspect will almost always be found 'guilty,' especially if the examiner is already biased in that direction" (p. 49). He also states, "Many persons working in the child protection field are untrained in play therapy and do not know about the projection-evoking properties of toys. The result has been that material produced by children in this manner can appear to confirm suspicions of sexual abuse when it may actually be no more than a normal reaction to the dolls and the situation" (p. 42).

In a study of nonabused children and their behavior with the dolls, Boat and Everson (undated) found that manual exploration of the sexual parts of unclothed dolls is not uncommon. A small number of nonabused older preschoolers will demonstrate explicit genital intercourse.

McIver, Wakefield, and Underwager (1989) compared 10 abused and 50 nonabused children in their responses to the dolls. Although they found no differences between these two groups, they report that two-fifths of the children spontaneously talked about and/or touched the dolls' genitals and three-fifths placed the dolls in clear sexual positions and/or played with the dolls in an overtly aggressive manner. Around half made spontaneous comments about what the doll did. They conclude that many of these spontaneous behaviors and comments could have elicited a suspicion of sexual abuse in an interviewer who accepts the assumptions that the doll play reflects actual experiences in a child's life.

King and Yuille (1987) point out that " . . . the dolls serve the function of a suggestive question with young children. The genitals and orifices of the dolls suggest a play pattern to children, and that play may be misinterpreted as evidence for abuse" (p. 31). Christiansen (1987) states that "the danger in the use of the dolls is that they will stimulate fantasy and not recall, and plant a falsified memory of fantasy to be recalled later as truth" (p. 711).

Herbert et al. (1987) used a standardized investigative interview approach and the dolls in studying 14 children, ages three to five with no suspicion of sexual abuse. Questions asked of the child when the dolls were in use were typical of the first level of questions asked in such interviews and then were followed by the use of leading questions.

All the children showed behavior that is often interpreted as demonstrating sexual abuse. The children mixed fantasy into their responses which was not detected by the interviewer. The authors regard this as troubling, demonstrating how easily an interview can be misinterpreted. Almost all children demonstrated suggestibility in responding to the interrogation. Evaluation of the interviews "as if" a sexual abuse allegation had been made resulted in half the sample being identified as probable victims of abuse.

The McIver et al. (1989) study also found that children could be easily influenced by the interviewer. Six of seven children who, following the initial portion of the interview, were given leading questions, cues, modeling, and reinforcement responded by performing the behaviors that were cued, modeled, and reinforced.

There have been efforts to standardize the procedure for using the dolls. White, Strom, and Santilli (1985) developed a protocol for interviewing preschoolers with the anatomically correct dolls. White (1986) observes that abuses in the use of these dolls are common and insists that appropriate caution be shown in their use and interpretation. Although White, Strom, Santilli and Halpin (1986) report that with their protocol, their sample of nonsexually abused children interacted differently with the dolls than did the abused sample, there is no information on other differences which may exist between the two groups (interviews about sexual abuse, previous therapy for sexual abuse, prior experiences with the dolls, etc.). Without this information, no conclusions can be drawn from their results.

The protocol suggested by White et al. was used by Jensen, Realmuto, and Wescoe (1986) with three abused and nine nonabused children. Following videotaped interviews by a single therapist, a panel of raters viewed the videotapes and rated the behaviors along White's scale from not at all suspicious to very suspicious. No differences between groups were found. Some of the nonabused children got the highest rating of very suspicious and some of the abused children got ratings of no suspicion of abuse.

Jampole and Weber (1987) investigated the presence or absence of sexual behavior with the anatomically correct dolls with ten sexually-abused and ten nonsexually-abused children. The researchers report a significant difference between the two groups in their demonstration or lack of demonstration of sexual behaviors in their play with the dolls and conclude that the anatomically correct doll is a reliable, valid instrument for use in sexual abuse investigations. The major problem with this study is that, although none of the children had been previously interviewed with the dolls, there is no information concerning the content of any interviews about sexual abuse, any therapy given to the sexually abused children, or what discussions were held with these children about sexual abuse by foster parents or social workers. Also, the criterion for determining the sample of abused children is a decision made by law enforcement personnel long before any determination by the judicial system. Thus this study does not really compare abused and nonabused children but rather children who have been interrogated by the system and children who have not been interrogated by the system.

August and Forman (1986) state that abused differed from nonabused children in their interactions with the dolls. The abused children tended to avoid engaging in storytelling while an adult was present but showed more interest in the private parts of the dolls when the adult was absent. However, the abused group was drawn from a population that was being treated for sexual abuse so the same criticisms apply to this study as do to the Jampole and Weber study.

Aman and Goodman (1987) claim that their study of nonabused three year olds and five year olds indicated that the use of the dolls does not lead to false reports of molestation in nonabused children. However, this is an overstatement and overinterpretation of this study. The real life event, an interaction with an adult male, was ten minutes long and included five play activities, permitting about two minutes for each activity. Such brief exposures are not analogous to the real life events likely to be the subject of an investigative interview using the dolls.

Although Aman and Goodman state that the dolls did not lead to an increase in false alarm errors, in responding to questions described as objective, the three year olds demonstrated an age X doll condition interaction. The three year olds in the doll condition were significantly less accurate in answering the objective questions than were the three year olds in the no doll condition. It is the younger children with whom the dolls are more likely to be used in real life interrogations. The questions described as objective by the authors are said to be nonleading. However, the five objective questions given as examples of questions that could lead to false reports are leading and suggestive.

False alarm errors, that is, errors that could lead to false reports of abuse, were significantly greater for three year olds than five year olds. One in five three-year-old children made such errors. The most important finding of this study is a clear age effect throughout. The younger children were consistently more suggestive across all variables.

The questions demonstrating false alarms and suggestibility were asked once. In the real world of child interrogations, children are asked leading and suggestive questions over and over again. (In one tape of a real interrogation the same types of coercive and leading questions are asked 80 times.) In the real world of child interrogations, children are pressured to interact with the dolls until the desired behavior is elicited. Questions are not asked once and then dropped if the child does not respond as desired. Children are not permitted to put the dolls aside. The Aman and Goodman study demonstrates the possibility of false reports from younger children. If one in five can be led to produce false alarms by asking questions once, the real world of interrogations in which children are pressured and coerced by repeated questions and demands for response will produce a much greater proportion of false reports.

An assumption underlying the use of the dolls is that the children will identify the dolls as male or female, use the dolls to symbolize actual people (generally themselves and the person accused), then use the dolls to demonstrate what has happened to them. The dolls are assumed to be useful because children can demonstrate actual behaviors with the dolls that they, because of limited verbal capacity, reluctance and/or fear, cannot talk about. But these assumptions are not supported. The McIver et al. (1989) study found that most young children were unable to identify the dolls as males or females on the basis of primary sexual characteristics and that very few used the dolls to symbolize persons in their lives. Herbert et al. (1987) also found that children showed inability to identify gender on the basis of the symbolic genitalia.

Sivan, Schor, Koeppl, and Noble (1988) found that although girls play with dolls more than boys and all children play with the dolls more when the interviewer is female, that overall the dolls are of little interest to children. They do not spontaneously choose to play with them. Herbert et al. (1987) report that the children did not approach the dolls spontaneously but required the interrogator to direct them to approach the dolls. None initiated undressing the dolls although all accepted the direction of the interrogator to undress them. This suggests the extent to which the interactions with the dolls are a result of the adult modeling and reinforcement.

Sivan and Schor (1987) report a study of 144 children, ages three to eight, on labeling of body parts using anatomically correct dolls. Younger children give more responses, but older children give clearer responses. Younger children are said to be willing to provide answers to questions when they have no meaningful response. The attitude and approach of the interviewer is a crucial factor in eliciting responses.

The use of the dolls can provide modeling to the child. One of the most powerful ways of teaching a child is by modeling (Bandura & Walters, 1963). Interviewers model handling the dolls, suggest that they be undressed (or undress them for the child) and label them for the child. They may say, "Let's pretend that this is you and this is Daddy," which invites the child to confuse fact and fantasy. They ask the child to show with the dolls what Daddy did and they may place the dolls in the sexually explicit positions for the child. This is a teaching experience for the child.

When an adult gives support and structure to a child in using dolls to tell a story, the child produces a story much different and at a higher developmental level than when left to produce a spontaneous story with little adult support. When actions are modeled by an adult using dolls the effect is to facilitate pretending and fantasy behavior (Watson & Fischer, 1977). This falsifies any claim that the dolls can be used with young children because then they can show something real with dolls that they can't talk about.

There has been no research to establish standardized procedures for using the dolls in an investigation. Although White et al. (1985) describe a protocol, there is no normative data to standardize it. Standardized procedures that can be repeated by others are a requirement before anything sensible can be said or any conclusions drawn. A California Appeals Court ruled in 1987 that the use of the dolls was not supported by the scientific evidence and their use did not meet the Frye test for admissibility. Testimony based upon the use of the dolls was therefore ruled inadmissible (Law Week, 1987).

The problem is exacerbated by the fact that persons actually using the dolls are untrained, unsophisticated, ignorant of child development, and widely variable in their interpretation of behavior with the dolls (Boat & Everson, undated). The American Psychological Association's Committee on Psychological Testing and Assessment determined in its March 1988, meeting that the dolls "are considered to be a psychological test and are subject to the standards when used to assess individuals and make inferences about their behavior" (Landers, 1988). This means that a psychologist who uses the dolls and reports conclusions based on their use without including appropriate cautions about their reliability and validity is behaving unethically.

There has been a vigorous national debate in the Netherlands, during which we cooperated with some Dutch psychologists by providing materials and consultation. This controversy has resulted in the highest court in the Netherlands (Hoge Raad) ruling that evidence gained from the use of dolls or doll play sessions cannot be admitted unless the judge can explain in that specific case why the objections to the dolls do not apply. This effectively means that the "anatomically correct" dolls are dead in Holland (Rossen, 1989).

A basic issue is the use of the dolls to elicit behaviors from young children that can be said to show abuse. Children are in a process of developing. They show various levels of capacity and ability throughout that process; this puts limits on what children are able to do at any given level of development. Adults want to break through developmental limits in order to attain their objectives. This means that whatever techniques adults use to overcome the limits of a child's developmental ability are at risk for producing mistaken information reflecting the adult agenda rather than the truth. The techniques used must be shown to avoid this risk. If they do not demonstrate validity and reliability, they must not be used.

The use of the dolls in interviews must not be viewed as a pursuit of truth but rather as a learning experience. To date there are no data that support a differential behavior of abused and nonabused children when the dolls are used to assess sexual abuse. The data that is available suggests that they cannot be used to distinguish abused from nonabused children.

CONCLUSIONS

The way children are interrogated when sexual abuse is suspected shows a common pattern. There are common techniques used to investigate the abuse and interview the children, but the way children are interviewed has a high potential for introducing error and reducing the reliability of statements that children make. Children, interrogated with suggestive approaches by adults who have no conception of their influence, are being taught. This raises serious questions about the possible role of adult social influence upon children's behavior. When there is no corroborating data or no admission from the accused, children's statements standing alone must be viewed with great caution.

Chapter 2

VIDEO- AND AUDIOTAPE ANALYSIS RESEARCH PROJECT

CHRISTINE SAMPLES BARTZ, ROSS LEGRAND,
HOLLIDA WAKEFIELD, RALPH UNDERWAGER

We are engaged in an ongoing research project of analyzing video- and audiotaped interviews from actual cases of alleged sexual abuse. To date, we have analyzed 36 cases plus a pilot study. We have reviewed additional tapes in many other cases; the cases where we performed the analysis are typical of the ones we have seen. In a second project, we have begun a preliminary analysis in order to investigate possible causal links between the behavior of the interviewers and that of the children.

PROJECT I: INITIAL ANALYSIS

Sample

The tapes were from cases on which we consulted. In each of the cases, the persons accused of the sexual abuse had denied the allegations. An attorney contacted us and we agreed to review the documents and available tapes. In three of the cases we also interviewed the children and in ten cases we evaluated the accused person(s). The tape analysis was done when the attorney requested this service.

The cases in which we formally analyzed tapes were typical of the cases in which we have been involved in the past five years. The analyzed cases came from Alaska, Florida, Kentucky, Hawaii, Indiana, Wisconsin, North Dakota, Massachusetts, Minnesota, Mississippi, Missouri, New Jersey, Nevada, North Carolina, Ohio, Rhode Island, Tennessee, Texas, Washington, and Vermont. Nine involved accusations in day care centers, thirteen were in divorce and custody situations, and fourteen involved accusations by neighbors, friends, students, or others. In only two of the cases was there an accusation of abuse in an intact family.

There were 99 total children in tapes we analyzed. In 15 cases there was 1 child; in 13 cases 2 children; in 3 cases, 3 children; and in 5 cases from 4 to 19 children. The larger numbers of children were from the day care cases. There were twice as many girls (65) as boys (34).

The children ranged from age 3 to 12 with a median age of 4 and a mean age of 4.9. There was no significant difference in the mean ages of the girls (4.8) and the boys (5.1). Four-fifths (80) of the children were ages 3 to 6 and one-fifth (19) were ages 7 to 12.

There were 150 interviews available for the 99 children. There was only one interview for each child in 19 of the cases; the others had two, three, or more interviews. However, internal evidence suggested that the taped interviews were seldom the first interview (for example, the interviewer said "Remember when we talked before?" or "Do you remember the other day when we were playing with the dolls?" or the child said "I forgot what I was supposed to say to you."). The recorded interviews took place anywhere from a few weeks to two years after the alleged event. The length of the interviews ranged from a few minutes in a couple of the cases to 117 minutes; most were from 30 to 50 minutes.

There were a total of 62 interviewers: 40 women and 22 men. The interviewers included social workers, police, psychologists, psychiatrists, and physicians. Two-thirds of the police officers were males (66%), but most of the social workers, psychologists, psychiatrists, and physicians were females (86%). In some of the interviews, the child was alone with one interviewer. In others two, three, or more interviewers were present. In several cases the mother and/or grandmother was present and participated in the questioning. Sometimes two children were interviewed at the same time. The anatomical dolls were used in two-thirds (24) of the tapes analyzed.

Procedure

In developing the analysis techniques, we first surveyed the research on children's memory capabilities, their ability to distinguish truth from falsehood or fantasy from reality, and how methods used to question witnesses can distort what adults and children recall. The studies indicate that not only what we regard as leading questions but specific questions that probe beyond witnesses' free recall can create false memories (see Wakefield & Underwager, 1988 for a discussion of this).

From this information, we developed categories of open-ended and closed questions. The pilot study included 7 interrogator behaviors and

6 child behaviors. We then added new scoring categories derived from what actually transpired in the interviews. For example, no ethical researcher would ever tell a child that he is a "fraidy cat," or "stupid," or "cowardly," but interviewers applied such pressure on the witnesses, so we added a category for that. We now have operationally defined 16 adult interrogator behaviors and 15 child behaviors. The rules for sorting observed behaviors into categories were defined as objectively as possible so that others could use them in similar research.

In the pilot study two college graduates, unacquainted with sexual abuse issues, were hired, trained, and did the rating. In subsequent analyses, scoring of the tapes was performed by three women and one man (two social workers, a mental health practitioner, and a research assistant) who were unfamiliar with the details of the cases. All but two of the tapes were analyzed by two raters. One of the women analyzed every tape along with one of the other three raters. The ratings were done independently by the two raters from a transcript of the interview while they viewed and/or listened to the tape.

The goal was to score every verbal act by the participants in the interviews. Some actions were entered into more than one category. For example, a closed question may be perceived as also applying pressure. The instructions for the rating system are included at the end of this chapter.

Six categories of interviewer behaviors were defined as potential error-inducing adult behaviors: closed questions, modeling, pressure, rewards, aids, and paraphrase. Closed questions and modeling can give information to the child on how to respond. Along with pressure and rewards, paraphrasing can reinforce the child's response, especially if the paraphrase is presented with nonverbal signs of approval. Aids such as the anatomical dolls, which were used in most of the interviews, can provide a modeling effect to the child and can potentially generate false information (refer to the discussion about the dolls and books in the previous chapter).

Results

Level of agreement between raters was calculated by dividing the number of agreements between raters by the number of agreements plus disagreements. The level of agreement ranged from 68 to 92 percent with a mean of 79 percent.

A summary of the results are given in Tables 1 and 2. The actual number of scored behaviors varies with the amount of material available.

In most of these interrogations, the adults are two to three times more active than the children ranging from 53 percent to 82 percent of the total interview (with a mean of 66%).

The behaviors of the adults that can convey information to the children on how to respond are closed questions, pressure, reward, modeling, use of aids, and paraphrase. When these categories are combined, they total from 45 to 80 percent (with a mean of 64%) of the interviewers' behaviors.

Discussion

The project did not attempt to determine the truthfulness or untruthfulness of the statements of the children. It examined the behaviors, statements, and questions of the participants in actual interviews. We obtained information on the interviewing process and the responses of children in a real world situation. The tapes are interrogations in actual cases. These are not laboratory analogs or attempted simulations.

The adults did most of the talking in the interviews. In most of the cases, the adults were from one and one-half to three times more active than the child. The picture that emerges is one in which the adult is active and task-oriented, and the child plays a more passive role.

Six categories of interviewer behaviors were defined as potential error-inducing adult behaviors: closed questions, modeling, pressure, rewards, aids, and paraphrase. The proportion of the total adult behaviors that were potentially error-inducing ranged from half to four-fifths of the interviews. The average was two-thirds. In the research studies on suggestibility, children are asked the leading questions once and the proportion of leading questions does not exceed 10 to 20 percent. In the real world children are subjected to much more misinformation, leading and suggestion, and coercion than in any research study.

The behaviors of the adults in these interviews does not appear geared to encourage free recall, allowing the children to tell their own accounts without pressure and suggestion. Closed questions, pressure, rewards, use of aids, and modeling are adult behaviors that teach a child what is expected, what story to tell, and what pleases the adult. The adult interrogators often appear to be trying to extract testimony that will substantiate abuse they have already concluded is real.

This picture is more disturbing because the children usually had been

TABLE 1
PERCENTAGES OF INTERVIEWERS' BEHAVIORS FOR 36 CASES

Interviewer Behaviors

Case	Open Questions	Closed Questions	Combin. Questions	Pressure	Reward	Modeling	Discuss	Irrelevant	Use of Aids	Ambig- uous	Para- phrase	Unscor- able	% of Total Interview
1	11	28	3	14	7	13	4	2	0	9	10	*	79
2	15	30	2	11	7	9	0	2	7	5	11	0	77
3	15	21	1	9	7	11	0	6	11	7	12	*	73
4	12	22	1	12	12	8	0	3	6	12	7	3	69
5	10	27	3	16	6	13	0	3	4	5	10	2	71
6	13	23	2	17	6	20	2	0	4	3	10	0	82
7	16	24	3	14	2	11	0	7	3	3	15	1	70
8	23	34	1	11	2	5	0	1	4	4	12	2	71
9	17	18	0	10	1	5	0	8	23	5	10	4	59
10	8	18	1	6	6	9	0	22	7	8	12	3	62
11	15	25	3	7	1	2	0	7	8	14	16	2	56
12	11	16	1	11	5	8	1	14	6	9	11	6	64
13	14	18	2	10	5	4	1	8	8	10	15	5	69
14	18	13	2	16	12	0	0	1	0	16	13	9	73
15	12	15	2	13	4	2	0	13	8	10	12	8	57
16	16	19	2	4	2	5	0	0	17	10	21	2	71
17	21	18	3	16	9	4	0	2	16	0	5	5	77
18	19	21	2	3	6	6	0	4	15	6	11	5	71
19	14	22	1	3	3	3	0	22	1	10	21	3	53
20	9	13	2	14	6	4	1	13	16	9	8	6	71
21	10	22	1	21	6	9	0	8	2	10	8	3	70
22	16	27	2	9	6	5	1	8	6	9	10	3	61
23	9	22	1	16	4	25	0	3	0	10	8	2	65
24	17	25	5	2	3	4	1	1	0	20	17	4	66
25	10	24	1	6	6	7	0	20	1	10	12	2	55
26	9	29	2	1	1	9	3	3	3	28	8	2	66
27	22	26	3	1	1	4	1	1	0	12	29	2	62
28	7	40	1	5	4	9	0	5	0	8	18	3	60
29	19	22	1	3	1	6	0	6	0	27	13	2	58
30	19	22	0	1	1	3	0	1	10	11	27	3	62
31	7	26	2	15	6	5	0	6	9	11	11	2	69
32	10	26	2	10	1	7	0	8	6	9	16	4	70
33	12	25	0	12	1	9	0	2	16	11	12	1	64
34	10	17	0	23	3	14	1	7	7	7	8	2	70
35	9	22	0	11	8	3	0	10	5	11	8	14	67
36	17	34	1	7	3	11	0	1	3	9	11	3	53
Mean %	14	23	2	10	5	8	0	6	6	10	13	3	66
Median %	14	22	2	11	5	7	0	6	6	10	12	3	68

(* Category not scored)

TABLE 2

PERCENTAGES OF CHILDREN'S BEHAVIORS FOR 36 CASES

Child Behaviors

Case	Affirm	Affirm-Describe	Affirm-Contradict	Disagree	Disagree-Describe	Disagree-Contradict	Describe	Refusal	Irrelevant	"Don't know"*	Upset*	Play	Move Away	Ask Question	Ambiguous	% of Total Interview
1	25	2	1	8	3	0	47	1	8	3	•	•	•	2	•	21
2	21	0	0	12	1	0	43	2	6	4	•	•	•	7	•	23
3	17	1	0	7	1	0	47	1	5	2	•	•	•	7	•	27
4	17	1	0	9	1	0	40	1	8	4	•	•	•	8	•	31
5	18	2	0	14	2	0	41	1	8	3	•	•	•	7	•	29
6	17	1	0	13	1	0	35	6	0	5	•	•	•	8	•	18
7	16	2	0	3	1	0	44	1	20	1	•	•	•	8	•	30
8	18	0	0	13	1	0	52	1	1	5	•	•	•	3	•	29
9	14	1	0	6	1	0	29	5	15	2	•	•	•	24	•	41
10	13	2	0	8	1	0	32	0	26	1	•	•	•	13	•	38
11	23	3	0	11	2	0	46	0	8	1	•	•	•	2	•	44
12	14	2	0	8	2	0	28	6	23	0	3	0	0	11	2	36
13	17	1	0	14	1	0	29	1	17	3	0	1	0	6	10	31
14	13	0	0	13	4	0	49	7	12	0	1	1	1	1	0	27
15	12	1	0	7	0	0	32	3	30	2	1	0	0	5	5	43
16	29	1	0	12	1	0	51	0	0	2	0	0	0	0	4	29
17	30	0	0	7	0	0	37	6	7	0	2	0	0	0	11	23
18	18	0	0	13	0	0	45	0	6	3	0	0	0	1	12	29
19	14	2	0	7	1	0	31	0	29	0	0	0	0	4	11	47
20	15	1	0	7	1	0	28	3	22	1	2	1	1	8	11	29
21	9	0	0	16	2	1	22	4	17	13	2	3	0	7	4	30
22	26	2	0	8	1	0	35	1	13	1	0	0	•	7	5	39
23	14	2	0	10	1	0	54	0	5	4	•	•	0	3	7	35
24	23	1	0	8	2	0	48	3	2	5	•	•	•	3	4	34
25	10	1	0	5	1	0	16	1	40	2	0	1	•	12	11	45
26	24	1	0	12	2	0	42	0	9	2	•	•	0	2	7	34
27	14	1	0	8	2	0	56	0	0	6	•	•	•	1	10	38
28	22	3	0	11	1	0	23	1	24	0	•	•	•	7	7	40
29	16	5	0	7	1	0	48	0	9	2	0	0	0	3	8	42
30	16	0	0	11	0	0	45	4	7	2	0	8	1	6	10	38
31	22	0	0	2	0	0	31	8	14	1	0	0	3	4	7	31
32	7	0	0	8	2	0	38	6	17	0	0	4	0	14	5	30
33	22	4	0	9	2	0	36	1	9	0	0	•	•	9	4	36
34	4	0	0	4	0	0	17	12	36	0	•	2	•	20	7	30
35	14	0	0	3	0	0	23	5	18	2	2	2	0	19	14	33
36	11	1	0	9	1	0	67	1	3	2	0	0	0	3	2	47
Mean %:	17	1	0	9	1	0	39	3	13	2	1	1	0	7	7	34
Median %:	17	1	0	8	1	0	39	1	9	2	0	0	0	7	7	32

(* Category not scored)

TABLE 3
PERCENTAGES OF INTERVIEWERS'
ERROR-INTRODUCING BEHAVIORS FOR 36 CASES

Interviewer Behaviors

Case	Closed Questions	Pressure	Reward	Modeling	Use of Aids	Para- phrase	% of Total Interview
1	28	14	7	13	0	10	72
2	30	11	7	9	7	11	75
3	21	9	7	11	11	12	71
4	22	12	12	8	6	7	67
5	27	16	6	13	4	10	76
6	23	17	6	20	4	10	80
7	24	14	2	11	3	15	69
8	34	11	2	5	4	12	68
9	18	10	1	5	23	10	67
10	18	6	6	9	7	12	58
11	25	7	1	2	8	16	59
12	16	11	5	8	6	11	57
13	18	10	5	4	8	15	60
14	13	16	12	0	0	13	54
15	15	13	4	2	8	12	54
16	19	4	2	5	17	21	68
17	18	16	9	4	16	5	68
18	21	3	6	6	15	11	62
19	22	3	3	3	1	21	53
20	13	14	6	4	16	8	61
21	22	21	6	9	2	8	68
22	27	9	6	5	6	10	63
23	22	16	4	25	0	8	75
24	25	2	3	4	0	17	51
25	24	6	6	7	1	12	56
26	29	1	1	9	3	8	51
27	26	1	1	4	0	29	61
28	40	5	4	9	0	18	76
29	22	3	1	6	0	13	45
30	22	1	1	3	10	27	64
31	26	15	6	5	9	11	72
32	26	10	1	7	6	16	66
33	25	12	1	9	16	12	75
34	17	23	3	14	7	8	72
35	22	11	8	3	5	8	57
36	34	7	3	11	3	11	69
Mean %	23	10	5	8	6	13	64
Median %	22	11	5	7	6	12	67

interrogated several times before the taped interview was recorded. Prior interrogations are not documented. The procedure of the interrogators appears to be to get the story down first and then tape it. It is likely that knowing the interview was being taped would result in the interrogator trying to avoid more obvious questionable behavior. The undocumented and unknown interrogations that precede the documented one are apt to be more coercive and suggestive than the ones we analyzed. Also, when a child has been interviewed several times previously, what appears to be a spontaneous statement or one elicited by an open question may have been learned in previous interviews.

PROJECT II
INTERACTION OF INTERROGATOR BEHAVIORS AND KEY STATEMENTS BY CHILD WITNESSES: A TIMELINE ANALYSIS

The second project is a preliminary analysis of the relationship of specific behaviors of the interviewers and specific behaviors of the children. Our hypothesis was that the child statements in interviews are functionally related across time to the interviewer behaviors.

While using the same scoring procedures, we divided the interviews into first and second halves in order to examine changes in the rates of behaviors with time. We also noted which categories preceded or followed one another. This is one way to search for possible cause-and-effect relationships. For example, we investigated whether some types of statements made by children were more likely to be rewarded than others.

We singled out those key statements by the children that may form the basis of a sexual abuse accusation. These types of key statements answer the questions Who, What, Where, and When, and can be assembled by social workers, psychologists, prosecutors, police, and investigators into a coherent account of alleged sexual abuse. For example, if the story line in an interview was that "Daddy touched me on my bottom while we were in the basement," all statements relating to this story, such as how often the child was touched, who else was home, the nature of the touch, a description of the clothing worn by the child and the accused assailant, and so on, were considered important to the accusation and were defined as key statements.

There are two primary questions about the information contained in the key statements. First, how was the information elicited? Was it offered spontaneously by the child or initially introduced by the interviewer? In the first instance, the adult may ask, "Did someone do something to you?" to which the child replies, "Daddy touched me." In the second instance, the adult may ask, "Did someone touch you?" and the child's reply is "Yes." In the first case, the important element of the child being touched was introduced by the child, whereas in the second, it originated with the adult and the child simply assented.

Both of these are examples of key statements which occur in interviews. Although the information gained is identical, the source is not. Knowing where the key statements originated is important in evaluating the weight to be given to children's statements in a sexual abuse situation. Our experience has been, in the reports and testimony of professionals who conduct interrogations, that it is often claimed that the child spoke spontaneously. However, when there is a tape available these claims are often falsified. If the source of the information is the adult, the value of the statement must be assessed cautiously.

Second, how is the information responded to? Is it accepted, rewarded, ignored, or reflected back by the interviewer? Does it cause certain interviewer behaviors to increase or decrease? What, then, happens to future statements by the child? The assumption is that the adult is in charge of the contingencies in the interview situation. We expected that behaviors such as rewards, pressure, modeling, and paraphrase should appear in relatively predictable patterns depending on statements and behaviors of children. For example, one might expect a reward such as "Good girl!" as a predictable response to a lengthy description of alleged events by a child. Children, in turn, should respond in similar ways to statements by the adults based on their perception of what the interviewer will reinforce. For example, if a child refuses to answer an interviewer's question a number of times, and is then successfully pressured by the interviewer to respond, one might expect a description, rather than another refusal.

We believe that analyses of the interrogation process in actual child sexual abuse cases offer greater clarification of what really occurs in these complex interactions than pallid laboratory simulation. Through investigating what happens in actual interviews, interview techniques can be improved.

Sample

Nine interviews were chosen from those included in this book. The tenth interview was not included because it was a play therapy session and contained no key statements by the child. The children were five males and four females, and their average age was 4.1 years old. The duration of the interrogations ranged from 15 to 50 minutes with an average of 36 minutes. A total of 15 interrogators were involved, including psychologists, social workers, a psychiatrist, relatives of the children, police officers, and a pediatrician. Four of the interviews involved more than one adult. Several of the interrogations are known to be part of a series of interviews of the same children by various investigators while others appear to be independent. It is impossible to determine the effect of interrogations preceding the taped session, therefore we cannot state to what extent the statements of the children might have been affected by their experiences prior to the session for which we have a tape.

Procedure

Categories for adults' and children's behaviors are described in the Rating Instructions at the end of this chapter. Each transcript of an interrogation was divided into first and second halves, and scored by one of the developers of the scoring system. The key statements were highlighted and it was determined whether their important elements originated with the adult or the child. Those child behaviors that preceded and followed the categories of adult pressures, reward, modeling, and paraphrase categories were tabulated. We selected only these four categories for this preliminary analysis. We also tabulated the different categories of adult behaviors that preceded and followed key statements by the children. "Preceded" and "followed" are defined as the statements directly adjacent to the categories of interest. If statements fell into more than one category, then all relevant categories were counted.

Results and Discussion

Tables 4–7 show the results of dividing the nine transcripts into first and second halves and examining where the adults' pressures, rewards, modeling, and paraphrasing occur in relation to children's statements. The tables present the frequencies with which the adult actions precede and follow each of the children's categories of statements and the percentages of the totals represented by those frequencies. The frequency of these four categories as a whole was greater in the second halves (2014) than in the first halves (1645) of the interviews.

In general, there were more pressure statements addressed by the adults to the children in the second halves (866) than in the first halves (558) of the interrogation sessions as shown in Table 4. There is not much difference between halves of the interviews in the adults' application of pressure before and after children's affirmations. In contrast, pressure was increasingly applied during the course of the interviews in regard to instances in which the children disagreed with adults' statements. The children's refusals were also surrounded by more pressure as the sessions progressed. The overall pattern could be explained as a reflection of a gradual loss of patience by the interrogators, who began to push the children harder for more descriptions and to respond more negatively to instances when the children did not provide what the adults desired.

There were slightly more rewards given in the second halves (254) than in the first halves (203) as shown in Table 5. Although adults relied on rewards far less frequently than on assertions of power through pressure (457 to 1424), the pattern may reflect the same loss of patience hypothesized for the table above. That is, the adults pushed for certain kinds of descriptions and when these occurred more frequently, rewards became more likely. Perhaps the scarcity of rewards in comparison with other interviewer behaviors made them more potent when finally earned. As the sessions progressed, rewarding statements by the adults decreased for the children's affirmations and questions, but increased for irrelevant statements. This might indicate a general encouragement of friendly interactions.

There was more modeling in the first halves (524) than in the second halves (489) as shown in Table 6. The pattern of modeling statements generally match what one would expect. Affirmative statements by the children often followed modeling by the adults (such as, "Is this what happened?" "Yes"). Modeling actions by adults surrounded children's disagreements more in the second halves of the interviews which may reflect added intensity on the part of the adults to shape children's responses as time passed. The pattern of modeling in regard to children's descriptions changed during sessions. In the first halves, modeling generally preceded descriptions, but in the second halves, modeling more often followed them. Does this suggest that modeling was likely to be used initially to prompt descriptions but later was a more corrective device?

TABLE 4
PRESSURE
BY INTERVIEWER

Child Behaviors	First Half						Second Half						Total	(%)
	Preceded by		Followed by		Total First Half	(%)	Preceded by		Followed by		Total Second Half	(%)		
Affirm	18	7%	26	9%	44	8%	35	8%	36	8%	71	8%	115	8%
Affirm-describe	1	0%	4	1%	5	1%	0	0%	5	1%	5	1%	10	1%
Affirm-contradict	0	0%	0	0%	0	0%	0	0%	0	0%	0	0%	0	0%
Diasagree	23	8%	27	9%	50	9%	50	12%	41	9%	91	11%	141	10%
Disagree-describe	2	1%	0	0%	2	0%	1	0%	6	1%	7	1%	9	1%
Disagree-contradict	0	0%	0	0%	0	0%	0	0%	0	0%	0	0%	0	0%
Description	44	16%	45	16%	89	16%	96	22%	90	21%	186	21%	275	19%
Refusal	34	13%	40	14%	74	13%	66	15%	80	18%	146	17%	220	15%
Irrelevant	50	18%	37	13%	87	16%	56	13%	69	16%	125	14%	212	15%
"Don't Know"	13	5%	23	8%	36	6%	23	5%	23	5%	46	5%	82	6%
Upset	0	0%	1	0%	1	0%	5	1%	5	1%	10	1%	11	1%
Play	3	1%	3	1%	6	1%	3	1%	0	0%	3	0%	9	1%
Move away	1	0%	0	0%	1	0%	0	0%	0	0%	0	0%	1	0%
Ask question	67	25%	61	21%	128	23%	59	14%	44	10%	103	12%	231	16%
Unscorable	15	6%	20	7%	35	6%	34	8%	39	9%	73	8%	108	8%
TOTALS:	271	100%	287	100%	558	39%	428	100%	438	100%	866	61%	1424	100%

TABLE 5
REWARDS
INTERVIEWER BEHAVIORS

Child Behaviors	First Half						Second Half						Total	
	Preceded by		Followed by		Total First Half		Preceded by		Followed by		Total Second Half		Total	
		(%)		(%)		(%)		(%)		(%)		(%)		(%)
Affirm	12	12%	20	20%	32	16%	9	7%	9	8%	18	7%	50	11%
Affirm-describe	2	2%	3	3%	5	2%	0	0%	0	0%	0	0%	5	1%
Affirm-contradict	0	0%	0	0%	0	0%	0	0%	0	0%	0	0%	0	0%
Diasagree	8	8%	6	6%	14	7%	5	4%	15	13%	20	8%	34	7%
Disagree-describe	0	0%	4	4%	4	2%	0	0%	4	3%	4	2%	8	2%
Disagree-contradict	0	0%	0	0%	0	0%	0	0%	0	0%	0	0%	0	0%
Description	25	25%	17	17%	42	21%	35	26%	21	18%	56	22%	98	21%
Refusal	14	14%	5	5%	19	9%	18	13%	10	8%	28	11%	47	10%
Irrelevant	4	4%	12	12%	16	8%	24	18%	24	20%	48	19%	64	14%
"Don't Know"	6	6%	6	6%	12	6%	9	7%	5	4%	14	6%	26	6%
Upset	1	1%	0	0%	1	0%	4	3%	1	1%	5	2%	6	1%
Play	3	3%	1	1%	4	2%	2	1%	0	0%	2	1%	6	1%
Move away	0	0%	1	1%	1	0%	0	0%	0	0%	0	0%	1	0%
Ask question	19	19%	22	22%	41	20%	17	13%	13	11%	30	12%	71	16%
Unscorable	7	7%	5	5%	12	6%	11	8%	18	15%	29	11%	41	9%
TOTALS:	101	100%	102	100%	203	44%	134	100%	120	100%	254	56%	457	100%

TABLE 6
MODELING
BY INTERVIEWER

Child Behaviors	First Half						Second Half						Total	(%)
	Preceded by	(%)	Followed by	(%)	Total First Half	(%)	Preceded by	(%)	Followed by	(%)	Total Second Half	(%)	Total	(%)
Affirm	21	9%	34	12%	55	10%	22	9%	29	12%	51	10%	106	10%
Affirm-describe	0	0%	4	1%	4	1%	2	1%	1	0%	3	1%	7	1%
Affirm-contradict	0	0%	0	0%	0	0%	0	0%	0	0%	0	0%	0	0%
Diasagree	19	8%	18	6%	37	7%	23	9%	35	14%	58	12%	95	9%
Disagree-describe	2	1%	3	1%	5	1%	3	1%	3	1%	6	1%	11	1%
Disagree-contradict	0	0%	0	0%	0	0%	1	0%	0	0%	1	0%	1	0%
Description	33	14%	80	28%	113	22%	73	30%	50	20%	123	25%	236	23%
Refusal	27	11%	25	9%	52	10%	18	7%	40	16%	58	12%	110	11%
Irrelevant	21	9%	14	5%	35	7%	33	14%	18	7%	51	10%	86	8%
"Don't Know"	17	7%	19	7%	36	7%	17	7%	15	6%	32	7%	68	7%
Upset	0	0%	0	0%	0	0%	8	3%	5	2%	13	3%	13	1%
Play	3	1%	5	2%	8	2%	0	0%	0	0%	0	0%	8	1%
Move away	0	0%	0	0%	0	0%	0	0%	0	0%	0	0%	0	0%
Ask question	81	34%	74	26%	155	30%	29	12%	21	9%	50	10%	205	20%
Unscorable	14	6%	10	3%	24	5%	14	6%	29	12%	43	9%	67	7%
TOTALS:	238	100%	286	100%	524	52%	243	100%	246	100%	489	48%	1013	100%

TABLE 7
PARAPHRASE
BY INTERVIEWER

Child Behaviors	First Half						Second Half						Total	
	Preceded by		Followed by		Total First Half		Preceded by		Followed by		Total Second Half		Total	(%)
				(%)		(%)						(%)		
Affirm	20	12%	43	23%	63	18%	31	15%	54	27%	85	21%	148	19%
Affirm-describe	4	2%	2	1%	6	2%	1	0%	1	1%	2	0%	8	1%
Affirm-contradict	0	0%	0	0%	0	0%	0	0%	0	0%	0	0%	0	0%
Diasagree	13	8%	10	5%	23	6%	29	14%	45	23%	74	18%	97	13%
Disagree-describe	2	1%	0	0%	2	1%	1	0%	3	2%	4	1%	6	1%
Disagree-contradict	0	0%	2	1%	2	1%	0	0%	1	1%	1	0%	3	0%
Description	91	53%	57	30%	148	41%	92	44%	38	19%	130	32%	278	36%
Refusal	8	5%	12	6%	20	6%	9	4%	6	3%	15	4%	35	5%
Irrelevant	12	7%	21	11%	33	9%	11	5%	12	6%	23	6%	56	7%
"Don't Know"	5	3%	10	5%	15	4%	12	6%	10	5%	22	5%	37	5%
Upset	1	1%	0	0%	1	0%	0	0%	1	1%	1	0%	2	0%
Play	0	0%	2	1%	2	1%	0	0%	0	0%	0	0%	2	0%
Move away	0	0%	2	1%	2	1%	0	0%	0	0%	0	0%	2	0%
Ask question	12	7%	19	10%	31	9%	11	5%	14	7%	25	6%	56	7%
Unscorable	5	3%	7	4%	12	3%	10	5%	13	7%	23	6%	35	5%
TOTALS:	173	100%	187	100%	360	47%	207	100%	198	100%	405	53%	765	100%

Table 7 indicates that the adults paraphrased children's statements more often in the second halves of the interviews (405) than in the first halves (360). Paraphrases appear more likely to have followed rather than preceded children's affirmations, whereas the reverse is true for descriptions. This may represent attempts by the adults to expand on relatively brief answers to questions in the case of affirmations and to elicit more complete descriptions. The paraphrasing of children's disagreements increased during interviews, which may also reflect the adults' efforts to increase the clarity of the children's statements.

Overall, the children made 1,857 scoreable statements. Of these, 451, or 24 percent, were considered key statements containing important information for constructing allegations of sexual abuse. The key statements fell almost entirely into the children's categories of affirmations and descriptions, as one might expect. Table 8 shows the distribution of the key statements during the interrogations and whether the important content originated with the adults or with the children.

Table 8 reveals that in the 158 of 451 key statements by children, the important elements within those statements originated with the adults. That is, 35 percent of the important elements in the children's accusations were first stated by the interrogators. This tendency of the adults to lead the children increased as the interviews progressed. In that this was the first official interview in only half (4) of the interviews, and there is an indeterminate amount of unrecorded, informal questioning by parents and others, this is likely an underestimate.

Table 9 shows that questions were more likely to precede children's key statements than to follow them (particularly closed questions). Pressure and modeling were also more likely to precede key statements. But rewards and paraphrases were more likely to follow the children's key statements. The use of aids such as drawings or dolls appears to have been less productive in eliciting key statements from first to second halves of the interrogations.

In the nine cases that were analyzed further, the interactions between adult interrogators and child witnesses suggest a meaningful pattern. Young children are not good at constructing detailed, extensive testimonies in response to general, open-ended questions. As a result, the adults become increasingly active. The timing of the adult behaviors in relation to children's behaviors suggests it is adult behavior that causes the child's behavior. It is likely that the adults have caused, increased, and

TABLE 8
KEY STATEMENTS OF CHILDREN

Child Behaviors	First Made by Interviewer		Direct Statement by child		Totals	(%)
First Half						
Affirm	31	20%	24	8%	55	12%
Affirm-describe	8	5%	1	0%	9	2%
Affirm-contradict	0	0%	0	0%	0	0%
Diasagree	2	1%	4	1%	6	1%
Disagree-describe	0	0%	1	0%	1	0%
Disagree-contradict	0	0%	0	0%	0	0%
Description	22	14%	102	35%	124	27%
Refusal	0	0%	0	0%	0	0%
Irrelevant	1	1%	1	0%	2	0%
Don't Know	1	1%	2	1%	3	1%
Upset	0	0%	0	0%	0	0%
Play	0	0%	0	0%	0	0%
Move away	0	0%	0	0%	0	0%
Ask question	0	0%	2	1%	2	0%
Unscorable	0	0%	0	0%	0	0%
Total First Half:	65	41%	137	47%	202	45%
Second Half:						
Affirm	44	28%	34	12%	78	17%
Affirm-describe	0	0%	1	0%	1	0%
Affirm-contradict	0	0%	1	0%	1	0%
Diasagree	5	3%	21	7%	26	6%
Disagree-describe	1	1%	3	1%	4	1%
Disagree-contradict	0	0%	0	0%	0	0%
Description	42	27%	92	31%	134	30%
Refusal	0	0%	0	0%	0	0%
Irrelevant	0	0%	0	0%	0	0%
Don't Know	0	0%	0	0%	0	0%
Upset	0	0%	0	0%	0	0%
Play	0	0%	0	0%	0	0%
Move away	0	0%	1	0%	1	0%
Ask question	1	1%	2	1%	3	1%
Unscorable	0	0%	1	0%	1	0%
Total Second Half:	93	59%	156	53%	249	55%
Total Interview:	158	100%	293	100%	451	100%

TABLE 9

INTERVIEWER BEHAVIORS IN RELATION TO
KEY STATEMENTS BY CHILDREN

Interviewer Behaviors	First Half						Second Half						Total (%)	
	Preceded by		Followed by		Total First Half		Preceded by		Followed by		Total First Half			
Open	56	22%	43	18%	99	20%	65	21%	57	20%	122	21%	221	20%
Closed	82	33%	60	25%	142	29%	104	34%	73	25%	177	30%	319	29%
Combination	24	10%	2	1%	26	5%	23	8%	5	2%	28	5%	54	5%
Pressure	15	6%	9	4%	24	5%	33	11%	22	8%	55	9%	79	7%
Reward	1	0%	9	4%	10	2%	1	0%	6	2%	7	1%	17	2%
Modeling	15	6%	6	2%	21	4%	31	10%	8	3%	39	7%	60	6%
Discussion	0	0%	1	0%	1	0%	0	0%	0	0%	0	0%	1	0%
Irrelevant	0	0%	2	1%	2	0%	0	0%	1	0%	1	0%	3	0%
Use of Aids	15	6%	8	3%	23	5%	2	1%	1	0%	3	1%	26	2%
Ambiguous	7	3%	29	12%	36	7%	9	3%	30	10%	39	7%	75	7%
Paraphrase	36	14%	71	29%	107	22%	36	12%	84	29%	120	20%	227	21%
Unscorable	0	0%	1	0%	1	0%	0	0%	2	1%	2	0%	3	0%
TOTALS:	251	100%	241	100%	492	45%	304	100%	289	100%	593	55%	1085	100%

shaped children's statements that could then be used in support of the abuse accusations.

IMPLICATIONS FOR INTERVIEWS
OF CHILD WITNESSES

These analyses do not prove that contamination has occurred but they point to where it might enter. They also call for further study of actual child interrogations or situations that closely approximate them. In the absence of any other data based upon real world interrogations, this analysis demonstrates the risk in relying upon interrogations as they are now done. Adult social influence must be considered in evaluating the weight given to results of interrogations of children.

Other professionals are recognizing the problem of suggestive and rehearsed interviews and the importance of a videotaped documentation. DeLipsey and James (1988) report that the original purpose of videotaping in Texas was to protect child witnesses by providing an alternative to the child testifying in court. However, these authors soon realized that videotaping protected the rights of the accused as well. They have observed numerous example of bribery and coercion during their review of videotaped interviews. Raskin and Yuille (in press) state that "a videotape is the only means whereby the procedures and data obtained during the interview can be fully documented."

Studies on eyewitness testimony, memory, and suggestibility of children use a much smaller proportion of leading questions than we found in the tapes we analyzed. In the real world children being interviewed are given much more error-inducing information than in laboratory research. There is a much higher level of coercion, pressure, and reward for responding in the desired manner. In tapes we have reviewed children were told they couldn't play with toys (or go to the bathroom, or go home, or get to see their parents again, or get a treat) until they gave the desired response. In one tape, the interviewer asked the child the same question 18 times and each time the child either denied or did not respond. In a day care case, the interviewer told several children that another child had already told him about being abused. But when tapes of these earlier sessions were examined, such statements were not there. The interrogator lied to the children. Children who did not affirm abuse are called "fraidy cat" or told "you must be stupid." Children who made statements about abuse were told that they were brave, courageous, and that their parents would be proud of them.

Our analysis of actual interrogations in sexual abuse cases shows that the real world is much tougher on children than is the research laboratory. Even research studies that attempt to duplicate real life situations fail to come close to the amount of pressure and coercion put on children in the tapes we have analyzed. Research manipulations that used interview procedures on the tapes we have studied would be unethical. Therefore, the applicability and generalizability of the research studies is limited. The findings of the research studies most likely greatly underestimates the effects of adult behaviors in actual interviews of children. (The problem of ecological validity is acknowledged by several researchers in Ceci, Toglia & Ross, 1987.)

While these findings do not invalidate the children's statements, they raise serious questions about adult influence on children's behavior. The interrogation process cannot be accepted as neutral, objective, or unbiased. In each case, what has actually been done with a child by all of the people who have talked to the child, including other children, must be carefully scrutinized as a possible source of error. From our analysis we conclude that it is not possible to interrogate children to get to the truth unless every effort is made to control contaminating influences. If this is not done, there can be no confidence that truth is available.

RATING INSTRUCTIONS

The following are examples of target behaviors which you are to identify. You will be asked to observe audio- and videotaped interviews, and note the interactions between child and interviewer.

On the transcripts provided, rate each statement, using one or more of any categories which apply. Use the following examples as your guideline. When you observe a behavior, write the number or letter for the behavior you observe after the appropriate statement on the transcript.

Interviewer Variables

1) Open questions

1a) Open-objective questions or statements to which the child can respond spontaneously, based upon his or her own personal experience. No information is provided by the interviewer, and no attempt is made to lead or influence the child's response.

Examples:

> Where were you when that happened?
> What happened next?
> How did you feel?
> What were you wearing that day?

Here the child is providing the information free of suggestions or potentially false information.

1b) Open-suggestive questions. These questions are open in nature, but are suggestive or leading in that they may provide or imply information which may in fact be incorrect, and may pertain to information or events to which the child has not previously referred.*

Examples:

> Who else was there? (There may not have been others present.)
> Whose house were you at when the big person touched you? (The child may not have been at a house.)
> What did the other big person do to you? (The other person may not have done anything.)
> How big was the bed that was in the room? (When there was no previous mention of a bed.)

2) Closed questions

2a) Closed-objective questions or statements in which some information may be supplied to the child by the interviewer. Minimal response (such as "yes" or "no") is required.

Examples:

> Does your daddy ever spank you?
> Was there anyone else there?
> Was there a bed in the room?
> Did the other person do anything?

2b) Closed-suggestive questions or statements which supply information to the child that may be incorrect or pertain to information to which the child has not previously referred. Minimal response is required. Questions in this category are leading or suggestive questions.*

Examples:

> Does he hurt you?
> Does this always happen in your room?
> Has it ever happened in daddy's room?
> Was it you that she caught him doing it to?

Here, the interviewer, *not* the child, provides most of the information.

3) Combination questions.

3a) Combination-objective questions. Questions which contain elements of both closed and open-ended questions. They may begin as open questions and end as closed questions, or vice versa. In addition, combination questions may ask for more than one type of response, and may give conflicting or confusing messages. Questions with multiple options (this or that) are also included here.

Examples:

> What else, (open) did he touch you again? (closed)
> Where, (open) down there? (closed)
> What kind of games did you play (open), good or bad ones (closed)?
> What room were you in (open), the bedroom? (closed)
> Did it happen at school or at home?

3b) As above, but leading or suggestive in nature. (For example, in a question with multiple option, only two of several possible alternatives are given.)*

4) Questions or statements which put the child on the spot and coerce or pressure him or her to respond as expected. Questions in this category demand a response and may contain stated or implied threats. Commands given by the interviewer should be included in this category. Nonverbal messages can also be used for this purpose.

Examples:

> All of the other children talked to us and they felt better.
> Last time, you told me that they hurt you. Is that true, or not?
> If you don't tell, you will feel yucky inside.
> If you don't talk to us, your mommy will be very disappointed in you.
> Tell us what you told your mommy.
> Answer my question right now!
> We can't play with the game until we finish.
> It's important.
> We need you to tell us so other children won't get hurt.
> You can't go outside until you finish telling me!
> Show me what happened with the dolls.

Nonverbal behaviors in this category can include using a cold or neutral tone of voice, moving away from the child, avoiding the child's eyes, and ignoring the child's responses or questions.

5) Various rewards—verbal, nonverbal, and material—which the child receives for responding as expected.

Examples:

> You're a good talker.
> Good — That's just right.
> You're so brave to tell us all of this!
> Mommy will be so proud that you told us.
> After you talk to us, then you can have an ice cream cone.

Nonverbal rewards can include smiling, touching, or moving closer to the child, head nods, and changing from a cold or neutral voice to a warm voice.

6) Other behaviors.

6a) Modeling or teaching by the interviewer. (Often used in conjunction with dolls, puppets, drawings, or books.) For example, the interviewer may identify the ages, gender, or identity of the dolls and instruct the child to demonstrate events.

Examples:

> This is boy doll.
> These dolls have all of the parts, if you want to take their clothes off.
> Pretend that this is you, and this is your daddy.

6b) Discussing case with parents or guardians while the child is present. The parents may be asked to provide details about the events while the child is present. If the child has not provided this information, these statements are also rated as modeling.

6c) Random, "irrelevant" play behavior, or statements and questions which have no direct relation to the focus of the interview. These statements or behaviors are difficult to rate, except in the context of the interview. For example, "What did you do over the weekend," may be rated as an open question (1a) if the child has mentioned that significant events occurred during that time. Irrelevant statements should also be rated as questions, rewards, etc., if appropriate.

Examples:

> Do you have any pets?
> What did you do over the weekend?
> Let's just play checkers now.
> How are you today?
> Did you like the show?
> This puppet has orange hair.

7) Use of interview aids during sessions. Life-like dolls, puppets, drawings, and books are used during interviews to elicit responses from the children. In sections involving the use of the aids, use the numbered categories (1–10) to record your observations on the rating sheet, as well as labeling with #7. Remember to include #6a in your rating if modeling or teaching has occurred. For audiotapes or transcript-only interviews, be careful not to use this category unless the aid is being referred to directly.

8) Ambiguous questions or statements which have more than one possible meaning or implication. Use this category to rate stylistic speech patterns, such as "Okay," and "Uh huh," following children's statements. This category is also used for inaudible or unfinished statements consisting of more than one word.

9) Repeating, clarifying, or paraphrasing of a question or statement given by the child which does not change, question, or add to the message intended by the child. This technique is used in many interviews to facilitate understanding for the listener. In many cases, paraphrases also serve as questions. If this is the case, use the appropriate rating for the question as well.

10) Questions or statements given by the interviewer which relate to the interview, but do not fall into any of the above categories. This category is used to score the statements about the logistics of the interview. For example, statements about the time, date, location, and references to audiovisual equipment fall into this category. This category is also used for inaudible or ambiguous statements of one word or less.

*These subdivisions of Open, Closed, and Combination questions are used in the individual analyses only, and are not listed separately in the tables shown in this volume.

Child Variables

In rating the children's responses, use the following categories as your guideline:

A) Affirming a question or statement.

a1) The child agrees with or confirms a question or statement given by the interviewer.

Examples:

Yes, that's right.
Right, just like that.
Yes, that's true.

a2) The child affirms a question or statement, and then goes on to describe the event.

Examples:

Yes, and then they took us in the car.
Right, and we played Ring Around the Rosie, too.
Uh huh. It was fun when we did that!
Yeah, that's true, and it really hurt.
Yup, and the other kids did the same thing.

a3) The child affirms a question or statement, and then goes on to contradict what he or she has already said. Since more than one statement may be involved, rate each statement separately and then include this category as well.

Examples:

Yep, just like that. Well—no, maybe it was not so big as that, and blue instead of red.
Sure, just like you said . . . well, not really, I was just pretending.
Yeah, just like I told you yesterday . . . uh, well, I guess I wasn't really telling the truth—here's what really happened.

B) Refuting a question or statement.

b1) The child disagrees with or negates a question or statement given by the interviewer.

Examples:

No, that never happened.
No, not like that.
That's not true.
Nope, no way!

b2) The child negates or confirms a question or statement, and then goes on to describe an event.

Examples:

No, it wasn't him, it was the other one—the one with red hair.
Uh uh, we never did that, but sometimes we went on picnics and stuff.
Nope, not as big as that.
No, never at night, only during the day.

b3) The child denies a question or statement, and then goes on to contradict what he or she has already said. Since more than one statement may be involved, rate each statement separately and then include this category as well.

Examples:

> No, not that kind of game. Oh, I guess we did play that one once or twice.
> Uh uh, never! Well except once when we were in the bathroom, but it was no big deal.
> No, I didn't say that. Well, maybe I did and I forgot. I guess I did say that.

C) Describing an event. The child volunteers information or responds at length about the circumstances of a particular event.

Examples:

> He took my hand and then we went into that room.
> We all played house until it was time to go.
> It was like this . . .
> All of the other children were outside on the playground, and I was inside.

D) The child does not wish to answer a question, and uses verbal messages to indicate this.

d1) Refusal to talk.

Examples:

> I don't want to say.
> I'm done talking now.
> I can't/won't tell you.
> I want to go now.
> I hate you.
> Go away and leave me alone.

d2) Irrelevant talk. The child may change the subject, and address something other than the statement or question given by the interviewer.

Examples:

> This one has green hair.
> I had bologna for lunch.
> You got a big box of toys over there.

d3) The child responds to a question or statement by saying, "I don't know," or "I don't remember."

E) The child does not wish to answer a question, and uses nonverbal messages to indicate this.

e1) The child may ignore the question by becoming visibly upset, crying, and whining.

e2) The child may ignore the question by engaging in "unfocused" or independent playing.

e3) The child may ignore the question by moving away from the interviewer, or by leaving the room entirely.

F) The child *asks* a question of the interviewer or addresses a command to the interviewer.

Examples:

You do it.
Can I have that doll?
Put that away.
I want that one now.
What did you say?

G) Ambiguous or unclassifiable statements given by the child. Use this category for inaudible statements of one word or less.

Chapter 3

GRANDMA GETS A CHILD

One of the most popular manuals on how to deal with accusations of child sexual abuse contains the following definition of "standard crisis intervention theory" applied to investigative interviewing of children:

> In many cases, especially where the perpetrator is not a parent, investigative and therapeutic interviewing can, in effect, be done simultaneously, so long as the interviewer is prepared to utilize standard crisis intervention theory. This includes observing the child's emotional style, establishing interviewer credibility, developing and then proceeding with the "request concept" and assisting and supporting the child in remembering facts and details that will aid the prosecution to establish a case against the perpetrator (Sgroi, 1978, p. 137).

The beliefs of the person doing the simultaneous work of investigation and therapy are a powerful determinant of what comes out of the interviews. When the goal of the interview is to produce facts that will aid the prosecution, the decision has already been made that abuse occurred. There is a set to believe accusations immediately and attend only to whatever affirms the prior belief.

Entering an interview with the aim of aiding the prosecution not only prejudices the outcomes, it also leaves the child protection, investigative and prosecutorial systems open to manipulation by unscrupulous or disturbed individuals. There are many opportunities for mischief in a system biased toward credulity, rush to judgment, and punitiveness.

We occasionally see situations that developed primarily out of the needs of emotionally disturbed individuals who were able to manipulate the entire system of child protection workers, law enforcement officials, county attorneys, and judges. The system is vulnerable to manipulation by complaining adults who may threaten agencies and prosecutors with publicity, political pressure, and the displeasure of groups organized around eliminating child molestation. The way the system is set up rewards and reinforces the making of an accusation. Persons making the accusation get acceptance of their claims, attention and support from a cadre of authoritative individuals, free legal advice and services, free therapy, financial support from welfare funds, and punishment of the person they seek to damage. In some instances the rewards include possession of a child.

The vulnerability of the system to manipulation is increased when a complaining adult takes advantage of different jurisdictions, the lack of communication between different county or state authorities, and professional jealousies or turf conflicts between counties, courts, states, or other political entities. The simple expedient of moving from one county to another may prolong the process for years while each county's agencies fumble about. If a competent worker in one county becomes cautious and questions the complaining adult more closely, a geographical move will bring a new person into the case who may be more susceptible to manipulation. Routine, habit, large case loads, overwork, and possibly relief at getting rid of a troublesome case can reduce the likelihood of effective communication between differing jurisdictions or agencies. We have observed lack of cooperation, disagreement, and even hostility between state police and local police, police and child protection, physicians and psychologists, state police and county sheriffs, and judges with other judges.

In the interview below, a grandmother manipulated the system successfully to get custody of her grandchild.

BACKGROUND

Mandy Schultz was an emotionally and physically abused child. Her parents were divorced when she was eight years old. She was so traumatized by the bitter divorce and her mother's constant hostility to her father that she did not want to go to school. That's when the whippings started. Her mother, Irene, whipped her to force her to go to school. Mandy would go, tell the nurse she was sick, and could then lie on a cot in a quiet room. Until three weeks short of her eighteenth birthday, she was beaten with switches, belts, and hairbrushes. Years later, the school guidance counselor described how Mandy would talk to him and cry about her situation at home, describing the beatings and being threatened by her mother with a shotgun. Finally, when she was nineteen, she married Donald Barnes, a young man who was twenty-two years old at the time of the marriage.

Donald and Mandy moved to another state and both got jobs. Their son, Billy, was born a year later. Mandy's mother, Irene, was delighted by Billy and for a short time the relationship between mother and daughter seemed improved. But it soon became apparent that Irene's interest was in the child, Billy, and not in her daughter. She was heard to say to various people that Mandy wasn't capable of properly raising a child and that she would take the child away any way she could. However, on the surface there was an uneasy truce between Mandy and her mother, and Billy spent much time visiting his grandmother.

In 1985, following continual conflicts, Mandy and Donald were divorced. The couple had joint custody of Billy and both saw him frequently. He also spent much time with his grandmother and in July 1986, Donald left Billy with Irene while he went on vacation. During this time, Irene made the charges of sexual abuse against Donald.

An unusual situation in this case developed because the grandmother resided in one state and the parents lived in another. When Irene first made the report of sexual abuse, she did it in the state she lived in. The investigation and the interrogation of the child took place in that state, not the state the parents lived in. This created jurisdictional issues and confused the whole situation. Another aspect of the case was the behavior of the grandmother, Irene, who had a long history of psychiatric illness, treatment with psychotropic medication, and hostile and aggressive behavior. She had had difficulties with coworkers on jobs and with her neighbors. She complained about older teenagers in her neighborhood sexually abusing children and reported them, but no charges were ever filed.

The day after Irene reported that Donald had sexually abused Billy, a taped interview was made. In this interview, Billy was interrogated by Trina Smith from social services and Deputy Scott Lipton from the Sheriff's Department. Irene was present and participated in the interview. Irene then persuaded the court to give her temporary custody of the child. Donald was arrested on criminal charges and ordered not to see his son. From that time on, Irene allowed Mandy to see her son only a few times. Although Mandy originally was slated as a prosecution witness, she sought out Donald's attorney because of the continuing difficulties she had with her mother in terms of seeing her son and getting information as to what was happening.

Deputy Lipton claims about the interview that "The child had a believable statement about the alleged molestation. It was not in any way coerced." However, the transcript shows something entirely different.

For several pages, Deputy Lipton asks Billy to "tell me about your Daddy." This is repeated over and over but Billy says nothing about abuse. Billy mentions a camera and Lipton asks a series of questions about what kind of pictures his daddy takes of him. It appears that Lipton is looking for statements about pornographic pictures. But nothing useful is obtained and Trina Smith, the social worker, brings out the anatomical dolls. Billy makes no statements about abuse.

Halfway through the interview, Trina Smith and Deputy Lipton change their strategy and begin asking Billy to tell them what he told his grandmother about what he did to his daddy. Billy says nothing about abuse. Then they ask him to tell about sucking on Daddy's wiener. Billy still says nothing about abuse.

They ask him to demonstrate with the dolls and put increasing pressure on him to tell ("Please? You can do it, can't you? Why? Don't know how? Or you're afraid to. Hmm. You know how. You're a big boy. It'd really help me out a lot if you'd show me").

Irene orders Billy to "Get up here now and say something," and to "Tell them what you told me." But Billy says nothing about abuse. He plays and changes the subject or denies what they are asking.

Finally the three interrogators turn the tape recorder off for an indeterminate length of time. (In Donald Barnes's criminal trial, Deputy Lipton testified that it was off for 15 minutes.) Lipton takes Billy into the bedroom and talks to him alone. The tape recorder is turned back on and the interrogation continues. Billy is now saying what they want. He agrees that his daddy sucked on his pee-pee and his butt, that he sucked his dad's wiener and that his daddy peed in his mouth. Deputy Lipton asks, "Did he say not to tell anybody?"

Billy replies, "He said to tell everybody."

This, obviously, is not want Lipton wants to hear. Now, for the first time in the interview, Billy is told that what is really wanted is the truth and a lecture about truth and lies is given.

The others come back in and Billy repeats the statements Lipton has finally coerced. After a few minutes the tape recorder is turned off. Immediately before this, there is a confusing babble of voices that sound happy and someone makes a remark about getting all of the facts.

Three-fourths (76%) of the total interviewer behaviors fell into the error-inducing categories.

INTERVIEW

Interviewers: Trina Smith, social worker, Department of Public Welfare, and Deputy Scott Lipton, County Sheriff's Department. Also present, Irene Schultz, grandmother.

Child: Billy Barnes

Trina Smith = Soc Wkr; Scott Lipton = Deputy; Irene Schultz = Grandma

Deputy: Tell me about your daddy.[4, 6A]

Billy: . . . [G]

Deputy: Billy, tell me about your daddy.[4, 6A]

Billy: I don't want to.[D1]

Deputy: Is he a big man?[2B]

Billy: Yeah, he can beat up anybody.[A2]

Deputy: Is that right.[8] Think he could beat up my daddy?[2A]

Billy: What?[F]

Deputy: Think he could beat up my daddy?[2A]

Billy: Yeah.[A1]

Deputy: Your daddy's a big man.[9]

Billy: My daddy could beat up anybody.[C]

Deputy: He play games with you?[2B]

Billy: No, I don't got no games.[B2]

Deputy: What?[1A]

Billy: I don't got no games.[C]

Deputy: I . . . but I'm talking about catch ball.[6C]

Billy: I can't catch nothing.[D2]

Deputy: Throw rocks.[6C] You live in the city?[2B]

Billy: On West 45th.[C]

Deputy: West 45th.[9]

Billy: What?[F]

Deputy: How about West 55th?[2B] You know all about that, don't you?[2B]

Billy: Where that?[F]

Deputy: West.[9] Who says funny?[6C] Billy, you said funny.[9] How?[1A]

Billy: Uh(?).[D2]

[Break in tape]

Billy: Evansville.[C] Evansville.[C]

Deputy: How old are you?[1A]

Billy: Four.[C]

Deputy: Four?[2A, 9]

Billy: Four.[C]

Deputy: Billy.[8] Billy.[8] Tell me about your daddy.[4, 6A]

Billy: Why?[F]

Deputy: 'Cause I want to know about your daddy.[4, 6A] I want to know how he treats you.[6A, 4]

Billy: He treats me bad.[C]

Deputy: Why's that?[1A]

Billy: 'Cause he always . . . 'cause he whips me.[C]

Deputy: Whips you.[9] Why's he whip you?[1A]

Billy: 'Cause I done something bad[C]

Deputy: Oh.[8] He whips you 'cause your bad.[9] What else does he do to you?[1B] Hmm?[1B]

Billy: Wanna play a game?[F, D1]

Deputy: Not now.[8]

[Noise, banging]

Deputy: Hey, Billy.[8] Billy.[8]

Billy: What?[F]

Deputy: You ever see your daddy without any clothes on?[2B, 6A]

Billy: What?[F]

Deputy: Did you ever see your daddy without any clothes on?[2B, 6A]

Billy: Yeah.[A1]

Deputy: You have.[9] You remember when that was?[2A] Look at that.[6C] Ripped (?) my tie.[6C]

Billy: It's not ripped.[D2]

Deputy: Please stop.[4] Billy.[4]

Billy: I got to take the sticker off.[D2]

Deputy: Oh.[8] I appreciate that.[6C] I don't like.[8]

Billy: Look it![D2]

Deputy: Hey, Billy.[4]

Billy: Here's something.[D2]

Deputy: Hey, Billy.[4]

Billy: This is my camera.[D2]

Deputy: Oh.[8] Okay.[8]

Billy: Here's your camera?[F]

Deputy: I got a little bitty camera.[6C] You got a big one.[6C]

Billy: Ha.[D2] Cheese.[D2]

Deputy: Cheese (laughter).[6C]

Billy: Say, "cheese," now.[D2] Say "cheese."[D2] Smile.[D2] Say "cheese."[D2]

Deputy: Hey, Billy.[4]

Billy: What?[F]

Deputy: I want to talk to you about your daddy.[4, 6A]

Billy: Picture.[D2]

Deputy: Hey, Billy.[4] Tell me about your daddy.[4, 6A]
Billy: Noooo.[D1]

Deputy: Please.[4] If I say pretty please, will you tell me about your daddy?[2B, 5, 4]
Billy: Noooo.[D1]

Deputy: Why?[1A]
Billy: What's that you're doing? (Lego blocks)[F]

Deputy: Just building something.[6C]
Billy: Looky.[D2] There's the roof.[D2]

Deputy: Hey, Billy.[4]
Billy: Chimney, windows.[D2] What?[F] Duck.[D2]

Deputy: Tell me about your daddy.[4, 6A]
Billy: Duck.[D2]

Deputy: Billy![4]
Billy: No.[D1] Duck.[D2]

Deputy: Billy![4]
Billy: It's a duck.[D2] See, he's standing up.[D2] Da, da, da.[D2]

Deputy: Eh, eh, eh.[6C]
Billy: . . . [G]

Deputy: Hey, Billy.[4] Billy.[4] How come you don't want to tell me about your daddy?[1A]
Billy: I just don't.[D1]

Deputy: Why?[1A] Billy![4] Why?[1A]
Billy: . . . [G]

Deputy: (indecipherable)[8]

Billy:	We was driving around.[C] Raining on my pants.[C] Everywhere on me.[C] And my shirt, too, and on my flip-flops.[C]

Soc Wkr: Billy, when you're with your daddy, who gets you ready for bed?[1A]

Billy: My dad.[C]

Soc Wkr: Yeah?[8] Do you take a bath before you go to bed?[2B]

Billy: Sometimes.[C]

Soc Wkr: Sometimes?[2A, 9] Are you a big boy?[2A] Can you take a bath by yourself?[2A] Or do you need your daddy to help you?[3A]

Billy: I can take a bath all by myself.[C]

Soc Wkr: Good for you![5]

Billy: Coo, coo, coo.[D2]

Soc Wkr: Does anybody ever help you?[2A]

Billy: Nobody.[B1]

Soc Wkr: Nobody?[2A, 9]

Billy: I'm gonna put (banging).[D2] I got a Garfield bubble bath.[D2]

Soc Wkr: You do![6C] Do you get to splash around as long as you want?[6C]

Billy: I am allowed to go down.[D2] I'm allowed to go down to (Evansville? basement?)[D2] Camera.[D2] Cam, cam, camera, cam camera.[D2] This is my camera.[D2] I got to make another.[D2] This is camera.[D2] They make cameras here, man.[D2] (Blocks falling on the floor) Camera, camera, camera, camera, camera, camera, camera (sing-song).[D2]

Soc Wkr: I want to know how your daddy treats you *bad* other than spanking.[4, 6A]

Billy: Here, Grandma, here's your camera.[D2] Take a picture.[D2] Say, "cheese."[D2] (Noise) Take a picture of me, now.[D2] Know what?[F] I'm going to get some bullets for my gun.[D2] Hum.[D2]

Deputy: Your daddy got a camera?[2A]

Billy: Yeah.[A1]

Deputy: He take pictures of you?[2A]

Billy: I took pictures of him.[C]

Deputy: Oh, you did.[9] He takes pictures of you, huh?[2B] I bet he's got them all over the house.[6A]

Billy: What?[F]

Deputy: I bet he's got pictures of you all over the house.[6A]

[Garbled-whispering]

Billy: He got?[F]

Deputy: Sometimes these don't stick together too good.[6C]

Billy: Nope.[D2]

Deputy: Hey, Billy, your daddy ever take pictures of you?[2A]

Billy: Sometimes.[C]

Deputy: What were you doing when he takes pictures of you?[1B]

Billy: (indecipherable) camera's (indecipherable).[G] You wasn't supposed to a messed your camera up.[D2]

Soc Wkr: I didn't know when I messed my camera up.[6C] When your daddy takes pictures of you, does he have you (indecipherable)?[2B]

Billy: This is an airplane, watch.[D2]

Soc Wkr: Does he have you play cheese?[6C]

Billy: No.[B1]

Soc Wkr: No?[2A, 9]

Billy: This could be a camera, watch.[D2]

Soc Wkr: Tell us some of the times he'd taken pictures of you.[4]

Billy: Take a picture![F]

Soc Wkr: Tell us how many times your daddy's ... your daddy's taken pictures of you.[4]

Billy: What?[F]

Soc Wkr:	Tell us some of the times your daddy's taken pictures of you.[4] What were you doing special that he wanted to take a picture of?[1B]
Billy:	You want this camera?[F]
Soc Wkr:	No, I want you to answer my question.[4] What were you doing special that he wanted to take a picture of?[1B]
Billy:	He took a picture of (garbled).[G] (indecipherable) got put on (indecipherable).[G]
Soc Wkr:	When he's taking pictures of you, Billy, did you have your clothes on or did you have your clothes off?[3A, 6A]
Billy:	On.[C]
Soc Wkr:	On?[2A, 9]
Billy:	See this?[F] Grandma?[F] I got a watch.[D2] Got to get some more pieces first.[D2] Look what I did.[D2]
Deputy:	Put the blocks down.[8]
Soc Wkr:	Now, Billy, does your daddy ever ask you to play games that you don't want to play?[2B, 6A]
Billy:	He never asks me to play games.[C]
Soc Wkr:	He doesn't![9, 4] You have all those toys there, he doesn't ask you to play with him?[2B, 4]
Billy:	He never wants to play.[C] With me ever again . . . ever.[C]
Soc Wkr:	Never again?[2A, 9] Never again.[9] Since when?[1A]
Billy:	'Cause I have another friend to play with now.[C]
Deputy:	Who's that?[1A]
Billy:	Jo Jo.[C]
Soc Wkr:	Jo Jo?[2A, 9] Jo Jo live real nearby?[2B]
Billy:	Not at my house.[C]
Soc Wkr:	Not at your house?[2A, 9]
Billy:	Nope.[B1]

Soc Wkr: Where does Jo Jo live?[1A]

Billy: At his mom's house.[C]

Soc Wkr: At his mom's house?[2A, 9]

Billy: Look what I did.[D2] Look it![D2] A . . . [G] What're you doing?[F]

Deputy: Have no idea?[6C] None.[6C] Hey, Billy.[4]

Billy: What?[F]

Deputy: Tell me about your daddy.[4, 6A]

Billy: I don't want to.[D1]

Deputy: Why not?[1A]

Billy: I got eight cartons full.[D2]

Deputy: Hey, Billy.[4]

Billy: What?[F] You gotta have the other words, the other pieces.[D2] The other pieces.[D2] What did you do with the other piece of this?[F]

Soc Wkr: You mean, over there.[6C] Like a wheel you mean?[6C]

Billy: No, other piece that I put on the wheel.[D2]

Soc Wkr: I don't know what it looks like.[6C]

Billy: Where's at?[F]

Deputy: Billy, can I help you find out?[6C]

Soc Wkr: (indecipherable)[8]

Billy: Where is it?[F]

Soc Wkr: Yeah, I'll look for it if you'll . . . that looks like a battery.[6C] Is that supposed to . . . ?[8]

Billy: No.[D2]

Soc Wkr: Oh.[8]

Billy: On there![D2]

Soc Wkr:	Now, okay.[8]
Billy:	I can't get it.[D2]
Deputy:	Hey, hey.[6C] Didn't (indecipherable) it yet.[6C]
Billy:	I wanna get it.[D2]
Soc Wkr:	Let me try it for you.[6C] Don't come apart, hmm?[6C]
Billy:	Nope.[D2] (indecipherable)[G]
Soc Wkr:	There.[6C]
Billy:	(indecipherable)[G]
Soc Wkr:	Now I think you need to answer some of Scott's questions.[4, 6A] He wants to talk to you about your daddy.[4, 6A] Do you have any dolls?[2A] Hmm?[2A]
Deputy:	Except that one?[2A]
Billy:	Other kinds?[F]
Deputy:	What?[1A]
Billy:	Other kinds?[F]
Deputy:	A bear?[8]
Billy:	Yeah.[G]
Deputy:	A tender heart bear or something like that.[6C]
Billy:	Uh.[D2]
Deputy:	You know, a little doggie.[6C]
Billy:	Dog?[F]
Deputy:	Little dog?[6C]
Billy:	One dog.[D2]
Deputy:	One dog.[9]
Billy:	And my grandma gave me.[D2] My grandma gave me one.[D2]

Soc Wkr: Are you going to be glad when your daddy comes to pick you up or are you going . . . [3B]

Billy: Good.[C]

Soc Wkr &
  Deputy: Why?[1A]

Billy: Real good![C]

Deputy: Real good.[9]

Soc Wkr: How come?[1A]

Billy: 'Cause I want to be with my dad.[C]

Soc Wkr: Now that's good.[5] Are there times you want to . . . ?[8]

Billy: No, I'm making a real big one.[D2]

Deputy: Yes, you are.[6C]

Billy: I make a real big (indecipherable).[D2]

Deputy: . . . block[6C]

Billy: I don't need no more blocks.[D2]

[Garbled conversation about blocks. Noise]

Soc Wkr: You want to draw a picture for us?[2A]

Billy: No.[D1]

Soc Wkr: No?[2A, 9] Of your dad?[2A]

Billy: No.[D1]

[Noise]

Deputy: . . . asked you that.[8]

Billy: Yup.[G]

[social worker evidently presents the anatomical dolls]

Soc Wkr:	This man doll's got a mustache just like your daddy.[6A, 7] Does your dad still have a mustache?[2B]
Billy:	Uh huh.[A1]
Soc Wkr:	Uh huh.[9]
Billy:	Is that a boy?[F]
Soc Wkr:	It's a man.[6A, 7] A grown-up.[6A, 7] I do have a little boy, though.[6A, 7] He's wearing blue jeans just like you are.[7]
Billy:	You got a baby (indecipherable)?[F] I got pieces that.[D2] Boom, boom, boom, I got (indecipherable) another.[D2] Boom, boom, boom, boom, boom, boom, boom.[D2] Look it.[D2] Look it, that's his toes exercising.[D2]
Soc Wkr:	Your toes are exercising, huh.[6C] Can't wait with the toes.[6C]
Billy:	One, two, one two.[D2]
Soc Wkr:	Maybe that one can be considered a baby, couldn't it?[6A, 7]
Billy:	...[G]
Soc Wkr:	He think's that's a grown-up doll.[9]
Deputy:	Let's play a game.[4, 6A]
Billy:	What?[F]
Deputy:	Now.[4]
Billy:	I know a game to play.[D2] Exercise at home.[D2]
Deputy:	Exercise.[6C] (Laughs) You're too good with that.[6C, 4]
Billy:	Look it.[D2] Can you play twirl around?[F]
Deputy:	Twirl around.[6C] Your toes fall off if you twirl around.[6C] Now.[8] I'll help.[6C] I'll help.[6C] Pretend this is you.[4, 6A, 7] Looks like you.[6A, 7]
Soc Wkr:	Who should the other people be?[1A, 7]
Billy:	What?[F]
Soc Wkr:	Who should the baby be?[1A, 7]

Billy: Nobody.[D1]

Soc Wkr: Nobody?[9, 2A] Shall I put the baby back on there?[2A, 7]

Deputy: What about the little girl?[1A, 7]

Soc Wkr: Or the baby?[1A, 7] Whichever you want.[5, 7]

Deputy: Or?[8] Yeah, this could be a lady.[6A, 7] I could be.[6A, 7] How many ladies wear pigtails this long?[1A, 7] It could be me.[7, 6A]

Soc Wkr: Who should that be?[1A, 7]

Deputy: Who should that be?[1A, 7] Billy?[4, 1A] Huh?[1A] Who should that be?[1A, 7] Billy.[4]

Soc Wkr: We may have to (indecipherable).[8]

Billy: What.[F]

Soc Wkr: Who should that be?[1A, 7]

Deputy: Billy.[4] Who should that be?[1A, 7]

Billy: Nobody.[D1]

Deputy: Nobody, why?[9, 2A] Don't you have somebody you don't like?[2B, 4, 6A]

Billy: She's garbage.[D2, D1]

Deputy: Garbage; you'll change your mind about girls later on.[9, 6A]

Billy: What?[F]

Deputy: (Laughs) Now, I think we'll make this your mom.[6A, 7] See, it's a girl one.[6A, 7]

Billy: It's big.[C]

Deputy: A few inches taller than you.[6A, 7] The mommy's taller than you.[6A, 7]

Billy: I'm big.[C]

Deputy: I know, but your mommy's a taller than you.[6A] Yes, she is, too.[6A, 4] You know she is.[4]

Soc Wkr:	(Noise) She lives in a different house, right?[2B]
Deputy:	Yes.[6A] Sometimes you visit with your mommy.[6A]
Soc Wkr:	Who's picture?[1A]
Billy:	Nobody.[D1]
Soc Wkr:	Nobody?[2A, 9] That look like anybody you know?[2A]
Billy:	Uh uh.[B1]
Soc Wkr:	Uh uh?[2A, 9]

[Banging noises for about 10 seconds]

Deputy:	(indecipherable) not in love with her?[8]
Soc Wkr:	(indecipherable)[10]
Deputy:	Billy, I want your attention.[4]
Billy:	No.[D1]
Deputy:	Please.[4] Please.[4]
Billy:	I'm almost done?[F]
Deputy:	(indecipherable).[10]
Billy:	Boom![D2]
Deputy:	Too late![6C]
Billy:	Boom![D2]
Deputy:	Billy.[4] Billy?[4, 1A] Billy?[4, 1A]
Billy:	What?[F]
Deputy:	Please.[4]
Billy:	NOPE![D1]
Deputy:	Please.[4] I want you to (indecipherable).[4, 6A]
Billy:	I'll break your heart out.[D1, D2]

Deputy:	You'll break my heart out.[9] I want to turn this (indecipherable).[10] Can you do it, please?[10] It's kind of cute and (indecipherable).[6C] Jumps around.[6C] Plays a (indecipherable).[6C] How?[1A] You (indecipherable).[8] Please.[4] Just (indecipherable).[8]
Billy:	Nope.[D1]
Deputy:	Please?[4] Hmm?[8]
Billy:	Stop it.[F, D1]
Deputy:	Stop what?[1A]
Billy:	Stop it.[F, D1]
Deputy:	Stop what?[1A]
Billy:	Now, who did this?[F, D2]
Deputy:	The little boy doll.[7, 6A]
Billy:	I'm going to hit him with it.[D2]
Deputy:	What?[1A]
Billy:	For doing that.[D2]
Deputy:	You're doing okay.[5] You made a nice little tower there.[5] Gray and yellow tower.[9] (indecipherable) head.[8] Billy?[1A]
Billy:	Look it.[F, D2]
Deputy:	(indecipherable)[10]
Soc Wkr:	Why did your grandma tell you we were coming out here to talk to you?[1A] Billy?[1A, 4] Did she tell you we were coming out to meet you?[2A]
Billy:	Yeah.[A1]
Soc Wkr:	Yeah?[2A, 9] What'd she tell you—what'd she say we were coming for?[1A]
Billy:	What?[F]
Soc Wkr:	Why'd she say we wanted to meet you?[1A]

[No answer—sounds of playing][G]

Soc Wkr:	Hmm?[1A] Billy, we heard you were a real smart little boy and we wanted to meet you.[5] Did she tell you that we wanted to talk to you about your mommy and your daddy?[2B, 6A, 4]
Billy:	(Sings)[D2]
Soc Wkr:	Hmm?[2B]
Billy:	Look it.[F, D2] A brand new building.[D2]
Soc Wkr:	Hmm.[8]
Billy:	Look, a brand new building.[D2]
Soc Wkr:	Yeah.[9] I think we can make anything, but we're going to do some talking.[4, 6A] (indecipherable).[10]
Billy:	My (indecipherable) a boy.[G]
Deputy:	These look like (indecipherable).[8]
Soc Wkr:	Grandma, maybe you can tell us what you said.[6B] About why we wanted to meet him.[6B]
Grandma:	(indecipherable)[10]
Soc Wkr:	That's fine.[5] (indecipherable).[10]
Billy:	That's the bear's gun.[D2]
Soc Wkr:	I'm looking for anything.[6C]
Billy:	The bear's gun.[D2]
Deputy:	(indecipherable)[10]
Soc Wkr:	Well, I think it's what we need to do at this point.[4, 6A]
Billy:	I'm going to make a bear's gun.[D2]
Deputy:	A what?[6C]
Billy:	A bear's gun.[D2]
Deputy:	Billy?[1A, 4]
Billy:	What?[F]

Deputy: The other day you were talking to your grandma and you told her about something that you did to your daddy.[4, 6A] Remember about that?[2B, 4, 6A]

Billy: What?[F] I got your gun.[D2, D1] Bang.[D2]

Deputy: You remember that?[2B, 4, 6A]

Billy: Let me see that.[D2, D1] You have my gun.[D2] (Indecipherable) Here's my gun.[D2] Hands up or freeze![D2]

Deputy: Hands up or freeze?[6C] (Laughs)

Billy: Pow![D2]

Deputy: Billy, you remember that?[2B, 4, 6A]

Billy: What?[F]

Deputy: You remember what you told your grandma that you did to your daddy?[2B, 4, 6A]

Billy: What?[F, D1]

Deputy: You remember?[2B, 4, 6A]

Billy: Why?[F]

Deputy: That you sucked your daddy's wiener?[2B, 4, 6A] You remember that?[2B, 4, 6A] I want you to tell me about that.[4] Huh?[2B, 4] What did you mean by that?[1B]

Grandma: Tell them with the doll.[4, 6A, 7] But don't tell his father; he can't play with dolls.[6B]

Deputy: Show me on the doll what you did to your daddy.[4, 6A, 7]

Billy: Huh?[F, D1]

Deputy: Show me on the doll what you did to your daddy.[4, 6A, 7]

Billy: The doll will tell you.[D1]

Deputy: The doll will tell me.[2A, 9] Okay.[8] (indecipherable).[10] You tell me.[4]

Billy: (Nonsense words) You got to shake her.[D2, D1] But you got to shake her like this.[D2]

Deputy: That's her eyes.[6C] You tell me what you did to your daddy, okay?[4, 2B, 6A] That's her eyes go open and shut.[6C]

Soc Wkr: Well, this doll might help, too.[6A, 7] You might be able to show us with this doll.[4, 6A, 7] This dolly has something on it.[6A, 7]

Deputy: This doll is just like your daddy.[6A, 7] Isn't it?[2B, 6A, 7]

Soc Wkr: It's just like daddy, it's just like you.[6A, 7]

Deputy: It's just like all (indecipherable).[6A, 7]

Soc Wkr: All of these guys have wieners.[6A, 7]

Deputy: Billy.[4]

Grandma: Now, Billy.[4] (indecipherable).[10]

Deputy: What's this mean?[1A]

[Long silence]

Deputy: It's got blue jeans on.[7]

[Long silence]

Deputy: Billy doll.[6A, 7] All right, what do you call that.[1A, 7]
Billy: A wiener.[C] (Laughs)

Deputy: Right?[5] You got one of them?[2B] Huh?[2B]
Billy: A girl doesn't.[C]

Deputy: A girl doesn't.[9] Girls don't have that.[9] Were you kissing the little wiener?[2B, 6A, 7]
Billy: (Giggles)[D2, D1]

Deputy: That's an old doll.[7]
Billy: It's my mom's.[D2]

Deputy: Yeah.[9]

Billy: I'm gonna shoot a bullet in her.[D2] Boom![D2] Got a bullet in her.[D2] Watch.[F, D2]

Deputy: Show me with the doll, Billy — Billy?[4, 6A, 7]

Billy: Freeze or I'll shoot.[D1, D2]

Deputy: Freeze or I'll shoot.[9] Billy.[4] Billy.[4]

Billy: What?[F]

Deputy: Show me with the doll what you did to your daddy.[4, 6A, 7]

Billy: Uh uh.[D1]

Deputy: Please?[4] You can't do it, can you?[2B, 4] Why?[1B, 4] Don't know how?[2B, 4] Or you're afraid to?[4, 6A] Hmm?[2B] You know how.[4] You're a big boy.[4, 5] It'd really help me out a lot if you'd show me.[4, 6A, 7]

Billy: Freeze or I'll shoot.[D2, D1] Pow! You're both dead.[D2] Freeze or I'll shoot.[D2]

Deputy: Billy.[4]

Billy: Pow![D2] Freeze or I'll shoot.[D2] Boom.[D2]

Grandma: Billy?[4, 1A]

Billy: What?[F]

Soc Wkr: Tell me what you told Grandma.[4]

Billy: What?[F]

Soc Wkr: Tell me what you told Grandma.[4]

Billy: No.[D1]

Soc Wkr: Please?[4] You're a good boy.[5]

Deputy: Just show me with the doll.[4, 6A, 7]

Billy: What?[F]

Deputy: Just show me with the doll.[4, 6A, 7]

| Billy: | My doll got (his) toes and fingers cut off.[D1, D2] Gonna toes and (indecipherable).[D2] Why don't you give me a (indecipherable) piggy back.[D2] Agh.[D2] Hurt my back.[D2] |

[Noise. Recorder goes off, then on]

| Deputy: | Billy, has your daddy ever touched you with his wiener?[2B, 6A] |
| Billy: | (Billy presumably shakes his head)[G] |

| Deputy: | Nowhere at all.[9] Hmm.[8] Has he ever made you touch his wiener?[2B, 6A] |
| Billy: | (Another gesture)[G] |

| Deputy: | You never touched his wiener at all.[9, 4] |

| Soc Wkr: | Oh, he has?[2B, 9, 5] Ah.[5] |

| Deputy: | What'd you touch it with?[1A] He said he did?[6B, 2B] |
| Billy: | No.[B1] |

| Deputy: | He just lay there and let you do it.[6A] Right?[2B, 4] You ever touch his wiener with your nose?[2B, 6A] |
| Billy: | (Giggles)[D2] |

| Deputy: | No.[9] How about your ear?[2B, 6A] How about your mouth?[2B, 6A] Never have.[9] |

[Tape recorder off then on again]

| Deputy: | You told your grandma that you sucked your daddy's wiener.[6A, 4] What's that mean?[1A] |
| Billy: | (indecipherable).[G] |

| Deputy: | Won't you what?[1A] Okay?[8] |
| Billy: | He has his clothes on.[D2] |

| Deputy: | Here.[10] |
| Billy: | Sure he has.[D2] You (indecipherable) give haircuts?[F, D2] |

| Deputy: | Did your daddy ever touch your wiener?[2B, 6A] |

Billy: No.[B1]

Deputy: Never has.[9]

Billy: No.[B1]

Deputy: Never.[4] (indecipherable)[10]

Billy: He going to (indecipherable) a haircut.[D2] Leave me alone![D1] Haircut is . . . [D2]

Deputy: How about a break?[5] (indecipherable) have pretty hair.[5]

Billy: I cut his hair.[D2] I got machine cutter.[D2] Here I go (makes shearing sounds).[D2]

Deputy: Hey, Billy,[4] he's not going to have any hair.[6C]

Billy: What?[F]

Deputy: Tell me what you mean when you say you sucked your daddy's wiener.[4]

Billy: No.[D1] (whining)

Deputy: Please?[4]

Billy: Noooo.[D1] (weak)

Deputy: Please.[4] You told your grandma.[4] Why can't you tell me?[1A, 4]

Billy: (indecipherable)[G]

Deputy: Put your baby down, Billy.[4] It's gonna take me a while.[4] Okay?[8] You showed your grandma.[4] Show me.[4, 6A, 7] You're a good boy.[5] How old you say you were?[1A]

Billy: Four.[C]

Deputy: Four.[9] That's all right.[5] You can do it.[5, 4] I know you can.[5, 4] We got lots of good boys that show Trina and I what happens between their mommies and daddies, neighbors, friends.[6A, 4] You can tell me.[4, 5]

Deputy: Show me.[4, 6A, 7] Show me what you showed your grandma.[4, 6A, 7]

Billy: I shot you.[D1, D2] Woo, woo, woo, woo.[D2]

Deputy:	Billy.[4] (Laughs) I'm dead.[6C] Hey, Billy.[4] Show me.[4, 6A, 7] Come on.[4]
Billy:	No.[D1]
Deputy:	We're getting serious this time.[4, 6A] Show me with the doll.[4, 6A, 7]
Billy:	It was (indecipherable).[G]
Deputy:	(indecipherable).[10]

[Ten seconds pass]

Deputy:	Hey, Billy.[4] Billy.[4] Billy.[4]
Soc Wkr:	I have a question, Billy.[4]
Billy:	What?[F]
Soc Wkr:	What is that?[1A, 7] (points to doll?) What do you have on the back of it?[1A, 7] What do you call that?[1A, 7] What do *you* call it?[1A, 7]
Billy:	. . . . [G]
Soc Wkr:	Can it move?[2B, 7]
Billy:	(indecipherable) in the back?[F]
Deputy:	The little bitty one in back.[9] Billy.[4] Trina asked you a question.[4] Billy?[2B, 4]
Billy:	You're dead.[D1, D2] Fall out.[D2]
Deputy:	Ha, ha, ha.[6C] We're down as far as we can go.[6C] Tell us what that is.[4, 6A, 7] Billy?[4] Billy?[4] What's this right here?[1A, 7] What is that?[1A, 7] What's your name for that?[1A, 7] What do you call that?[1A, 4, 7]
Billy:	Hm hm hm (giggles).[D1, D2]
Deputy:	You know what it's called.[4] It's not dirty.[4, 6A]
Billy:	He (indecipherable) with his hand.[G]
Deputy:	What?[1A] What do you call that?[1A, 7] What's your name for that?[1A, 7]

94 *The Real World of Child Interrogations*

Billy: (Giggles) [D2]

Deputy: What do you call that when you have to go to the bathroom and wipe yourself?[1A, 7] What do you call that?[1A, 7]

Billy: (Giggles)[D2]

Deputy: Huh?[4, 1A] Huh?[1A, 4] I'm not going to touch it.[6C]

Billy: (Hums four-word, five-note song)[D2]

Soc Wkr: Does Grandma know what he calls it?[6B]

Grandma: His butt, I think.[6A]

Deputy: That what you call it?[2B]

Soc Wkr: Oh.[8] That's what lots of people call it.[8] Lots of people have different names for a lot of different things.[8]

Billy: What are you making?[F]

Soc Wkr: I'm just fiddling.[6C]

Billy: That's a truck.[D2]

Deputy: Billy?[4]

Billy: With this machine gun?[F, D2]

Deputy: Billy.[4]

Billy: Choo, choo, choo, choo.[D2] Ah![D2] Billy![D2] (choking noise)

Deputy: (indecipherable) all play with it (indecipherable).[6C]

Soc Wkr: Quiet![6C] Quiet please![6C] (laughs)[6C] Quiet please.[6C] Well![4] Billy.[4]

Deputy: Please put it down.[4]

Soc Wkr: Looks like we might have to.[8]

Deputy: Oh.[8] Somebody shot him.[6C] Billy, you all right?[6C] I'll have to call the Rescue Squad.[6C] Billy.[4] (indecipherable).[10]

Soc Wkr: You know, it might be kind of scary to talk about this, Billy.[4, 6A]

Billy:	(makes crying sounds)[G]
Soc Wkr:	Hey, Billy.[4]
Billy:	(continues to make crying and laughing sounds)[G]
Deputy:	Hey, Billy?[4, 1A] Come here, Billy.[4]
Soc Wkr:	We really do need to have you talk to us about this.[4] Billy?[4]
Grandma:	No kidding![4, 6A] Get up here now and say something.[4, 6A]
Billy:	I want got a mustache.[D1, D2]
Soc Wkr:	You got a mustache like your daddy, huh?[6C]
Billy:	Yeah.[D2] I'm the po-lice.[D2]
Deputy:	Police?[6C]
Grandma:	Get that out of your mouth.[4] Don't put that in your mouth.[4] Get up off the floor![4]
Billy:	Noooo.[D1]
Grandma:	Tell them what you told me.[4] Please.[4]
Billy:	Uh uh![D1]
Grandma:	Come on now.[4] Why not?[1A, 4]
Billy:	They're dummies.[D1]
Deputy:	We're dummies?[2A, 9]
Billy:	Yes.[A1]
Deputy:	Well, help us out then.[4]
Billy:	They're dummies.[D1]
Soc Wkr:	We can't be smart until you teach us.[4, 6A]
Deputy:	We'll all be just as smart as you.[4, 5] You know something that we don't know.[4, 6A] Okay.[8]
Billy:	Here.[D2] Here, Grandma.[D2]
Deputy:	Billy.[4]

Billy: What.[G]

Deputy: Billy.[4]

Billy: What.[G]

Deputy: You know something we don't know.[4, 6A] You're smarter than I am, okay?[4, 5, 6A]

Billy: Grandma asked me.[D2]

Soc Wkr: Huh?[1A]

Deputy: You going to tell me?[4, 2B]

Billy: Noooo.[D1]

Deputy: Please.[4]

Billy: I can come.[D1] I can come to my bedroom?[D1, F]

Deputy: How's your bedroom?[1A] What's in your bedroom?[1A]

Billy: I'll show you.[C]

Deputy: Huh?[1A]

Billy: I'll show you.[C]

Deputy: Okay.[8]

Soc Wkr: Do you need a doll, Scott?[6B]

Deputy: No.[6B] If I do, I'll give you a holler.[6B]

Soc Wkr: Do you need the, uh?[6B]

Deputy: No.[6B] If I do I'll holler.[6B]
   [*Tape Recorder is shut off. Subsequent testimony establishes that this was for around 15–20 minutes. Deputy Lipton took Billy alone into Billy's room and talked to him and then turned the tape recorder back on.*]

[Conversation between Deputy Lipton and Billy in conspiratorial whispers]

Deputy: My name is Scott Lipton.[10] What's your name?[1A]

Billy: Billy.[C]

Deputy: No (indecipherable).[10]

Billy: Billy.[C]

Deputy: Billy what?[1A] What's your last name?[1A]

Billy: Daniel.[C]

Deputy: Billy Daniel?[2A, 9]

Billy: Billy Daniel Barnes.[C]

Deputy: Billy.[9]

Billy: Daniel.[C]

Deputy: Harrell?[2A, 9] What's your last name?[1A]

Billy: Barnes.[C]

Deputy: Okay.[8] Now.[8] Tell me about your daddy.[4, 6A]

Billy: I already did.[D1]

Deputy: Tell me again.[4, 6A] Please?[4, 2A]

Billy: You can talk on anything you want to talk on.[D2]

Deputy: That's right.[5] Tell me, tell me—tell me about your daddy.[4, 6A]

Billy: (whispering) I sucked his wiener.[C]

Deputy: You sucked his wiener?[2A, 9]

Billy: (whispering) Yes.[A1]

Deputy: How many times you done that?[1A]

Billy: Once.[C]

Deputy: Once.[9] Did he like it?[2B, 6A]

Billy: (Gestures?)[G]

Deputy: Does that mean no or yes?[3A]

Billy: No.[B1]

Deputy: What else did you do to your daddy?[1B, 6A]

Billy: Do you got another tape for that?[D2, D1]

Deputy: This isn't run down.[10] Hey, Billy, what else did you do to your daddy?[1B, 6A]

Billy: Nothing.[C]

Deputy: Oh, yes, you said you did.[4, 6A] Remember?[2B, 4, 6A]

Billy: What?[F]

Deputy: Remember?[2B, 4, 6A]

Billy: Sucked his butt.[C]

Deputy: That's right.[5, 9] Did he like that?[2B, 6A]

Billy: Yeah.[A1]

Deputy: He did.[9] Now, did your daddy ask you to do that?[2B]

Billy: No.[B1]

Deputy: Did he have his clothes on?[2B]

Billy: Yeah.[A1]

Deputy: He had his clothes on when you did it?[2A, 9] How much clothes did he have on?[1A]

Billy: All of them.[C]

Deputy: He had his pants on?[2A, 9] His wiener—how'd you see his wiener?[1B, 6A]

Billy: (indecipherable).[G]

Deputy: Huh?[1A]

Billy: I saw it before.[C]

Deputy: Okay, when you sucked your daddy's wiener, did he pull out the zipper, or did he take his pants off?[3B, 6A]

Billy: He pulled out the zipper.[C]

Deputy: He pulled out the zipper.[9]

Billy: That's it.[A1]

Deputy: And where were you at?[1A] In your room or his room?[3B]

Billy: In my room.[C]

Deputy: In your room.[9] Is that?[8] How many times you done that?[1A]

Billy: One.[C]

Deputy: Just one time?[2A, 9] What'd your daddy say?[1B, 6A] He tell you
            not to tell anybody?[2B, 6A] He didn't tell you not to tell any-
            body?[2B, 6A]

Billy: (No answer)[D1]

Deputy: Did you ever see—Did your daddy suck your wiener?[2B, 6A] Did
            he suck your butt?[2B, 6A]

Billy: (Gestures)[G]

Deputy: No, he didn't do any of those things.[9] Did he play with you?[2B,
            6A]

Billy: No.[B1]

Deputy: Did you play with him?[2B, 6A] You said you touched your daddy's
            wiener with your hands, remember?[2B, 4, 6A] Did you do that
            that day?[2B, 6A]

Billy: (Tremulous) No.[B1]

Deputy: You didn't?[2B, 4]

Billy: That's a winder.[D2, D1]

Deputy: I know.[10] It's working, too.[10]

Billy: Yeah?[F]

Deputy: It's taking down every word you say, so you want to tell the truth.[4,
            6A]

Billy: Are you going to turn it off?[F]

Deputy: No, not yet.[10]

Billy: When?[F]

Deputy: I'll let you know in a minute, after you answer my questions,
            okay?[2B, 4]

Billy: Yup.[G]

Deputy: Now, you sucked your daddy's wiener.[9] Did you put his wiener in your mouth?[2B, 6A] Did it hurt?[2B, 6A]

Billy: (Whispers) No.[B1]

Deputy: It didn't hurt.[9] Did anything come out of it?[2B, 6A] Did you feel anything white and sticky?[2B, 6A]

Billy: (Apparently gestures with his head)[G]

Deputy: Nothing at all.[9] Nothing.[9] Did he say not to tell anybody?[2B, 6A]

Billy: (Whispers) He said to tell everybody.[C]

Deputy: He said to tell everybody?[2A, 9] Did he really?[2B, 4] Have you told everybody?[2A]

Billy: (Whispers) Yeah.[A1]

Deputy: Hey, Billy.[4]

Billy: What?[F]

Deputy: I want you to tell me the truth.[4, 6A] Now look at me![4] Look![4] Billy![4] I want you to tell me the truth and the whole truth and nothing but the truth, okay?[4, 2B, 6A] You know what the truth is?[2B, 4] You know what a lie is?[2B, 4] A lie is when you tell something that didn't happen.[6A, 4]

[Lots of noise. Low speed voice recording about 14 seconds]

Billy: Can we turn it off now?[D1, F]

Deputy: Go ahead.[5]

Billy: What?[F]

Deputy: Sing![4]

Billy: No, you got to put it on first.[D2]

Deputy: It's on![6C] Go ahead![6C] It's running![10]

Billy: But you got to turn it on like we had it on.[D2, F]

Deputy: You sing it and I'll play it back to you.[6C] Go ahead.[6C]

Billy: Well, turn it on![F] You got to press the button down.[F]

Deputy:	The button's down.[10]
Grandma:	Did you sing, Billy?[2A]
Billy:	Yes.[A1]
Deputy:	Hey, Billy, what was you singing?[1A]
Billy:	The wiener on it.[C]
Deputy:	Billy (indecipherable) on it.[8] What was that song you sang about wiener?[1A]
Soc Wkr:	Would you sing it for me?[2A, 4]
Billy:	No. (makes a singing tone)[D1]
Soc Wkr:	Was that what you were singing to your grandma yesterday when I was talking to her on the phone?[2B]
Grandma:	Song singing about (indecipherable) weren't you?[2B, 4]
Billy:	He's in the (indecipherable).[G]
Soc Wkr:	Okay, your grandma just asked you something and I got kind of mixed up so you can help me, Billy.[4]
Grandma:	Can you show them, Billy?[2B, 4]
Billy:	What?[F]
Deputy:	They won't tell.[4] They don't (indecipherable).[8]
Billy:	(indecipherable)[G]
Deputy:	You want to show them?[2B, 4]
Billy:	Uh uh.[D1]
Deputy:	What did your daddy do to your wiener?[1B] Billy?[4]
Billy:	Nothing.[C]
Deputy:	Yes, he did.[4, 6A]
Billy:	What?[F]
Deputy:	You told your grandma he did.[4]

Billy: What?[F]

Deputy: Well, you tell me.[4]

Billy: He sucked my pee-pee.[C]

Deputy: Oh, he sucked your pee-pee.[9]

Billy: He sucked on my butt (almost singing it and laughing)[C] (indecipherable) wee-wee?)[G]

Soc Wkr: He sucked on your pee-pee and he sucked on your butt, is that what you said?[9, 2A] Yep? [2A, 9] And what about you?[1B] What have you done to your daddy?[1B]

Billy: Sucked his wiener.[C]

Soc Wkr: You sucked his wiener.[9] You told your grandma that he peed in your mouth.[4, 6A]

Billy: (Giggles)[D2]

Soc Wkr: Did that happen?[2B]

Billy: Yeah. (still giggling)[A1]

Soc Wkr: Yeah?[2A, 9]

Billy: I was in the (indecipherable) when Grandma.[C]

Grandma: (indecipherable) [10]

Billy: What?[F]

Grandma: (indecipherable) [10]

Billy: What is it?[F]

Grandma: (indecipherable) [10]

Billy: What?[F]
     [*Low voice speed—34 seconds*]

[Spoken dialogue, garbled voices.]

Soc Wkr: Okay, it was white, huh?[2B]

Billy: You sit in my rocking chair while I go pee-pee.[F, D2]

Soc Wkr:	Could you swallow it, Billy?[2B, 6A] No.[9] What'd you do?[1A] When he peed in your mouth, what did you do with his pee?[1B]
Billy:	I spit it.[C]
Soc Wkr:	You spit it.[9]
Deputy:	Was it sticky?[2B, 6A]
Billy:	Yeah.[A1] This is my cave.[D2]
Deputy:	Hey, Superman.[6C, 5]
Soc Wkr:	Well, something else that your grandma was saying and I got kind of confused about, on the sofa when you were getting ready for bed?[6A, 2B] You remember.[4]
Grandma:	I asked if you (indecipherable) your daddy.[9] And you said your daddy did it all by himself.[6A] (indecipherable).[10]
Billy:	Could be (indecipherable) it.[G]
Deputy:	Billy.[4]
Billy:	I can jump over.[D2] Up.[D2] Up.[D2]
Deputy:	Billy, Billy, come here.[4] This is something different that he keeps trying to . . . [6B]

[Indecipherable conversation]

Soc Wkr:	Made a drop come out?[2B]

[Indecipherable conversation]

Soc Wkr:	Oh, okay, testicles.[6A]
Grandma:	(indecipherable) [10]
Irene:	Didn't you, Billy, you said daddy showed you (indecipherable).[4, 6A]
Billy:	Yeah.[A1]
Deputy:	That's good.[5]

Soc Wkr: That would be in April.[6A] That he (indecipherable) happen?[8]
                Okay.[8]

Deputy: There's certainly more (indecipherable) before that (indecipherable)
                about my age.[8]

Billy: (sings in the background)[D2] Shut up![D1] Shut up![D1]

[Confusing babble of voices.]

End of interview

AFTERMATH

When the case eventually came to trial a year and a half later, this interview was presented in court. It took the jury 20 minutes to acquit Donald Barnes.

However, because the state in which Irene lived had substantiated the abuse charges, Donald had been placed on that state's central registry of child sexual molesters. The substantiation of the charge was based on this taped interview by Trina Smith and Deputy Dalton. Donald's name remains there today, listed as a child sexual abuser, in spite of his acquittal and his efforts to expunge the record. He has been told in writing that since the state substantiated the allegation, if he wants to proceed any further he must go through the full-scale appeals process set up by the state to get expungement from the central registry. This is, in effect, a retrial of the entire case, and requires thousands of dollars in attorney's fees. Donald no longer has any resources to combat his continued listing on the central registry as a child abuser. This means any agency that inquires about Donald's past will be told he is on the central registry.

Donald is depressed and discouraged. He now avoids any friendly contact with women and shies away from children if he encounters them in the supermarket or at church. He grieves for his missing child. Mandy is in much the same state. Donald and Mandy talk occasionally and commiserate with each other.

The system was manipulated by a disturbed woman with her own avowed agenda of getting custody of her grandchild. Despite her problems, she used the system and its power to accomplish her goal.

Because of continuing evidence of pathological behaviors of the part of the grandmother, custody of Billy was awarded to Mandy. However, in the meantime, Irene Schultz took Billy and disappeared.

To date, Billy has not been returned.

Chapter 4

TRAINING TO BE PSYCHOTIC

When a nonabused young child is taught by adults to produce false accounts of sexual abuse, the stories may become bizarre and fantastic. The child is required to repeat the account to many interviewers and the mere repetition may lead to increased embellishment and to subjective credibility. The child may come to believe events happened and are real that did not happen and are not real. This is an assault upon a developing child's ability to distinguish reality from unreality. It runs the risk of training a child to be psychotic.

A basic adult responsibility toward young children is to help them understand the reality of the world in which they live. When adults elicit preposterous accounts from children, fail to exercise any critical rationality, but instead lend credence to a child's improbable accounts, those adults are abandoning one of their fundamental responsibilities to children. Reinforcing and rewarding a child's fantasies as if they were true makes the world into a confusing and threatening place for the child.

In several cases we have reviewed, young children, as a result of repeated interrogations from adults, gradually produce accounts of unusual and improbable behaviors including ritual murder and torture, animal sacrifice, devil worship, rides in airplanes, helicopters, submarines (in a farm pond in semi-desert terrain), anal and vaginal penetration with spoons, knives, and lighted candles, and sex with animals. Following the chronological development of such accounts suggests that children are driven by those adult behaviors deeper and deeper into their fantasy world.

Police spent a month looking for a garage in which an elderly grandmother who worked as an aide at a day care center was said to have hidden the helicopter she used to transport children to a church in the mountains where they were given rifles to shoot bears. The grandmother had never learned to drive a car.

Social workers and police spent two weeks driving children around the countryside looking for a barn with a purple polka-dotted silo. The

107

children were said to have walked from a day care center to the barn while they were tied up in a line. In a secret room beneath the barn floor they were forced to dance around a fire and witness sacrifices of animals and children.

Sheriff's deputies explored a series of caves in a ten-mile radius of a farmhouse looking for a cave in which children were placed in wooden boxes, doped, and kept for days. Orgies and human sacrifice were said to have been performed by a series of strange adults who wore animal skins and had animal masks covering their heads.

In testimony under oath a child told a tale of children in a day care center being taken in buses to a graveyard where they dug up and opened coffins. The perpetrator then cut an arm off a body, which bled, and then told the children this is what would happen to them if they told. The prosecution hired an archaeological firm to search for evidence of buried bodies.

Some in the law enforcement community have become convinced there is a worldwide conspiracy of satanic worshipers who sexually abuse, murder, and breed children for these purposes. Conferences for police officers have been held at which this satanic conspiracy has been described and presented as real. Instruction is given on how to look for behavioral indicators of satanic worship (Diaz, 1987).

Charlier and Downing (1988) investigated 36 cases involving claims of bizarre ritual abuse. They found that key elements in these cases include runaway investigations, children's stories that are uncorroborated by any physical evidence, stories spread from city to city through the network of police and social workers, and a flawed child protection system in which there is no accountability for investigators and no safeguards for innocent people. A concluding statement of their investigation is that it "documented case after case in which charges of multiple child sexual abuse were the products of public hysteria and unprofessional investigation" (p. A26).

A consistent problem in these cases is that the adults doing the investigation and interviewing of children appear unaware of what child abusers actually do (Erickson, Walbek, & Seely, 1988; Wakefield & Underwager, 1988). If the investigators considered the known frequencies of the alleged behaviors, they could use this information to assess the likelihood of the statements about abuse. Instead, the adults accept as true uncorroborated accounts of highly unusual and low base rate behaviors.

The issue for children caught in the system is the effect of adult credulity and reinforcement of their darkest fantasies and fears. Part of growing up is to reach a point where the world is fairly comfortable. There are not monsters hiding in the closet at night, or goblins behind every bush, or witches poised to snatch children from the playgrounds. For a culture to continue, children must grow up to believe they can get along with most other people, expect others to behave fairly orderly and regularly, and know there is a relatively predictable pattern of interaction. A child exposed to years of adult belief in improbable events, adult interest in and attention to repeated telling of cruel, random, and fearsome events, may come to believe it is real. Such a world is not a good place to be.

BACKGROUND

In the following case, a four-year-old girl, Tammy Morgan, eventually produced accounts of urophagia and coprophagia (interest in and sexual arousal with urination and defecation). Her father, aunt, grandparents and her aunt's boyfriend were accused of sexually assaulting her in a group, taking photographs during this orgy, urinating and defecating on her and her thirteen-month-old brother, forcing the children to drink urine in a baby bottle, and making her eat "pooky" sandwiches made from feces. Enough people believed this account that it received wide newspaper publicity and was investigated for four years before all of the charges were permanently dropped.

Joe and Tina Morgan had been married for nearly seven years and had two children, Tammy, age four, and Steven, age thirteen months. Tammy was an attractive and imaginative child who received much attention from her parents and relatives. Her grandparents, who were in their 70s, often cared for her, and her aunt, Carole Morgan, was active in her upbringing. Carole entered her niece in child beauty pageants, which Tammy often won, and the family agreed that Tammy was a budding actress who loved attention.

The bond between Carole and Tammy was very close. Carole often brought Tammy unusual presents from the trips she took with her boyfriend, Bob Wilcox. They both had good jobs with a large corporation and were able to travel frequently.

In the fall of 1983, Tina and Joe's marriage had become troubled and they had been discussing divorce for several months. One afternoon Tammy was with Tina's sister and supposedly said to the sister, "Let's kiss like in the movies." The sister went to Tina with this information and added that Tammy had told her that this was the way that Carole had kissed her.

Tina then called a pediatrician's clinic in the city. The pediatrician was not available, but the counselor told Tina that the child was definitely showing signs of sexual abuse and advised her to notify the police. Tina did. Over the next several weeks, the child was interviewed by police and therapists and the stories grew to include Carole, Joe, the grandparents, and Bob Wilcox. A few months later, charges were filed against all five and warrants were issued to search for photographs, slides, snapshots, and equipment believed to have been used in pornographic productions with the children. Although nothing was found, all five were arrested and incarcerated for over two weeks. There was no child pornography found and no physical evidence. During a preliminary hearing, Tammy was ruled incompetent to testify and the charges were dropped. The press picked up the story and the charges came to the attention of the corporation which employed Carole and Bob. Approximately two months after the case was dismissed, both were summarily terminated.

Carole and Bob attempted to be reinstated in their jobs because the charges had been dropped. They raised objections to the improper manner by which they had been discharged. However, the corporation reacted by flying both children to a psychiatrist, Dr. Helen Jefferson, whom they considered to be a child sexual abuse expert. Dr. Jefferson spent several days interviewing Tammy several months after the events were said to have taken place. At the request of the corporation who had hired Dr. Jefferson, no notes nor tapes were made of these interviews. However, Dr. Jefferson later flew to the home city and a videotape was then made in the offices of Tammy's therapist, whom she had been seeing for sexual abuse therapy since the allegations were made.

In this videotape, anatomical dolls are used, and Dr. Jefferson is obviously encouraging Tammy to repeat the statements from the earlier, undocumented interviews. On the basis of the interview with Dr. Jefferson, a Grand Jury indictment was sought. But exculpatory evidence from this videotape was kept from the Grand Jury and when the omission was brought to the judge's attention, the indictment was dismissed.

A month later, the same Grand Jury was impaneled which resulted in another indictment, but yet another dismissal. While the defendants had been in jail, they had all passed polygraphs, but the prosecutor did not submit this exculpatory evidence to the Grand Jury resulting in the dismissal of the indictment.

The case then went before the State Supreme Court whereby the lower Court's decision was upheld. Once again, the case went back to the Grand Jury for a third indictment which was again dismissed.

This decision was appealed to the State Supreme Court. Finally, in 1987 the Supreme Court ruled that if the State was to proceed with this case, the polygraphs and all relevant exculpatory evidence must be submitted to a different Grand Jury.

The Morgans lost their homes, were bankrupted, and Joe had not seen his children for over three years. The family was told that the prosecution would no longer pursue the case if Joe would terminate his parental rights, and their attorneys urged them to accept this. The family resisted, despite the fact that they were facing life imprisonment. They retained new attorneys who were willing to fight for them.

The State did proceed in pursuit of the fourth Grand Jury hearing. In compliance with the Supreme Court's ruling, in preparation for the hearing, a mound of exculpatory evidence was compiled and given to the District Attorney. In response, the District Attorney stated that they would not pursue the case further and memorialized this in writing.

In the meantime, we had become involved in this case and performed extensive psychological evaluations on all five individuals. They were all interviewed for several hours and given a variety of psychological tests. All were psychologically healthy and normal individuals who had held up under their ordeal remarkably well.

In our report, we stressed the improbability of five normal, functional adults engaging in extremely low frequency and sadistic behaviors.

> The allegations against the five persons evaluated in this report include repeated acts of coprophagia, urolagia, and repeated penetration of the infantile genitalia of the two children. These assaults supposedly occurred with all five of the persons present and/or with at least two or more present. The two children would have been approximately eight months and three and one-half years old at the time of the attacks.
>
> It must be understood that the behaviors alleged are not sexual in nature but rather sadistic. The interactions alleged are sadomasochistic in nature. At no point in the accusations is there indication that there was sexual intent or purpose nor is there any indication of sexual gratification experienced by the adults. The acts are concerned with inflicting physical pain, dominance, and humiliation of the children. Such acts of sadism need not be connected with eroticism. If eroticism

is alleged, it remains the case that the acts described are sadistic in nature (Langevin, 1983). In this case the adults are the sadists, the donors of noxious experience, and the children are the masochists, the recipients.

Sadistic behaviors are extremely rare (Langevin, 1983). A study of the sexual experience and sexual behavior of 18,000 people showed not a single instance of sadistic behavior directed toward children (Gebhard, 1965). While Kinsey (1953) reports that three percent of females and one percent of males report erotic response to sadistic stories and fantasies, very few ever actually carry out any actual sadistic practices. The incidence of coprophilia and urophilia is so rare that there are no estimates of frequency. While these behaviors are said to be a part of a sadistic behavioral repertoire, they are more rare than sadistic behaviors such as bondage, torture, and physical assault of various sorts. The American Psychiatric Association's *Diagnostic and Statistical Manual of Mental Disorders* (Third Edition-Revised) (1980) gives no information and does not include these behaviors as specific sexual paraphilias. They are mentioned as being included in the diagnostic category (302.90) Atypical Paraphilia, a residual category for paraphilias that cannot be classified anywhere else.

Sadistic behaviors are connected with high levels of emotional disturbance (Ellis & Abarbanel, 1961; Tollison & Adams, 1979; Langevin, 1983; Karpman, 1954; Siomopoulos & Goldsmith, 1976). The most common view is that schizophrenics or, in the case of violent assaultive sadism, character disorders, are the kinds of persons that show sadism. Normal people do not engage in sadism. It is even less likely that normal people would engage in coprophagia and urophagia which are part of a sadistic behavior pattern. The odds that one person would engage in such behaviors are very low. The odds that five people would all engage in such behaviors in a group setting are even lower. The odds that five normal people with no evidence of pathology in any part of their life would engage in a group orgy of coprophagia and urophagia are astronomical.

The effect upon the children had they, in fact, been forced into repeated acts of sadomasochism of the kind alleged would have been evident. Simple learning theory would say that the children would have shown a marked and obvious aversion to excrement. They would have shown a response to pain that would have been evident and unusual. They would have shown a marked and obvious alternating aversion and attraction to the adult agents of the sadomasochistic experiences.

A much more common, indeed, highly normal behavior, is for children the age of the female child at the initial stage of the development of these allegations to have rich and vivid fantasies about eating, violence, pissing, and shitting (Cott, 1983; Bloch, 1978). It is much more likely that the allegations represent the more typical fantasies of children about excrement and elimination. Their fantasies are scatological. They think, talk, giggle, and make jokes about elimination processes and products. The statements made are most parsimoniously understood as the production of child fantasies in response to the pressure and stress of interrogation. The research in developmental psychology shows that when children are expected to say something about unknown events or matters they are unfamiliar with, they respond with fantasy material.

The tragedy with the children is that if adults believe such statements and reinforce fantasies as if they were real, the children are being trained to be psychotic. Their ability to distinguish fact from fantasy and to sort out the real world is impaired, possibly permanently. Taking seriously highly improbable allegations and fostering confusion of fantasy with reality is neither a benign nor innocuous process. It constitutes emotional abuse of the children. In this specific case, if the allegations are determined to be false, the pursuit of these allegations across such a length of time and the consequent involvement of the children in this process are most assuredly damaging and harmful to the children.

This potential for damage to the children is strengthened by the behavior of adults toward the child, Tammy, in the videotapes made available. Analysis of the adult behaviors toward the child show a high level of coercion, leading, and pressuring of the child to extract the statements the adults desire. The child has been taught by the adults to make the statements that fit the adult purpose and bias. This is most clearly evident in the videotape of Tammy giving testimony before the second grand jury.

This means that any statements made by the child under the condition of the adult interrogations must be viewed very cautiously. The effect of adult influence upon the child must be included in any assessment of the weight to be given to the child's statements. The research evidence on the functioning of human memory, and specifically the function of children's memory, shows that when such coercive and leading procedures are followed children's memories are destroyed and error-based reconstructed tales are substituted. After going through the process of interrogation, putative therapy, and testifying, it is impossible for the child Tammy to have any personal knowledge of the events.

The interview selection is a portion from the taped interview with Tammy by Dr. Jefferson following the untaped and undocumented interviews made earlier at the behest of the corporate officers. Tammy had also been interviewed by others, including her mother, child protection, and a local psychologist (trained in educational psychology) whom she was now seeing for therapy.

The interview is leading and goes over material that appears to have been covered many times before. The anatomical dolls are used throughout the interview and are labeled by Dr. Jefferson (for example, "This one is Carole, make believe, and this one is you"). Tammy shows no evidence of disturbance or anxiety as she talks. She laughs and readily relates what is wanted.

Tammy states that a friend, Anne, was involved in one of the orgies. Anne, who was 18 months older, stoutly denied anything happening when she was later jointly interviewed with Tammy by the therapist who had been treating Tammy. In the later interview with Anne, Tammy responds to Anne's denial of any abuse by tempering and withdrawing her own accounts.

The portion of the interview that is reproduced is taken from the middle of the lengthy interview. The portions that precede and follow it are similar. For all of the interviews analyzed in this case, the percentage of error-inducing statements by adults was 66 percent. This particular interview was taped almost a year after the alleged event and after the three days of untaped and undocumented interviews by Dr. Jefferson. The early interviews with the therapist were also not taped.

INTERVIEW

Interviewer: Dr. Helen Jefferson

Child: Tammy Morgan

Psychiatrist: Have you ever been to Carole's house?[2A]

Tammy: Um hmm, but I don't remember the house.[A2]

Psychiatrist: But you've been to Carole's house?[2A, 9]

Tammy: Yes.[A1]

Psychiatrist: Uh huh.[9] What did you do while you were at Carole's house?[1A]

Tammy: Oh, I been, umm, I been doing, umm, umm, I been doing . . . I been doing, I been playing with Carole.[C]

Psychiatrist: Can you show me what you and Carole play?[2A, 4, 7]

Tammy: Okay.[8] Who's Carole?[F]

Psychiatrist: This one is Carole, make believe, and this one is you.[4, 6A, 7] What are you doing there?[1A, 7]

Tammy: She kissed me there.[C] (Indicating with dolls)

Psychiatrist: She kissed you there?[9]

Tammy: And there, she kissed me[C] (Indicating with dolls)

Psychiatrist: She kissed you where else?[1A, 7]

Tammy: On the pee-pee and the butt and the . . . [C]

Psychiatrist: She kissed you on the pee-pee?[9, 2A]

Tammy: (Nods head)[A1]

Psychiatrist: Show me how she kissed you on the pee-pee?[4, 7]

Tammy: (Indicates with dolls)[C]

Psychiatrist: Uh huh.[8] And where else has she kissed you?[1B, 7]

Tammy: (indicates with dolls)[C]

Psychiatrist: What's that?[1A, 7]

Tammy: Legs.[C]

Psychiatrist: She kisses you on your legs?[9]

Tammy: Everybody kiss my feet.[C]

Psychiatrist: Uh huh.[8] Where else did Carole kiss you, can you come and show me, Tammy?[1B, 4, 7]

Tammy: I don't know.[D3]

Psychiatrist: Yes, you do.[4]

Tammy: (Laughter into microphone)[E2]

Psychiatrist: Show me where else she kissed you.[4, 7] What's that?[1A, 7] She kissed you where?[1A, 7]

Tammy: Oh . . . (Indicates with doll) On the butt.[C]

Psychiatrist: On the butt.[9] So she kissed you on the mouth?[2A, 7]

Tammy: Um hmm.[A1]

Psychiatrist: Where else did she kiss you?[1A, 7]

Tammy: Umm, she kissed me on the, you know, the boobies and the . . . and the . . . [C]

Psychiatrist: The boobies and what else?[1A, 7]

Tammy: And, and the . . . [C]

Psychiatrist: You have to come back over here, Tammy.[4]

Tammy: How come?[F]

Psychiatrist: So that they can see us on television.[10]

Tammy: But why, they can see us any time.[D2]

Psychiatrist: Yeah, they're taking a special picture of you.[10] Did you know that?[10]

Tammy: Um hmm.[G]

Psychiatrist: Yeah.[5] So Carole kissed you on the boobies?[1A, 9, 7]

Tammy: (Nods head)[A1]

Psychiatrist: Where else does she kiss you?[1A, 7]

Tammy: And then she kissed me on the pee-pee.[C]

Psychiatrist: She kissed you on the pee-pee?[9]

Tammy: And she put her finger in my butt, in my pee-pee.[C]

Psychiatrist: She put her finger in your butt and in your pee-pee?[9, 2A]

Tammy: Uh hmm.[A1]

Psychiatrist: Aw, we have to come back over here, yeah.[4] Did that hurt, Tammy?[2A]

Tammy: Yup, you betcha, that hurt.[A2]

Psychiatrist: Did you cry?[2A]

Tammy: Yes, I cried.[A2]

Psychiatrist: Tell me, what comes out of the butt?[1A]

Tammy:	Pookies.[C]
Psychiatrist:	Pookies?[9]
Tammy:	Hello.[D2] Hello.[D2] Hello.[D2] Hello.[D2] (Playing with microphone)
Psychiatrist:	You come back over here, Tammy, you can't play with those things; they're expensive equipment.[4]
Tammy:	Why not?[F]
Psychiatrist:	And we don't want to break it.[4] What comes out of here, the pee-pee?[1A]
Tammy:	Umm, pee-pee.[C]
Psychiatrist:	Pee-pees?[9] Uh huh.[8] Okay.[8] Do you know somebody by the name of Bob?[2A]
Tammy:	Uh huh.[A1]
Psychiatrist:	Do you remember Bob?[2B] You do remember Bob.[5] Uh huh.[8]

(Child is out of the picture)[E3]

Psychiatrist:	Come show me something on the dolls here, okay?[4, 7]
Tammy:	That's not Bob.[F] Oh . . . [G]
Psychiatrist:	What's that?[1A, 7]
Tammy:	The pee-pee.[C]
Psychiatrist:	The pee-pee?[9, 2A]
Tammy:	Yeah.[A1]
Psychiatrist:	Does Bob have a pee-pee?[2A, 7]
Tammy:	Yeah.[A1]
Psychiatrist:	Did you see Bob's pee-pee?[2A, 7]
Tammy:	Um hmm.[A1]
Psychiatrist:	You did see Bob's pee-pee?[2A, 7]
Tammy:	Uh huh.[A1]

Psychiatrist: Can you come back over here, Tammy?[4]

Tammy: Yes.[G]

Psychiatrist: That's a good girl.[5] What does Bob do with his pee-pee?[1A, 7]

Tammy: He puts it in my mouth.[C]

Psychiatrist: He puts his pee-pee in your mouth?[9, 2A]

Tammy: Yes.[A1]

Psychiatrist: Can you show me how he put his pee-pee in your mouth?[4, 7]
                  Show me with the dolls, please, Tammy.[4, 7]

Tammy: Umm, okay.[G] And he put it in my pee-pee . . . [C]

Psychiatrist: He put it in your pee-pee?[9]

Tammy: And then he put it in my mouth.[C]

Psychiatrist: And then he put it in your mouth.[9] Uh huh.[8]

Tammy: (Indicating)[C]

Psychiatrist: Did the pee-pee come out in your mouth?[2A]

Tammy: Yes.[A1]

Psychiatrist: What did it taste like?[1A]

Tammy: Oh, it tastes like yuck.[C]

Psychiatrist: It tastes like yuck?[9]

Tammy: (Nods head)[A1]

Psychiatrist: Um hmm.[8] What about the pookies?[1B, 6A]

Tammy: Oh, what about the pookies?[F] Well, I, umm . . . everybody done
                  . . . [C]

Psychiatrist: Everybody did the pookies?[9, 2A]

Tammy: Yeah.[A1]

Psychiatrist: Uh huh.[8] Who is everybody, can you tell me?[3A]

Tammy: You know, Daddy . . . [C]

Psychiatrist:	Daddy?[9]
Tammy:	Carole . . . [C]
Psychiatrist:	Carole?[9]
Tammy:	Bob . . . [C]
Psychiatrist:	Bob?[9]
Tammy:	Grandma . . . [C]
Psychiatrist:	Grandma?[9]
Tammy:	And Grandpa.[C] Grandma.[C]
Psychiatrist:	And Grandpa.[9] They all did the pookies?[2A, 9] What did they do with the pookies?[1A]
Tammy:	Umm, they all put it in my mouth.[C]
Psychiatrist:	They put it in your mouth?[9]
Tammy:	And they put it in my . . . um . . . and they put it in my, umm, and then they put it in my, umm, pee-pee.[C]
Psychiatrist:	Um hmm.[8]
Tammy:	And then . . . oh, geez . . . right here, and then they did, then they took off my panties.[C]
Psychiatrist:	They took off your panties?[9, 2A]
Tammy:	Um hmm.[A1]
Psychiatrist:	And what else did they take off?[1B] Can you come back over here, Tammy.[4] That's a good girl.[5] What else did they take off besides your panties?[1B, 6A]
Tammy:	Umm, they took off everything.[C]
Psychiatrist:	They took off everything?[9, 2A]
Tammy:	Yeah.[A1]
Psychiatrist:	Uh huh.[8] So you had no clothes on?[2A]
Tammy:	No.[B1]

Psychiatrist: Um hmm.[8] Was Steven there?[1A]

Tammy: Yes, the first day.[A2]

Psychiatrist: And Anne was there?[1B, 6A]

Tammy: Yeah.[A1]

Psychiatrist: Uh huh[A1] Did they do anything to Anne?[2A]

Tammy: No.[B1]

Psychiatrist: Can you remember . . . [8]

Tammy: Yes.[A1]

Psychiatrist: They did?[9, 2A]

Tammy: Um hmm.[A1]

Psychiatrist: What did they do to Anne?[1A] Can you show me what they did to Anne?[4, 7]

Tammy: He did the same thing like me.[C]

Psychiatrist: They did the same thing like you?[2A, 9]

Tammy: Yeah.[A1]

Psychiatrist: Well, can you show me what Bob did to Anne.[4, 7]

Tammy: Who is this?[F]

Psychiatrist: That's a little boy.[6A, 7]

Tammy: It's not Anne.[C]

Psychiatrist: That's Steven, uh huh.[6A, 7] Can you show me what they did to Steven?[4, 7] Okay.[8] You're a good little girl.[5] Show me what they did to Steven.[4, 7]

Tammy: You know . . . what Carole did.[C]

Psychiatrist: Carole did?[9] What Carole did?[1A]

Tammy: She put her pee-pee in Steven . . . so Steven put his pee-pee in her, only in (noises, indicating)[C]

Psychiatrist:	So she kissed Steven, she put her pee-pee in Steven's and then she kissed Steven?[9, 2A]
Tammy:	Um hmm.[A1]
Psychiatrist:	And what did they do to Anne?[1A]
Tammy:	They did the same thing just like Steven.[C]
Psychiatrist:	Uh huh.[8] They did the same thing just like Steven.[9] Did she cry?[2A] Did she cry?[2A]
Tammy:	(Nods head)[A1]
Psychiatrist:	What did they do with the pookies with Steven?[1B]
Tammy:	Oh, what they did, they . . . umm, they did, they, umm, I don't know.[D3]
Psychiatrist:	Um hmm.[8]
Tammy:	I don't remember.[D3] They . . . I throwed in the trash, so they were doing things again.[C]
Psychiatrist:	What did you throw in the trash?[1A]
Tammy:	I throwed in the trash, I throwed . . . (Child writing) . . . I throwed, umm, pookies.[C]
Psychiatrist:	You threw the pookies in the trash?[9, 2A]
Tammy:	Yeah.[A1]
Psychiatrist:	Why did you throw the pookies in the trash?[1A]
Tammy:	Because.[C]
Psychiatrist:	Because why?[1A] What did they want you to do with the pookies?[1B]
Tammy:	Don't throw it in the trash.[C]
Psychiatrist:	They didn't want you to throw it in the trash?[9, 2A]
Tammy:	No.[B1]
Psychiatrist:	What did they want you to do with the pookies?[1A]
Tammy:	Umm, they want me to do with the pookies is, is, umm, is, umm, is, umm, is umm, umm . . . what did you say again?[F, E2]

Psychiatrist: I said, what did they want you to do with the pookies?[1A]

Tammy: They didn't want me to throw it away.[C]

Psychiatrist: They didn't want you to throw it away?[9, 2A]

Tammy: No?[B1] Not now.[G]

Psychiatrist: What did they want you to do with them?[1A]

Tammy: They want me to do with them, they want me, umm, to do with, umm, umm, they want me to do, with . . . Daddy and them, they didn't want me do it, but now they do.[C]

Psychiatrist: What did you do with the pookies?[1A]

Tammy: I throwed it in the trash.[C]

Psychiatrist: Before they . . . you threw it in the trash, what happened to the pookies?[1A]

Tammy: What?[F]

Psychiatrist: Before you throw it away, what did you do with the pookies?[1A]

Tammy: Umm, I, umm, did, I did, umm, I throwed it away and out in the sink, so they can't . . . or in the toilet, I mean and they never, never, never, never, find it.[C] Let's take a break now.[D1]

Psychiatrist: I know it's hard for you to remember all of this but you're being such a good girl to remember all of this.[5] Yes.[5] Did Bob have his pookies, too?[2A]

Tammy: Um hmm.[A1]

Psychiatrist: And what about Carole, did she have pookies?[3A]

Tammy: Um hmm.[A1]

Psychiatrist: What about Daddy?[1A]

Tammy: Daddy had his pookies, too.[C]

Psychiatrist: Daddy had his pookies, too.[9, 2A]

Tammy: Um hmm.[A1]

Psychiatrist:	What about Grandma and Grandpa?[1A]
Tammy:	Yeah.[C, E3]
Psychiatrist:	Did they have pookies, too?[2A]
Tammy:	Yeah.[A1] You know.[D1]
Psychiatrist:	Oh, Tammy, you have to come back here because they won't be able to see your picture.[4] Is this the first time you have your picture taken?[6C]
Tammy:	Yes . . . or no.[D2]
Psychiatrist:	No?[6C]
Tammy:	I never take a picture.[D2]
Psychiatrist:	You never take pictures but has anybody else ever taken a picture of you?[2A]
Tammy:	No.[B1]
Psychiatrist:	No?[9]
Tammy:	Only Daddy and them.[C]
Psychiatrist:	Only Daddy and them?[9, 2A]
Tammy:	Yeah.[A1]
Psychiatrist:	What pictures did they take of you?[1A]
Tammy:	Umm, umm . . . I don't know, maybe when I come back.[D3]
Psychiatrist:	When you come back?[1A]
Tammy:	Yeah.[A1]
Psychiatrist:	What do you want to do now?[1A]
Tammy:	Umm, I want to play a game.[D1]
Psychiatrist:	Want to play a game?[6C]
Tammy:	Yeah.[D2]
Psychiatrist:	Uh huh.[8] Do you remember some movies?[2A]
Tammy:	Yeah.[A1]

Psychiatrist: Uh huh.[8] Were you in the movies?[2A]

Tammy: I don't know.[D3]

Psychiatrist: Hmm?[1A]

Tammy: No.[B1] No.[B1]

Psychiatrist: Uh huh.[8] You see this camera here?[2A] Look at it.[4] They're taking movies of us.[10]

Tammy: They can't be taking movies of us.[D2]

Psychiatrist: Hmm?[6C]

Tammy: They can't be taking movies of us.[D2]

Psychiatrist: They can't?[6C] Why not?[6C]

Tammy: Because.[D2]

Psychiatrist: Because why?[6C]

Tammy: Because.[D2]

Psychiatrist: Do you want to take a break now?[10]

Tammy: Umm, I think so.[D2]

Psychiatrist: You think so.[6C]

Tammy: Yeah, I'll take a break.[D2]

Psychiatrist: You'll take a break.[6C] Okay.[8] Let's take a break.[5]

[Recess]

AFTERMATH

Four years after this interview was taped, Tammy, now nine years old, firmly believes the accounts of abuse. She has been separated from her father, aunt, and grandparents and subjected to continuous therapy for five years. The therapy is feeling-expressive, insight-oriented, and keeps Tammy repeating her feelings about the abuse and the abusers week after week. In a recent deposition (part of a civil suit by Carole Morgan and Bob Wilcox against their corporation) she reports what she has learned but only remembers what she has been taught in the interviews.

It is now part of her reality that these people whom she once loved are evil monsters who penetrated her anally and vaginally, urinated and defecated on her and her baby brother, and then forced them to eat feces and drink urine.

This training to believe in grotesque falsehood cannot fail to harm this child. It may result in permanent damage to her contact with reality. It may cause her to perceive herself always as a victim, helpless and dependent and unable to resist any intrusion. She has learned to regard unusual and deviant behavior, such as group orgies, urophilia and coprophilia, as almost routine daily events. She has been desensitized to horribly degrading behaviors, sexual perversions, and lack of privacy. Her capacity to engage in healthy and rewarding sexual relationships once she becomes an adult is likely to be permanently diminished.

The five adults accused of these horrendous acts struggle to recover from their five-year ordeal. A matrimonial domestic referee declared that Joe was an innocent man who had not abused his children and ordered reunification with his children, but to date, this order is being stonewalled. The grandparents are now in their late 70s and have not seen their only grandchildren in five years. Carole and Bob are presently involved in employment reinstatement proceedings for unlawful termination from their corporation. Joe, the grandparents, Carole and Bob have filed a civil complaint against the corporation, Dr. Jefferson, and the others who were involved in the false accusations. Due to numerous delays, this lawsuit has not yet been settled. All five keep their spirits up through their faith in God and their conviction that the truth will prevail and they will ultimately be vindicated.

Chapter 5

TRAINING TO HATE FATHER

An antimale attitude is often found in documents, statements, and in the writings of those claiming to be experts in cases of child sexual abuse. Many men describe behaviors they experience as "male bashing" or "father bashing." Some professionals believe that there is an undercurrent of radical feminist rhetoric and concepts involved in the way accusations of child sexual abuse are dealt with by the system. Some attorneys believe that radical feminists are the assistant district attorneys deliberately assigned by the chief prosecutor to handle sexual abuse cases.

Child protection workers are predominantly women. Child protection is a high stress and rapid burnout job and many child protection workers are young and inexperienced (Borman & Joseph, 1986). Some accused men say the child protection workers showed no awareness of what it means to be a parent, much less a father, and take a hostile and punitive stance toward them without ever talking to them. An almost universal complaint by the men in the cases in which we have been involved is that no one on the investigating team ever talked to them or tried to get their side of the story. Instead, they were believed to be guilty from the beginning, then were treated as already judged and sentenced.

We have reviewed notes, reports, and testimony of child protection workers, law enforcement officials, and mental health professionals in over 300 cases. Many of these professionals use techniques that teach children a negative and critical view of men in general and fathers in particular. These adult influences range from telling the child that Daddy is sick and needs help, to years of therapy in which the child is encouraged to use dolls to act out telling Daddy he is bad and should apologize. The child is repeatedly reinforced for fantasizing throwing Daddy in jail and is trained to hate and fear him.

When children are given therapy for sexual abuse, in every instance we have encountered, it is therapy based upon the belief that children must express and act out feelings about being abused and understand a number of cognitive propositions about themselves and the abuser. There

127

is, however, no evidence to support the effectiveness of this procedure with children. Children lack the cognitive and emotional capacities to benefit from this therapeutic approach. What it does accomplish is to teach children the emotions reinforced by the therapy, usually anger, aggression, and hostility. It teaches children about deviant sexual behavior and may reinforce them for sexual acting out. It may teach children to harbor resentments and hatred toward their father and men generally. If the child has not actually been abused, there is a risk of harm to all concerned.

Most sexual crimes are committed by men. Most sexual paraphilias are male behaviors. Most sexual abusers of children are men. However, a generalized bias against men does not permit an individualized or realistic appraisal of a basically good person who happens to be male. A readiness to lump all men together as potential aggressors and abusers may result in a situation where an antimale attitude is taught to a child whose father is innocent. This can only result in confusion for a child, disastrous consequences for the relationship between father and child, and irreversible damage to the father.

This is what happened for Allen, Michelle, Amy, and Jodie.

BACKGROUND

The divorce of Allen and Michelle Westlund lasted longer than their marriage and was much more conflicted. Michelle's mother had opposed the marriage and predicted it would fail. Michelle had recently graduated from a women's college of high status but insisted on marrying Allen. Her wealthy, powerful, and cultured family saw Allen as a hopeless, ill-mannered boor, far below their social status. His parents worked in factories and Allen was their seventh and last child. Allen, a tall and handsome man, had earned his General Education Diploma a few years after leaving high school at age sixteen for a job. He had worked hard, saved, invested in real estate, and, by the time he met Michelle, was financially well off.

Michelle had become involved in a counterculture life style during her last two years of college. She met Allen in a bar in a working-class neighborhood and was immediately attracted to him, seeing him as a diamond in the rough. Michelle's sophistication, culture, and self-assurance represented the world to which Allen aspired and Michelle introduced Allen into her circle of wealthy young friends who were rebelling against their parents' values by choosing everything their parents abhorred. These young people impressed Allen with their wit and brilliance, borrowed money from him, and tried to get him to use drugs. He refused drugs but drank beer with them while they sipped white wine from gallon jugs.

After the wedding, a large and conspicuous social event to which Michelle agreed in order to placate her parents, their honeymoon was one long battle about Allen's social ineptitude at the reception. They first lived in a small apartment in one of the houses Allen owned. Then Michelle convinced Allen to move to a small shack in the country with no electricity or running water. Their two daughters were born in this setting. Toward the end Michelle was estranged from her parents, fighting with Allen, and trying to manage two children in a primitive environment.

They had been married for four years, and their two daughters, Amy and Jodie, were ages three and one when Michelle's mother surprised her with a visit. The next day Michelle forced Allen out and filed for divorce. By this time, the couple was extremely angry at each other. There were bitter disagreements over the stipulations of the impending divorce, custody of the two children, and the visitation schedule. Each hired lawyers and continued the fight in court.

At one point, Allen brought the children to the hospital emergency room, after he had picked them up for his visit, because of severe diaper rash he observed on Jodie. The doctor reported that the rash was so bad that "whomever had been (supposedly) attending to the health care needs of this child was either a moron or *grossly* neglectful of her health care needs."

Allen blamed Michelle for neglecting the children and the situation was reported to child protection. However, the child protection team never contacted the doctor and never investigated Allen's complaint. Allen protested, wrote letters, and complained to county commissioners, but by this time Michelle had moved into a house her parents bought for her, and a telephone call from Michelle's father stopped any investigation.

The fighting escalated when Michelle, following a court hearing over visitation, took Amy to the hospital complaining that Allen had sexually abused her. A physician reported no physical findings but nevertheless made a diagnosis of possible sexual abuse based on the history provided by Michelle who said that Amy was having nightmares and showing sexually suggestive play with dolls after coming home from a visit with

Allen. This time, when the report was made, child protection reacted with alacrity. A court order was issued preventing Allen from seeing his children, and Amy was placed in therapy for the abuse. He wasn't able to see them for over a year but eventually was granted supervised visits after several legal actions.

Two years after the report and suspension of contact, when the case finally was due to come to trial, criminal charges were dropped. However, an agreement was reached in family court in which there was a judicial finding of no abuse by Allen, but he was still required to see his children under supervision. The claim was that he had been separated from them so long that there was no bond between them, and they had to be reintroduced to each other gradually. Allen agreed to this because he was emotionally exhausted, broke, and desperately wanted to see his children. Michelle by now was behaving more like a middle class mother and he did not think they were physically neglected anymore.

When we saw Allen, he was bitter and frustrated over his four-year battle with child protection and the system. He said that because the charges were dropped, his side of the case was never heard. He complained that reports had been written about what he was supposed to have done, although the individual writing the report never spoke to him. He had undergone several evaluations (both with and without his children) in which the professionals stated that they did not believe that he had abused his children, but these professionals were never contacted by the child protection investigators.

Although his legal bills had bankrupted him, he was still attempting to remove the requirement for supervision of his visits. He also wanted to remove Amy from the sexual abuse therapy, which consisted of weekly sessions focused on getting her to talk about the abuse and to express anger about him. He said repeatedly that his children were extremely important to him and that he would do whatever was necessary to fight the charges of sexual abuse and have a workable arrangement of visits.

As part of our involvement in this case, we reviewed the reports, the taped therapy sessions, and the therapy provided to Amy by two mental health professionals—a psychologist and a social worker. We also analyzed 12 of the interviews of the children, including several sessions of the social worker with Amy. Amy is four years old in the interviews reproduced here.

The social worker, Ms. Susan Sherman, first saw Amy by referral from the child protection workers. Ms. Sherman's practice consists mostly of children referred by the protection workers for sexual abuse evaluation and treatment. After eight sessions, including those reproduced here, she stated that she believed Allen did sexually molest Amy on at least one occasion. She based this opinion upon the mother's reports of nightmares and Amy's suggestive play with dolls. After telling Amy what her mother said about her doll play, Ms. Sherman reported that she questioned the child saying, "I know that when children play that way it usually means that a bigger person has been touching them 'there,' (pointing to the genital area of the girl dolls) . . . "

Ms. Sherman said Amy was preoccupied with "play about her father" and was worried that he was angry with her but could not explain why she feared he was angry. The report says that Amy's play also centered on a baby doll needing special attention and a Little Miss Muffet doll who talked to Daddy on the phone in the pretend telephone calls. Amy is described as playing "getting married to Daddy." Michelle reported that Amy was now saying she has two daddies, a good daddy and a bad gorilla daddy who hurts her. In an interview observed by two police officers behind a one way mirror, Amy said that Mommy told her that Daddy was a monster. The only allegation coming out of these sessions was that Allen "bad touched" Amy. No specificity about the touching was obtained.

For the 12 interviews we analyzed the proportion of error-inducing statements made by the interviewers was 57 percent. The primary focus of the therapy sessions was play therapy, predicated upon the assumption that the sexual abuse was real. Therefore, less time was spent in attempting to elicit statements to validate the abuse, but more was spent in encouraging Amy to express her feelings and work through the assumed trauma through her play therapy.

However, the play therapy engaged in by this therapist is not play therapy as originally intended. In traditional play therapy, the therapist is relatively quiet and observes the child playing at whatever the child chooses. No interpretations of the child's behavior are given to the child but rather the play therapist reflects back to the child whatever is judged to be the theme of the play. The child is the active and initiating person while the therapist is the passive observer (Axline, 1969).

In contrast, the social worker for Amy takes an active role in modeling the aggression toward the punching doll, symbolizing Allen. In prior sessions, the social worker taught Amy to pretend the punching doll was the bad Allen who did bad things to her. This identification appears in this interview as well. Note the guidance and reinforcement the social worker gives the child for aggressive and hostile acts toward the doll. The child's ambivalence about pretending the punching doll was Daddy is seen in her wanting to put Band Aids on it after punching and kicking it.

In all the sessions for which we have tapes, the social worker uses role playing, role modeling, and role reversal procedures extensively. There are frequent pretend telephone calls using play telephones. She has the child pretend to be various people or characters and then has her act out scenes or behaviors. The child is often confused by this, mistakes the directions of the social worker, or corrects the social worker who has slipped in her own agenda. This procedure is a powerful teaching technique as the social learning and social modeling research demonstrates (Bandura & Walters, 1963). It is also a technique frequently used by parents and teachers in the expectation that children will learn the attitude or behavior desired by the adult.

Susan Sherman had over 100 sessions of therapy with Amy. The transcripts reproduced here are typical of the ones we reviewed.

INTERVIEW

| Interviewer: | Susan Sherman, Social Worker. |
| Child: | Amy Westlund |

Soc Wkr:	I thought maybe you wanted to have it set.[10]
Amy:	No, when we have a long play we can set up.[B2]
Soc Wkr:	When we have a long play.[9] Sometimes near the end I have to set it just so I can remember when it's time to put the toys away and go upstairs.[10] It gets to be time for Amy to go to school after awhile, doesn't it?[2A]
Amy:	Hey, where's did . . . go?[F]
Soc Wkr:	Where did you leave her last week?[1A] Where do you usually leave her?[1A] You know where you usually leave her when we finish, when we put things away?[2A] I think she's probably right near where you left her.[10] There she is, there she is.[8]
Amy:	(Giggling) She needs her ba ba. [D2]
Soc Wkr:	Got have her ba ba . . . right?[6C]

Amy:	Yeah.[D2]
Soc Wkr:	Okay.[8]
Amy:	And a blanket.[D2]
Soc Wkr:	And a blanket.[6C]
Amy:	Pretend you're the bad guy today.[F]
Soc Wkr:	I'm going to be the bad guy today?[9, 2A]
Amy:	Yeah.[A1]
Soc Wkr:	Okay.[8] We don't need the wastebasket over there, probably.[6C]
Amy:	No.[D2]
Soc Wkr:	Is it in your way?[6C]
Amy:	Yeah.[D2] Let's pretend we're playing and our bottle will be right there.[F] And we should get the guns out, and um, and get the cash register out.[F]
Soc Wkr:	Get the cash register and the guns out?[9, 2A]
Amy:	Yeah.[A1]
Soc Wkr:	Okay.[8] I don't see the guns.[10] (inaudible) . . . the cash register.[10]
Amy:	The money is still there![D2]
Soc Wkr:	That new money that we found last time, isn't it?[9] We never did find the old money, I don't know where it was.[10]
Amy:	Ow, it's heavy.[D2]
Soc Wkr:	Is it heavy?[9, 2A]
Amy:	You bring that stuff, I'll bring this stuff.[F]

[Child crawls under easel]

Soc Wkr:	(Inaudible exchange while toys are being arranged) Are you all set up over there?[2A] With your baby, cash register, guns . . . [10] And my job is what, to be a bad guy?[2A] My job is to be a bad guy.[9] Let's see, should I take over these guns next?[10] Which one should I take?[1A] Okay?[8]

Amy: Yeah.[A1] You shot my baby, okay?[F] And I'll shoot you with my gun.[F]

Soc Wkr: So the way we're going to play today is I'm going to pretend to shoot your baby?[9, 2A]

Amy: Yeah.[A1]

Soc Wkr: I'm the bad guy.[9]

Amy: And I will shoot you![C]

Soc Wkr: Then I get shot.[9] You're the baby's mommy?[2B]

Amy: Yeah.[A1]

Soc Wkr: You're the baby's mommy.[9] And who am I?[1A]

Amy: The bad guy.[C]

Soc Wkr: I'm the bad guy.[9]

Amy: And then you're the bad He-Man and then you're going to be the good He-Man.[C]

Soc Wkr: Well, next after that I'll be the bad He-Man and then I'll be a good He-Man.[9] Okay.[8] And that's the baby and I'm going to shoot the baby.[9] Why do I shoot her?[1A]

Amy: Because you want her.[C]

Soc Wkr: Because I want her?[9, 2A]

Amy: Yeah.[A1]

Soc Wkr: Why do I want her?[1A] Do you think I should take her away after I shoot her?[2A]

Amy: Yeah.[A1]

Soc Wkr: Take her away, okay.[9] (Social worker makes shooting sounds.) I take the baby away now?[2A]

Amy: Yes.[A1]

Soc Wkr: I'm going to take the baby away.[9] All right.[8] So I hide over here somewhere?[2A]

Amy: Yeah.[A1]

Soc Wkr:	Where should I hide?[1A]
Amy:	Under the table.[C]
Soc Wkr:	Take the baby away.[9] All right.[8] Oh, I think I'm going to get shot.[6A] I guess Mommy is mad at me that I took the baby away.[6A] Baby's mommy is mad.[6A] (Inaudible) . . . shot.[10] Mommy is taking the baby away from the bad guy.[9]

[Child takes doll and crawls back under easel]

Amy:	And you take her away again.[F]
Soc Wkr:	You want me to take her away again?[9, 2A]
Amy:	Yeah.[A1] And get your gun.[F]
Soc Wkr:	. . . my gun too, huh?[9, 2A]
Amy:	Yeah.[A1]
Soc Wkr:	Where did my gun go?[1A] Here it is.[10]
Amy:	And you don't give her to me.[F] Okay?[F] And I chased you and you don't give her back to me.[F]
Soc Wkr:	I don't give her back to you?[9, 2A]
Amy:	And you're under arrest, okay?[F]
Soc Wkr:	Under what?[1A]
Amy:	You're under arrest.[C]
Soc Wkr:	Oh, I'm under arrest.[9] Okay.[8] Shoot, bang, bang, bang,[6A] I'm going to get that baby.[6A] Take the baby away from her mommy, take her away from her mommy.[6A] Baby's crying.[6A] Baby really upset, do you think Baby's upset?[6A, 2B]
Amy:	No.[B] Don't talk![F]
Soc Wkr:	Maybe the baby wanted to go with me.[6A]
Amy:	She's upset.[C]
Soc Wkr:	She is upset.[9] I bet she misses her mommy.[6A]
Amy:	And you, and I . . . and you run away.[F]

Soc Wkr:	And I run away.[9]
Amy:	But take her with you.[F]
Soc Wkr:	I'll take her and run away, all right.[9] And you can't find me?[9, 2A]
Amy:	Yeah, and I . . . you.[A2]
Soc Wkr:	(Inaudible)[10]
Amy:	And I chase you.[F]
Soc Wkr:	Okay, I'm going to run away.[9] I hope I don't get caught, I hope that Mommy doesn't catch me.[10]

[Child is chasing her around the room and giggling.]

Soc Wkr:	Should I let you catch me?[2A]
Amy:	Yeah.[A1] And I shoot you.[C]
Soc Wkr:	You're going to shoot me?[9, 2A]
Amy:	And when I chase you.[C] And then you go around here, like this.[F]
Soc Wkr:	Around here, like this.[9] Okay.[8]

[Child chases interviewer around a post and then shoots her.]

Soc Wkr:	I think I'm going to get shot.[10] Oh, I got shot.[10]
Amy:	Got shot.[G]
Soc Wkr:	I got caught.[10]
Amy:	Punchy did it![C]
Soc Wkr:	Was it Punchy that did it?[9, 2A]
Amy:	Yeah![A1]
Soc Wkr:	Oh, I thought it was the bad guy.[10] Is Punchy the bad guy?[2A]
Amy:	Punchy shoot you.[C]

Soc Wkr:	Did Punchy shoot you?[2A]
Amy:	No.[B1]

Soc Wkr:	I mean the baby, oh me, *I'm* the bad guy.[2A] Punchy shot me.[9]
Amy:	Yeah.[A1]

Soc Wkr:	Punchy shot the bad guy, Punchy's a good guy today?[9, 2A]
Amy:	No, he's a bad guy today.[B2]

Soc Wkr:	Today he's a bad guy.[9]
Amy:	Tomorrow he'll be a good guy.[C]

Soc Wkr:	Tomorrow he'll be a good guy.[9] So, you got your baby back.[9] Um.[8]
Amy:	I'm gonna shoot Punchy.[C] Now you're the good He-Man.[F]

Soc Wkr:	Baby's mommy is pretty mad that Baby got taken away.[6A] Um.[8] Maybe she wants to say something to the bad guy.[6A] Do you think Mommy wants to say something to the bad guy?[2A]
Amy:	Hey, I have to get the dinner.[B2]

Soc Wkr:	After you get dinner.[9] Okay.[8]
Amy:	What happened?[F]

Soc Wkr:	You shot me, didn't you?[9, 2A]
Amy:	No, Punchy did.[B2]

Soc Wkr:	I mean, Punchy shoot me.[9]
Amy:	What happened?[F]

Soc Wkr:	What do you mean, what happened?[1A] I don't know.[10] You'll have to tell me what happened, Amy.[4] 'Cause you're the one that tells the story so good.[5]
Amy:	Did Punchy shoot you?[F]

Soc Wkr:	I think Punchy shot me, yeah.[10]
Amy:	Does it hurt?[F]

Soc Wkr: Um, I'll pretend it does.[10] Do you want me to pretend that it hurts?[2A]

Amy: No.[B1]

Soc Wkr: No.[9] Okay.[8] Do you want me to say I'm all better?[2A]

Amy: Yeah.[A1]

Soc Wkr: Okay, I'm all better now.[10] Um, wonder what happens when the bad guy takes the baby away?[1A]

Amy: Punchy did it.[C]

Soc Wkr: It was Punchy that did it.[9] Well, what happened when Punchy took the bad guy, took the baby I mean?[1A] Did Punchy take the baby?[2A]

Amy: Yes.[A1]

Soc Wkr: Oh.[8] Let's find out.[4] Why don't we ask the baby what happened?[4, 6A]

Amy: Let's shoot Punchy.[C]

Soc Wkr: We could ask the baby.[6A]

Amy: Here's the gun.[C]

Soc Wkr: Is the baby still upset?[2A]

Amy: Yeah.[A1]

Soc Wkr: Baby is upset.[9] I wonder if we should help the baby feel better?[2A, 6A]

Amy: Yeah.[A1]

Soc Wkr: Should we?[2A]

Amy: Well, . . . [G]

Soc Wkr: Do you know how to help the baby?[2A]

Amy: Get your gun.[F]

Soc Wkr: Get my gun.[9]

Amy: And shoot Punchy.[C, F]

Soc Wkr:	We have to shoot Punchy, 'cause he's a bad guy.[6A] And he took the baby away.[6A] (Shooting sounds) Bad guy Punchy.[6A]
Amy:	Yours doesn't click.[G] Pretend your's clicks.[F]
Soc Wkr:	I have to pretend mine clicks.[9] Punchy, you're a bad guy and we're going to shoot you.[6A] (More shooting sounds) 'Cause you took the baby away.[6A]
Amy:	Don't![F] Don't talk.[F] (lots more shooting, child is looking at interviewer) He's all dead now.[C]
Soc Wkr:	Is Punchy all dead?[2A] Is the baby all right?[2A]
Amy:	Now we should make Gumby.[D2] He doesn't have any glasses.[D2] Make Gumby now.[D2] Put your guns in here.[F]
Soc Wkr:	Make Gumby on the blackboard?[9, 2A] Okay.[8]
Amy:	And put your guns all right here.[F]
Soc Wkr:	We're not going to playing with Baby anymore right now.[10] Baby, you're just laying there on the floor, right?[2A]
Amy:	And while you do Gumby, I'll go and get dinner ready.[C]
Soc Wkr:	And you'll take care of Baby.[6A] Is she still upset, Amy?[2A]
Amy:	Not yet.[B2] No, my name is the mother, Betty Westlund.[B2]
Soc Wkr:	Betty Westlund's Mommy, taking care of Baby?[9, 2A]
Amy:	Yeah.[A1] And you're the daddy.[F]
Soc Wkr:	I'm the daddy, huh?[9]
Amy:	We don't need a brother.[F]
Soc Wkr:	We don't need any brother.[9] And you wanted me to draw Gumby on here.[6C] Okay.[8] You want me to draw a picture of Gumby?[6C]
Amy:	Yes.[D2]
Soc Wkr:	All right, let's see, what does Gumby look like?[6C]
Amy:	No glasses![D2] He doesn't have no glasses.[D2]
Soc Wkr:	Yeah, Gumby doesn't have any glasses.[6C] All right.[8]

Amy: It's in the kitchen.[D2]

Soc Wkr: What kind of face does he have?[6C]

Amy: Ah, round, and a round, and a round, and some eyes.[D2]

Soc Wkr: Those look like eyes?[6C]

Amy: Yeah, no, no, those are his eye glasses.[D2]

Soc Wkr: You want round eyes.[6C] Okay.[8] Like that.[9] How about his mouth, what kind of mouth should we give him?[6C] A straight across mouth like this?[6C]

[Inaudible discussion continues at the chalkboard]

Amy: Where's Gumby?[D2] Let's make him again.[D2, F]

Soc Wkr: Should we make him again?[6C]

Amy: Yeah.[D2]

Soc Wkr: Okay.[8]

Amy: I can't do the legs.[D2]

Soc Wkr: (Inaudible) [6C]

Amy: . . . not going to be again, like Daddy's not scary.[C] Me, Benjy, Mama, John.[C] Okay?[F]

Soc Wkr: You want Mommy, let's see, say it again.[9]

Amy: Mom.[C]

Soc Wkr: Mommy, and you, and Benjy, and John.[9]

Amy: And Daddy.[C]

Soc Wkr: And Daddy.[9] But what about scary?[1A]

Amy: Not scary.[C]

Soc Wkr: Not a scary daddy?[9, 2A] And you want Daddy to look, how should we make Daddy look?[1A]

Amy: Nice.[C]

Soc Wkr: Nice.[9] Happy?[2A]

Amy:	Yep.[A1]
Soc Wkr:	Nice and[9]
Amy:	Happy.[C]
Soc Wkr:	Okay, let's see, what kind of face should this be, this will be laughing.[1A]
Amy:	My mommy.[C]
Soc Wkr:	That will be Mommy, all right.[9] So we want long hair on Mommy, like that.[10]
Amy:	Yeah.[A1]
Soc Wkr:	What kind of mouth should we give your mommy?[1A]
Amy:	I can do the mouth.[C]
Soc Wkr:	You like to do the mouth, don't you?[9, 2A] Okay.[8] You like to do that.[5]
Amy:	Like that.[C]
Soc Wkr:	... nose, right?[2A]
Amy:	A sad mouth.[C]
Soc Wkr:	Mommy has a sad mouth, is Mommy feeling bad in this picture?[2B]
Amy:	Yeah.[1A]
Soc Wkr:	Okay, Mommy feels bad, I wonder why she's sad?[9, 1A]
Amy:	Because she wants to get married with Allen.[C]
Soc Wkr:	She wants to get married with Allen, and she's sad?[9, 2A]
Amy:	Yeah.[A1]
Soc Wkr:	Oh, dear, why can't she get married with Allen?[1A]
Amy:	I want *her* to get married.[C]
Soc Wkr:	*You* want her to get married.[9]
Amy:	Two eyes.[C]
Soc Wkr:	Good eyes.[5] Nice big eyes.[5]

Amy: . . . we need an eye.[C]

Soc Wkr: That's an eye.[9] Okay.[8]

Amy: I don't like it.[F]

Soc Wkr: You don't like it, you want a different kind?[2A] Okay, who's this going to be?[1A]

Amy: A daddy.[C]

Soc Wkr: Okay.[8] A daddy.[9] I'm going to write down this is Mommy.[10]

Amy: Write it down.[C]

Soc Wkr: This is Mommy, sad because she want to get married.[9] You want her to get married.[9]

Amy: Yeah, with Allen.[A2]

Soc Wkr: With Allen.[9] She's sad because Amy wants her to be married to Allen.[9] Amy wants her family back together.[6A] Right?[2B]

Amy: Yeah.[A1]

Soc Wkr: Amy wishes her family would get back together and people wouldn't be getting mad anymore.[6A]

Amy: I'm going to step on the chalk.[D2]

Soc Wkr: No, because that would get it all mashed up.[4] Then we won't be able to use it.[10] You have to tell me what kind of a picture you want me make next.[4] Which person in your family should we have this one be?[1A]

Amy: Daddy.[C]

Soc Wkr: That'll be Daddy, all right.[9] You want to put on the mouth, what kind of a mouth do you want to give Daddy?[1A] Okay, that's the kind of mouth Daddy's going to have.[9] Um.[8] What does that mean, how's Daddy feeling?[1A]

Amy: Good.[C]

Soc Wkr: He's feeling good, huh?[9, 2A] Let's write down Daddy.[10]

Amy: Daddy Butch.[C]

Soc Wkr: Daddy what?[1A]

Amy:	Daddy Butch.[C]
Soc Wkr:	Daddy Butch, who's Daddy Butch?[1A]
Amy:	He's kinda my friend.[C]
Soc Wkr:	Is that your friend, Joey?[2B] Is Joey's last name Butch?[2B]
Amy:	No, my dad.[B2] Allen.[C]
Soc Wkr:	I thought his name was Westlund.[4]
Amy:	His name is Westlund.[C]
Soc Wkr:	But who's Butch?[1A]
Amy:	I don't know.[D3]
Soc Wkr:	Someone of your friends you said, huh?[9]
Amy:	Yeah.[A1]
Soc Wkr:	All right.[8] So Daddy, you said he feels good, right?[9, 2A]
Amy:	Yeah.[A1]
Soc Wkr:	I wonder why he feels good.[1A] What's he happy about?[1A]
Amy:	He's happy about getting married.[C]
Soc Wkr:	He's happy about getting married.[9] Who's he going to marry?[1A]
Amy:	Um, Nancy.[C] No, no she's not.[B1]
Soc Wkr:	Not going to marry Nancy, he wants to marry somebody?[1A]
Amy:	Yeah, me . . . [A2]
Soc Wkr:	Amy wants him to marry Nancy, but he wants to marry Amy?[2B] Is that the way it is?[2A]
Amy:	Yeah, because Punchy's Allen.[C]
Soc Wkr:	Now we need to have a picture of Amy here.[6A] Do you think we should?[2A] Have a picture of Amy on the chalkboard?[2A]
Amy:	Yeah . . . Mary.[A2]

Soc Wkr:	Amy has a lot of hair, so we got to give Mommy and Daddy, Daddy a little bit of hair like that.[10] And Mommy has a lot of hair and Amy has a lot of hair.[10] Okay.[8] I want to know if Amy can make a mouth on this picture over here.[2A]
Amy:	No, my name is Betty and Punchy married me.[C]
Soc Wkr:	Punchy married you.[9]
Amy:	Punchy Allen.[C]
Soc Wkr:	Punchy is Allen, right?[9, 2A] I'm getting kinda mixed up about who's marrying who.[10] I guess I'm having a hard time understanding who's gonna marry who.[10] Amy would like to have Mommy and Daddy married.[9]
Amy:	No, I'm gonna get married now.[B2]
Soc Wkr:	You're gonna get married, okay.[9] Can you show me what it's like to get married?[2A]
Amy:	No.[B1] I'm doing dinner now.[C, D1]
Soc Wkr:	'Cause I'm not sure what you mean about getting married.[4] I'm not sure what you mean.[4]
Amy:	Now you're the dada sister . . . watch TV.[F]
Soc Wkr:	Watch TV.[9]
Amy:	Watch over there.[F]
Soc Wkr:	Over there?[2A]
Amy:	Yeah.[A1] Baby's sleeping.[C]
Soc Wkr:	Baby's sleeping over here.[9] Baby stays over there.[9]
Amy:	And then I can do pay for something.[C]
Soc Wkr:	And then you can pay for something.[9]
Amy:	. . . ice cream cone . . . and bring them over there.[F]
Soc Wkr:	Oh, okay.[8] You want me to go and watch TV, I'm the daddy, no, I'm the sister, right?[9-2A]
Amy:	Yeah.[A1]

Soc Wkr:	I'm the sister.[9] Over here.[2A] Is this where I watch TV?[2A] And there's Punchy.[10] Punchy is Allen?[2A] I can't remember whether Punchy is Allen or not.[10]
Amy:	It's going . . . (inaudible)[G]
Soc Wkr:	Um[8]
Amy:	I better get it out of the refrigerator.[C]
Soc Wkr:	You need to get it out of the refrigerator.[9]
Amy:	We're making jam for dinner.[C]
Soc Wkr:	Making some jam for dinner.[9]
Amy:	Pretend you're the policeman now.[F]
Soc Wkr:	Oh, I'll be the policeman now.[9] Okay.[8]
Amy:	And I'll have my phone, okay?[F, D2]
Soc Wkr:	Now you have your phone, okay.[9]
Amy:	And you call me.[F]
Soc Wkr:	You want me to call you this time, huh?[9, 2A] You're Betty, the mommy?[2A]
Amy:	Yeah.[A1] And the phone rings and you call me.[F] Pretend you're Bozo the Policeman.[F]
Soc Wkr:	Hello, I'm the policeman.[10]
Amy:	Hi.[C] My baby had a bad dream.[C]
Soc Wkr:	Your baby had a bad dream.[9] Oh, what did she dream about?[1A]
Amy:	Well, the monster here and it's real.[C]
Soc Wkr:	It's a real monster?[9, 2A]
Amy:	And I'll get your gun, okay?[F]
Soc Wkr:	And I need to have a gun?[9, 2A] You want me to come and help?[2A]
Amy:	Yeah.[A1] I'll get your gun.[C]

Soc Wkr: Okay.[8] I guess I better hurry over there and help.[6A]

Amy: No, no.[F] We're still talking.[F]

Soc Wkr: Oh, okay.[8]

Amy: I got your gun.[C] I got your gun.[C]

Soc Wkr: You have my gun all ready for me?[10]

Amy: Yeah.[A1]

Soc Wkr: All right, what do you want me to do when I come to the house?[1A]

Amy: Well, shot him.[F] And then kill him.[F]

Soc Wkr: Shoot the monster and then kill him, huh?[9, 2A]

Amy: Yeah.[A1]

Soc Wkr: And what about the baby?[1A]

Amy: Well, I'm going to hold her in case she's hungry and wants some dinner.[C]

Soc Wkr: Is she upset?[2A]

Amy: Yes, she wants me.[A2]

Soc Wkr: She wants her mommy to hold her.[9]

Amy: Yeah.[A1]

Soc Wkr: Um hum.[8]

Amy: Are you on your way?[F]

Soc Wkr: Yeah, I'll be on my way.[10] I would like to talk to the baby though when I come, do you think I could do that?[6A, 2A]

Amy: I don't know.[D3] She doesn't want to talk.[C]

Soc Wkr: She doesn't want to talk?[9, 2A] Oh, I see.[8]

Amy: . . . your gun.[F]

Soc Wkr: I'll take my gun and shoot the monster, right?[9, 2A]

Amy: Yeah.[A1]

Soc Wkr: All right.[8] Okay.[8]

[Short inaudible exchange]

Amy: Come right now.[F]

Soc Wkr: Right now, okay.[9] Bye.[8]

Amy: Bye.[C]

Soc Wkr: I'd better hurry over to that house where that baby had a bad dream . . . [10]

Amy: Now you drive.[F]

Soc Wkr: I drive.[9] All right.[8]

Amy: No, this is not the door, the door is over there.[F]

Soc Wkr: Okay.[8] (knock, knock) Anybody home?[2A]

Amy: Yeah.[A1] (pretends to open the door) Hi![C]

Soc Wkr: Oh, you're opening the door for me.[9] I need to come and find out if the baby is all right and is the monster here?[10]

Amy: And it's a real monster.[C] I better get it though because he's scared of you.[C]

Soc Wkr: Oh, you were scared of him, too.[6A] Not just the baby, but you were, too.[6A]

Amy: Well, he's not scared of you.[C]

Soc Wkr: He's not scared of me.[9] Oh, well, what do you want me to do?[1A]

Amy: Just get him off of the bedroom.[F]

Soc Wkr: Get him out of the room, huh?[9, 2A]

Amy: Well, just look at my hair.[D2] It's in a tight ponytail.[D2]

Soc Wkr: Your mommy fixed it for you with blue and red, what are those things on there?[6C]

Amy: (Inaudible)[G]

Soc Wkr: Maybe I better go get Punchy in now.[6A] Should we pretend that Punchy is the monster?[2A]

Amy: Yeah.[A1]

Soc Wkr: Punchy, you did a bad thing.[6A] You were scaring the baby and even scaring the mommy.[6A]

Amy: Talk to Punchy and knock him over with the bat.[F]

Soc Wkr: We gotta knock you over, Punchy, with the bats.[9]

Amy: I gotta help, too.[C] I need bat.[C]

Soc Wkr: Punchy, you were doing scaring Baby, making her have bad dreams.[6A]

Amy: Knock him over now.[F]

Soc Wkr: Okay, let's knock him over now.[9] Okay?[8] He didn't go over yet.[10] There he goes.[10]

[Amy throws herself on top of the punchbag.]

Soc Wkr: Get right on, hon, and hold him down.[9]

[Amy stands on top of punchbag.]

Soc Wkr: Stand right on him.[9] I guess you're showing him that you don't want him to do that anymore.[6A]

Amy: Because I'm dead you get the doctor stuff out.[F]

Soc Wkr: Oh, Mommy got hurt this time.[9] She was trying to get Punchy down on the ground and she got hurt, she needs to be fixed now.[9] We have so many things to do today.[10] Taking care of mommies and taking care of babies, and it's hard to know who's the best person to help.[8] The doctor, the policeman, or the daddy, or the He-Man . . .[8] Mommy got hurt, we'll fix her up.[10] We'll put a magic Band Aid on her.[10] Where should we put the magic Band Aid?[1A] Right on your knee?[9] That's where the magic Band Aid goes 'cause that's where she got hurt.[6A] I wonder if she's all better yet?[2A] (inaudible) Take the mirror and look.[10]

Amy: No, no, I do it.[B2]

Soc Wkr: You do it.[9]

Amy: You tried to get Punchy and you do it, okay?[F]

Soc Wkr: And now I should get Punchy.[9] Okay.[8] (Strikes Punchy with fist) Punchy, you've been a bad guy.[6A]

Amy: And you get hurt.[F]

Soc Wkr: And I get hurt, huh?[9, 2A] I want you to stop being a bad guy with the baby.[6A] The baby gets scared and upset.[6A]

Amy: Now you fall down and get hurt.[F]

Soc Wkr: We've got to take better care of that baby.[6A] (Strikes punchbag and they fall on the floor together) Oh, I got hurt that time, ugh.[10]

Amy: Don't open your eyes, don't open your eyes.[F] Where does it hurt?[F] Open.[F] get a mirror.[F] Say aah.[F]

Soc Wkr: Aah.[10] (inaudible)...be a good guy after this.[10] Will I be a good guy?[2A]

Amy: Take you glasses off because put them up there.[F]

Soc Wkr: Put them up there?[9, 2A]

Amy: (inaudible)[G]

Soc Wkr: (inaudible)...will I be a good guy after I get fixed?[2A]

[Inaudible exchange.]

Amy: Now we try to get Punchy again.[F]

Soc Wkr: (Inaudible)...dangerous trying to get Punchy, we get hurt sometimes.[9]

[Inaudible exchange.]

Amy: Okay.[G]

Soc Wkr: ...better now?[8]

Amy: One more thing we have to do.[F]

Soc Wkr: Um hum.[8]

Amy: (laughs)

[Inaudible exchange.]

Soc Wkr: . . . tiny baby.[10] (Inaudible)[10] Am I all better now?[2A]

Amy: Yep.[A1]

Soc Wkr: Oh, that feels good, Doctor.[5]

Amy: (Stands on Punchy)[D2]

Soc Wkr: Now what are we going to do?[1A] Are we still trying to make
                Punchy better?[2A] Make him stop being bad?[6A, 2A]

Amy: Get this off of me.[F]

Soc Wkr: What's that, the Band Aid on your shoe?[6C] I thought it was on
                your knee.[6C] How did it get down there on your shoe?[6C]

Amy: (standing on Punchy—making loud noises)[D2]

Soc Wkr: Should we put a Band Aid on Punchy?[2B]

Amy: No.[B1] (she continues to stand and bounce on Punchy, then jumps
                off)

Soc Wkr: Amy, I want to talk to you for a minute about something real.[4]
                Maybe you can help me with.[4] Because your mommy's been
                telling me that lots of times lately you've been kind of upset about
                visiting Daddy.[4, 6A] When you get back home, or when you go in
                the car with him.[4, 6A] When I talk with your daddy or when with
                somebody that will talk to him, I need to tell him how he can help
                you.[4] So that you aren't so upset.[4] Or maybe you can tell me how
                Mommy can help.[4]

Amy: No.[D1]

Soc Wkr: Who do you think can help you most, Mommy or Daddy?[3A]
                With these visits?[1A]

Amy: Mommy.[C]

Soc Wkr: Mommy can help?[9, 2A] What can Mommy say or do to make you
                feel better about visits?[1A]

Amy: . . . phone.[G]

Soc Wkr: . . . a Band Aid on the phone?[6C]

Amy: Take it off.[F]

Soc Wkr:	Maybe it has something to do with Mommy being mad at Daddy?[6A] Is that what makes visits hard, Amy?[2B]
Amy:	(child hangs up her phone) No.[B1] No.[B1] Take this off.[F] (indicates Band Aid on phone)
Soc Wkr:	You want it off, huh?[9, 2A] I'll get it started and you pull it off.[10] (hands phone back to child) There you go.[5] All better, no more tape.[5]
Amy:	No more tape.[D2]
Soc Wkr:	No more tape.[6C] Oh my goodness.[6C]
Amy:	(inaudible) phone . . . [G]
Soc Wkr:	Can I talk on the other telephone?[9, 2A] Where is the other phone?[1A]
Amy:	I don't know.[D3] Don't look for it, I got this phone.[F]
Soc Wkr:	Okay.[8] You don't want me to talk on the other phone.[9]
Amy:	(pretend phone conversation) Well, well, you want to talk to Daddy?[C] Well, pretend your kinda tired now and you're sleeping.[F] (addressed to therapist)
Soc Wkr:	Oh, okay, where should I be sleeping?[1A]
Amy:	That's your bed and lie down.[C, F]
Soc Wkr:	Oh, you want me to lie down over there.[9]
Amy:	Lie down for real.[F]
Soc Wkr:	Okay.[8] I got . . . my office . . . [8]
Amy:	(into phone) He's sleeping.[C] What . . . he's sleeping.[C] Well, I'm cooking dinner . . . I might wake him up when I'm talking on the phone.[C] Daddy, wake up![C]
Soc Wkr:	Okay.[8]
Amy:	Somebody wants to talk to you.[C]
Soc Wkr:	Oh, all right.[10] Hello.[10] Hello.[10]
Amy:	No, it's this phone.[F]

Soc Wkr:	Oh, you want me to talk over there?[2A] Should I leave this here?[2A]
Amy:	(Inaudible)[G]
Soc Wkr:	I wonder who it is on the telephone.[10]
Amy:	It's your business.[C]
Soc Wkr:	Hello, Who are you?[1A] Oh, you're Susan.[6A] Is this Susan calling?[6A] You wanted to talk to me about Amy getting kinda scared about visiting.[4, 6A]
Amy:	No, I'm Betty.[B2] Her name is Amy.[F, D1]
Soc Wkr:	Okay.[8] But I think Susan wanted to talk to Daddy about Amy.[6A, 4] You're Daddy Allen, aren't you?[6A, 4] Well, Amy's been feeling kinda scared, kind worried about visits.[4] Yeah.[8] Do you know what she might be scared about?[6A] You want Amy to tell you?[6A, 4] Okay.[8] Amy, will you tell your daddy what it is that makes you feel kinda scared sometimes about visits?[2A, 4]
Amy:	No, her name is Amy[F, D1] (points to other side of room).
Soc Wkr:	Over there, oh, okay.[9] Amy, can you talk to Daddy?[2A, 4]
Amy:	It can't reach.[F] Talk to her.[F]
Soc Wkr:	I guess it's really hard for Amy, maybe she needs to have the grown ups talk about her.[6A]
Amy:	I can't do this one.[D1]
Soc Wkr:	You want Michelle to talk?[2B] Michelle, okay, Michelle, what do you think makes Amy upset?[1A, 4]
Amy:	No, my name is Betty.[F, D1] That's Amy over there.[F, D1]
Soc Wkr:	Oh, all right.[8] Let's ask Betty then.[4, 6A] Betty, would you tell Allen what you think would make Amy feel better?[4, 6A]
Amy:	. . . (inaudible) no, you do this part.[F, D1]
Soc Wkr:	Okay, I'm getting dinner ready over here . . . [9]

[Inaudible exchange]

Soc Wkr: Oh, boy, I think it's really hard to talk about . . . [4, 6A] I think so especially, 'cause Daddy says things . . . Daddy says that Mommy is bad or Daddy says that Mommy is bad.[6A, 4] That's really hard for Amy.[6A, 4] Daddy says that Mommy is a bad person.[6A, 4]

Amy: Well, pretend that you're talking to someone and you're the mama and I'm the daddy.[F]

Soc Wkr: Allen, I want to tell you Amy's sleeping, I mean, Betty's sleeping right now.[10]

Amy: No, you're Mama Betty.[F]

Soc Wkr: Oh, I'm the mommy Betty.[9] All right.[8] I'm concerned, I need to be sure my baby is safe.[6A] Taken care of good.[6A]

Amy: I'm Betty.[C] And my baby comes over and you bring her over and she wants, I mean.[F]

Soc Wkr: You want me to bring the baby over to you?[9, 2A]

Amy: Yeah.[A1]

Soc Wkr: Okay.[8] Goodbye.[10] I'll talk to you later.[10] I think the grownups have to have a serious talk about . . . to make sure Amy feels better.[6A] Okay.[8] Goodbye.[10]

Amy: No, my name is Betty.[F, D1]

Soc Wkr: I know, but we were talking about Amy.[4] And now we'll get the baby over to Betty's 'cause the baby misses Mommy.[6A] Baby really wants to see her mommy.[6A] Oh, guess what, Amy, I forgot to set the timer and here it is time for us to put the toys away.[10] Here you are, Betty, you take good care of baby . . . all the Play Dough and all the dishes.[6C] Can you help me put things away?[6C]

Amy: Yes.[D2]

Soc Wkr: We've got to be going upstairs, 'cause your mommy's waiting for you I bet.[6C] Punchy, we'll put you back over here.[6C] What should we tell Punchy when we put him away?[1A] Um?[2A]

Amy: I forgot to pay for my ice cream cones.[D2]

Soc Wkr: We have to put the cash register away, Amy.[6C]

Amy: . . . in the cash register.[D2]

Soc Wkr: All right, all right, you put the dollar . . . Amy and Daddy after we did Gumby.[6C] We did so many things today.[9] So many important things.[9, 6C]

Amy: I'm so tired.[C]

Soc Wkr: You get all tired out from . . . in the play room, don't we?[9, 2A]

Amy: Yeah.[A1]

Soc Wkr: All tired out.[9] Sometimes we get all tired out.[9] We work so hard to make things better.[6A] Trying to help make things better.[6A] Play about feelings, play about bad feelings and getting better feelings.[6A]

Amy: I fell down.[D2]

Soc Wkr: Yeah.[8] Fell right down on your knee.[6C]

Amy: I got a booboo.[D2]

Soc Wkr: You got a booboo?[6C]

Amy: Yeah.[D2]

Soc Wkr: What do we need to make you feel better?[6C] Can you push the, Amy, it isn't quite time to go yet.[4] Can you put the cash register in the cabinet?[6C] Maybe you can put the doctor kit in there, too, can you find room for it?[6C] We are just about, oh, we have the Play Dough left to put away, and the dishes, and the guns.[6C] (inaudible) Putting things away nice and.[6C] Only the Play Dough left.[6C] Can you carry the Play Dough?[6C]

Amy: Before we go home, can I get some paper up in your office?[F, D2]

Soc Wkr: I think there's some down here that you left another time.[6C]

Amy: Well, I wanted to get your kind.[D2]

Soc Wkr: This is the kinds, some other day you forgot to take them home.[6C] And that's your special color.[5, 6C] Isn't it?[6C]

Amy: I got it here last time.[D2]

Soc Wkr: I know it.[6C] There we go.[5] We worked so hard today that we're all tired out.[5]

Amy: All tired out.[C]

Soc Wkr:	We worked so hard . . . [5]
Amy:	I can't . . . the door even.[D2]
Soc Wkr:	You need some help opening the door?[6C]
Amy:	Yep.[D2]

[End of Interview]

The next session with Amy included the following portion. It shows the continued modeling and reinforcement of aggression toward her father. This behavior by the social worker is evident in all the sessions for which we have tapes. We did not include the entire session simply because of length.

Amy:	. . . talk to him[G] (child is sitting under table, hands telephone to interviewer)
Soc Wkr:	You want me to talk about the baby being pushed in the face?[2B]
Amy:	No. I talked about that already, he's on the way.[B2]
Soc Wkr:	Hello, I'm the daddy, you want to ask me something?[2A]
Amy:	He wants . . . (whispering) . . . Bozo.[C]
Soc Wkr:	You're the police and you're Bozo.[F]
Amy:	Yeah, and you'll get your phone out and call me, okay?[A2, F]
Soc Wkr:	Pretty soon we'll have to stop playing games, it'll be time for you to go back home and go to school.[10] (Hands phone back to child.)
Amy:	Okay.[G]
Soc Wkr:	Oh, hi, I'm the policeman.[10]
Amy:	You should be way, way over there. (Points to other side of room).[F, C]
Soc Wkr:	Do you want to tell me something?[2B]
Amy:	I'm not Bozo.[C]
Soc Wkr:	Who are you then?[1A]
Amy:	You're Bozo.[F] I'm Betty Adams.[C]

Soc Wkr: Okay, Betty, do you want to tell me something about what happened?[2B]

Amy: No, I'm not talking about *that* thing.[B2]

Soc Wkr: No?[9]

Amy: And you're Bozo.[F] Are you on your way?[F]

Soc Wkr: Are we only going to talk about good things?[2A]

Amy: Yeah.[A1]

Soc Wkr: Okay, okay.[8]

Amy: Are you on your way?[F]

Soc Wkr: Well, if you need any help with anything bad . . . [6A]

Amy: . . . touched my back, my . . . um, baby.[C]

Soc Wkr: Somebody touched your baby and wants to?[9, 2A]

Amy: Yeah. . . . making ice cream for . . . somebody.[A2]

Amy: . . . bad dreams . . . [C]

Soc Wkr: . . . bad dreams, she . . . [9]

Amy: No, she didn't have bad dreams and she wants to sit on my lap, and the bad guy came . . . over my house and punched her.[B2]

Soc Wkr: . . . that sounds like a really hard time.[10] Your baby must be very scared.[6A] Do you need me to help?[2A]

Amy: No.[B1]

Soc Wkr: Are you sure?[2A, 4]

Amy: No.[B1]

Soc Wkr: Okay, well, you tell me if you need me . . . [6A]

Amy: My baby helps.[C]

Soc Wkr: All right, do you want me to come to your house now?[2B]

Amy: Are you on your way?[F]

Soc Wkr: Yeah, I'll come to the house right now.[10] All right?[2A]

Amy: Drive your car.[F]

Soc Wkr: I'll drive my car.[9] Okay.[8] See you in a few minutes.[10]

Amy: Okay.[G]

Soc Wkr: Bye.[10] (Social Worker and child hang up phones. Social Worker makes car sounds) Here I come.[10] I'd better bring my gun.[6A] Should I bring a gun, Amy?[2A]

Amy: Yeah.[A1]

Soc Wkr: This has to be taken care of.[6A] It's not good for that little girl to be scared like that.[6A]

Amy: What am I supposed to do?[F]

Soc Wkr: Gee, maybe we should talk with that bad guy . . . [6A] (Social Worker is handling a toy gun)

Amy: (Inaudible)[G] (Child comes out from under the table.)

Soc Wkr: And tell him that he has to stop hurting her.[6A] No more hurting.[6A]

Amy: He's over there.[C]

Soc Wkr: Who is?[1A]

Amy: Punchy, the bad guy.[C]

Soc Wkr: Oh, oh, he's the bad guy.[9] You didn't tell me that Punchy was going to be the bad guy now.[10] All right.[8] We've got to finish our story because pretty soon we've got to go upstairs.[4] We've got Punchy here, are we going to shoot him?[2B, 6A] Me, too, do you want me to shoot him, too?[2A, 6A]

Amy: Yeah. (Lots of shooting noises)[A1]

Soc Wkr: You are bad, bad guy.[6A] You've been hurting and scaring that little girl . . . baby.[6A]

Amy: The baby's a girl.[C]

Soc Wkr: Is it a girl baby?[9, 2A] . . . Now that baby's all mixed up and scared.[6A] That's it, I can see you know how to take care of bad guys.[5]

Amy: He fell down.[C]

Soc Wkr: That's one way to take care of that bad guy.[6A, 5] Pushed him right down.[5] Right?[2A, 5]

Amy: You make him get up again.[F]

Soc Wkr: Even if he's bigger than you, right?[2A, 6A]

Amy: You make him stand up again.[F]

Soc Wkr: Okay, I'll see if I can get him to stay.[10] Now stay there.[6A] I can make him stay.[10] Okay.[8] There he is, push him right over with the bat.[6A, 4] Take a bat and make him fall right down.[4, 6A]

Amy: I'm going to jump on him.[C]

Soc Wkr: Um hum.[8]

Amy: I'm . . . because I'm a Betty Adams doctor.[C]

Soc Wkr: You're a Betty Adams doctor?[9, 2A]

Amy: . . . 'cause she's mine.[C]

Soc Wkr: We're going to fix him up real fast 'cause it's time to finish playing.[9] Just about time to finish playing. Fix him up real fast.[4] I'm going to be putting some of the toys away pretty soon because it's time to finish here.[10] And you can be fixing Punchy, 'cause you like to make him all better after we've killed him, don't you, huh?[4, 2A, 6A]

Amy: (Inaudible)[G]

Soc Wkr: You like to make him all better when you can.[6A]

[Both child and interviewer are picking up toys]

Soc Wkr: Maybe we should talk to that bad guy Punchy, too, before we finish up here, huh?[4, 2A, 6A] Sometimes he needs to be told how to behave, how to be a good guy.[6A] Can you tell him how to be a good guy?[2A, 4]

Amy: Yeah, . . . you be the good guy next time, okay?[A2, C] He says, okay.[C]

Soc Wkr: And I don't want you to get that little baby all mixed up about getting married.[6A] Sometimes she gets all mixed up.[6A]

Amy: Yep.[A2]

Soc Wkr:	It's makes her mixed up because that's grown up stuff, getting married.[6A]
Amy:	(inaudible)[G]
Soc Wkr:	So I'm going to watch and to make sure you're a good guy.[6A] And try to help you be a good guy.[6A] Try to help.[6A]
Amy:	(inaudible)[G]
Soc Wkr:	Think so?[2A] Is he getting better?[2A]
Amy:	Yeah.[A1]
Soc Wkr:	Did you?[6C] (opens door) That's what we heard, Mommy, we heard Mommy.[6C]
Amy:	(inaudible)[G]
Soc Wkr:	Do you want to show Mommy the bandage you put on Punchy?[2A]
Mother:	Are you fixing him, oh, good.[2A, 5]
Amy:	Could you help me . . . over there?[D2]
Soc Wkr:	Amy painted a picture, it's still drying.[6B]
Mother:	Isn't that pretty![5]
Amy:	Where's . . . [F, D2]
Mother:	He's waiting in the car.[6C]
Soc Wkr:	Do you know anything about some doll, a Cabbage Patch doll her dad gave her?[6B]
Mother:	Um hum.[6B]
Soc Wkr:	She brought them home?[6B]
Mother:	Um hum.[6B]
Soc Wkr:	I was unsure if she brought them home or they were to stay there.[6B]

AFTERMATH

Allen sees his children under supervision. He says that Jodie does not show any affection towards him and acts like he is a friendly uncle. Amy is hesitant and withdrawn when the visits begin. She talks about how

Allen did bad things to her and hurt her. After a time she seems to relax and does not continue asking or talking about it. Allen is confused and saddened by this. He cannot talk to her about it because child protection has told him he cannot tell her she is wrong or that it didn't really happen. Although there has never been a finding of abuse, they maintain that the child must be believed in order for her to feel secure and safe. Therefore, since she said he "bad touched" her, he cannot challenge or deny it. Allen fears he will never have a normal, easy, affectionate relationship with his children.

Allen lost his real estate holdings because of the expenses of the protracted legal battle. He has a good job and hopes to recover and begin again. He is involved with a woman whom he loves and whom he believes loves him. She knows all about the accusations and the struggle and believes he did not abuse his child. They will marry soon.

Allen says now that he does not want any more children.

It hurts too much.

Chapter 6

WHEN THERAPY BECOMES INTERROGATION

An accusation of sexual abuse sometimes emerges when a child has been in therapy for a different problem. But accusations developing in this fashion may not always be true. The therapist may have adopted the unfounded dogmas characteristic of the system that finds actual abuse in all accusations. The therapist may have accepted the concept of behavioral indicators uncritically and may not understand the danger of too many false positives in using nondiscriminating signs to make a diagnosis of sexual abuse. The therapist may be unaware of feelings of like and dislike developed toward patients (negative or positive counter-transference) and may not realize how those feelings can produce a positive bias toward one patient and a negative bias against another. Mix these factors together and an accusation of sexual abuse against the disliked patient unwittingly developed out of the therapist's biases becomes possible.

A report by a professional carries more weight with child protection and law enforcement officers than do reports by nonprofessionals, even when no investigation of the allegations has yet been made. Although the accusation has not been dealt with by the justice system, the workers involved may agree that it is real abuse. When this happens, the child may receive therapy for sexual abuse for months because the therapist believes it is real. The therapist then becomes an interrogator, questioning and pressuring the child to describe the abuse in the therapy sessions. These statements elicited by the therapist are later used in a trial or hearing as evidence in the determination of guilt. What began as therapy has now changed into interrogation and no one, including the therapist, sees that this is a questionable, and perhaps unethical, procedure.

In the following case, the allegations were originally made by the therapist, Dr. Marie Draper, a psychologist trained in educational rather than clinical psychology but who was in private practice. The allegations surfaced after several months of therapy in which Dr. Draper saw all of the members of the family in differing combinations for marital, family,

161

and individual therapy. Following the separation of the couple, Dr. Draper interpreted behavior of the five-year-old daughter to mean that she had been sexually abused by her father.

BACKGROUND

Andrea and Kent Erickson met at a company-sponsored picnic at the large company where both worked. They began dating and Andrea moved in with Kent a few months later. Six months after this they were married and eventually had two daughters, Jill Ann and Molly.

Conflicts started soon after the girls were born. The couple had radically different ideas as to how the children should be handled and disciplined and disagreements over this were the source of many heated arguments. Kent perceived Andrea as lax in discipline and unable to set appropriate limits, and Andrea saw Kent as rigid and punitive.

In February, when Jill Ann and Molly were five and two, Andrea began individual therapy with Dr. Marie Draper for the stress she reported from the stormy marriage and for help with her plan to get a divorce. After two sessions with Andrea, Dr. Draper asked Kent to come in for joint sessions of marital therapy while she continued to see Andrea for individual therapy. She then worked with the two of them on child management and marital therapy. Her therapy notes indicate that in every session she tells Kent something critical about his parenting behaviors which she saw as inappropriate, mistaken, or stupid. Despite therapy, the marriage difficulties continued and four months later, at the beginning of June, the couple separated.

During the marriage, both girls had been awakening the parents up to three or four times a night and Jill Ann was sleeping in her parents' bed for a portion of each night. Kent was bitterly opposed to this behavior while Andrea could not see what the big fuss was about. These episodes resulted in heightened emotions and a steady escalation of the conflicts. Dr. Draper worked with Andrea and Kent on a behavior management program to control Jill Ann's awakening her parents and encourage her to sleep in her own bed. After the separation, Andrea and Kent frequently accused each other of sabotaging the behavioral program. At this point, the girls spent approximately 50 percent of their time with each parent.

Jill Ann was showing signs of stress and in July, Andrea started her in individual therapy with Dr. Draper. Jill Ann told Dr. Draper that she was angry at both parents for separating, but that she was angriest at her mother. She also said that she believed that she was the cause of her parents' divorce because she would not sleep in her own bed. The notes of the first session include statements by Andrea as to how the children were mistreated and neglected by Kent. Dr. Draper accepts these reports from Andrea as fact.

Because the parents had joint physical custody, Kent occasionally brought Jill Ann to a therapy session. At the end of August when he brought her, Dr. Draper observed that Jill Ann had a bag of makeup and plastic clip-on earrings. She had been excited about coming to therapy and asked to get dressed up for it, however, Dr. Draper said makeup and earrings were inappropriate for a five year old. In talking before the session, Kent said he might take Jill Ann to a Loretta Lynn concert at the fairgrounds that night. In a later report, Dr. Draper wrote, "This concerned me because of his seeming inability to hear the message that he was not choosing appropriate activities, nor was he having appropriate expectations for a child of the age of barely five years old."

Kent left and Dr. Draper began to question the child about possible molestation. She asked Jill Ann about sleeping in her own bed. The notes say the child said she was doing okay and that daddy had called her into his bed. Jill Ann said nothing suggesting molestation, but Dr. Draper called Andrea and said she wanted another session in two days to get more information about possible abuse. Andrea, in the midst of a bitter and angry divorce, was quick to believe that Kent had sexually abused Jill Ann and agreed.

Dr. Draper saw Jill Ann two days later and taped this session. As a result of the questioning, Jill Ann made statements about sitting on her father's tummy and penis. The report of sexual abuse was made and Kent was prohibited from seeing his children. Criminal charges were filed and grew to include penile insertion into Jill Ann's vagina.

Kent Erickson's version of the events was that on the morning in question, Jill Ann had awakened early and went to the bathroom. When he heard her, he told her that she could come into bed with him at that time instead of waiting for the alarm which was to go off in a few minutes. (Jill Ann received 25¢ for every morning that she waited for the alarm to go off before coming to bed with her mother or father.) Jill Ann came to bed but was uncomfortable because she was afraid that she had not followed the rules and would not get her quarter. Kent told her that they didn't have to tell her mother about it. He believes that this is why she was anxious in response to the pressure from Dr. Draper to discuss the events of that morning. Kent admitted to holding and cuddling both children and to sometimes bathing with them but denied any sexual arousal or sexually abusive behaviors.

This situation is typical in that a sexual abuse allegation began with an ambiguous event. The ambiguous event is seen as suspicious of sexual abuse, with the result that the adult questions the child in a way to elicit statements about the hypothesized abuse. Dr. Draper was ready to believe that Kent abused Jill Ann once she was confronted with the initial statement from Jill Ann that her daddy had asked her to come to his bed. Her reports indicate that she had taken Andrea's side in the marriage battles and in the conflicts over discipline. She concluded that Kent was not behaving appropriately in allowing Jill Ann to appear for a therapy session wearing makeup and plastic jewelry. She interpreted the distress that Jill Ann was showing over her parents' divorce as behavioral indicators consistent with sexual abuse. Once having decided that Kent had abused Jill Ann she tried to get the child to describe the abuse.

Dr. Draper was using a feeling-expressive therapy which assumes that the child must repeatedly describe abuse in order to get her feelings about it out and thus be cured from the trauma of the abuse. This therapy, which was adapted from the therapy used to treat adult rape victims, has no proven efficacy for treatment of child sexual abuse but is the modality most frequently used when there is an allegation of abuse. Dr. Draper has also confused the roles of the investigator with that of the therapist with a probable iatrogenic effect for Jill Ann.

The following transcript is of the taped session that led to the report of sexual abuse. This was a therapy session and much of the exchange between Jill Ann and Dr. Draper is irrelevant to the question of sexual abuse. Despite the high proportion of interviewer behaviors categorized as irrelevant, over half (56%) of the interviewer behaviors fell into the error-inducing categories for this interview and a later one that we analyzed.

Dr. Draper begins the session by asking Jill Ann if her daddy did something that made her mad in the session two days ago. Jill Ann replies that she just wanted to be silly and adds that she always shows her bottom to her daddy. This remark suggests the effect of the reinforcement for such statements in the earlier, unrecorded session.

A few minutes into the interview, Dr. Draper asks Jill Ann if her daddy tells her that it is okay to sleep in his bed and Jill Ann replies,

"No," and, in response to a further question, states, "Yeah, he did but only in the morning." This is consistent with the explanation given by Kent.

Dr. Draper tells Jill Ann that it is all right to cry when talking about sleeping with her dad and states that she would feel better if she talked. She asks several leading questions and when she gets no response about sexual abuse, assumes that Jill Ann doesn't want to talk because she is anxious and afraid to talk about it.

She repeatedly asks what happened in Daddy's bed and says to Jill Ann, "You know when you said that you sleep in Daddy's bed, and that you are uncomfortable there, that it makes you uptight . . . " although Jill Ann has not said this. She puts pressure on Jill Ann to tell what happened and when she asks, "Are you afraid to tell me, Jill Ann?" Jill Ann finally replies, "Yeah, I think." Jill Ann is giving Dr. Draper the answer she believes the psychologist wants. Dr. Draper is assuming that something bad happened and that Jill Ann is afraid to talk about it and this assumption determines the course of the session.

Dr. Draper tells Jill Ann, " . . . you're going to be uptight and you're going to feel bad inside about it as long as it's happening. Is that true?" Jill Ann replies, "No," and Dr. Draper asks, "Why won't you tell me?" Jill Ann says, "Because I don't want to tell you" and that she wants "to keep it a secret." Although this is consistent with Kent's account, it is also confirms Dr. Draper's theory that Jill Ann is keeping a dreaded secret about sexual abuse.

Dr. Draper thus far has obtained no useful statements about abuse and requests Jill Ann to draw a picture of "what happens in bed." The report by Dr. Draper states that Jill Ann drew a picture of her father, herself, and Molly lying down in bed with their arms spread out and smiles on their faces. In response to the innocuous picture, Dr. Draper says, "You didn't show me what the secret was." Jill Ann draws a heart and Dr. Draper pressures her, "I want to know the secret that you have in Daddy's bed." She repeats this request several times.

Finally, Jill Ann says, "And he'll let me cuddle. And that's it." But Dr. Draper persists, "What else do you play, Jill Ann?" This gives Jill Ann the clear message that she has not given Dr. Draper what the therapist wants. When an interviewer says, "What else?" this tells the child that she has not yet produced what the adult wants to hear.

Dr. Draper persists and Jill Ann finally adds, "I bounce on Daddy's bed." Dr. Draper replies, "Do you bounce on Daddy?" Jill Ann says that she and Molly do this and then adds the "really secret," "I sit on Daddy's tummy," and in response to a request for elaboration adds, "I rub his tummy." Dr. Draper immediately asks, "Do you rub anything else?" and Jill Ann states, "No. Heavens no." This is not what Dr. Draper wants to hear, and she says, "Are you sure?"

When Jill Ann answers, "Yeah," she increases the pressure on the child, "You know, Jill Ann, I think maybe that you're not telling me the whole secret . . . I know you aren't."

This is extremely coercive. The child is told she is lying, that she has not yet produced whatever Dr. Draper wants and the message is that she'd better produce it. When adults believe that a child has been sexually abused and that children keep abuse a secret, any denial by the child is ignored and treated as being consistent with abuse. The child is therefore pressured to tell the secret. The adult believes that because the child has a secret about sexual abuse the adult must keep pressing in order to break the child's resistance. What this does is to make it impossible for the child to say anything that the adult will accept as evidence against abuse. No matter what the child does, as in this interview, the adult keeps pressing until some response is obtained that may be interpreted as indicating abuse.

Dr. Draper repeats this type of coercion, and when she gets no statements about sexual abuse, finally tells Jill Ann what she wants the child to say, "Did you ever rub his penis, Jill Ann?" Jill Ann says, "No, but I sit on it."

This leads to a series of questions about sitting on her dad's penis and Dr. Draper asks, "Does it feel better to have told me?" Jill Ann says, "No." Still attempting to confirm her assumptions about what has happened, she tells Jill Ann that the child knew that she shouldn't be doing this with her daddy and this is why she is not as comfortable at daddy's house. The interview ends a few minutes later.

INTERVIEW

Interviewer: Marie Draper, Psychologist

Child: Jill Ann Erickson

Psychologist: Jill Ann, you were not very happy with your daddy last time, huh?[2B, 9]

Jill Ann:	Yeah.[A1]
Psychologist:	Pushed him right out the door, didn't we?[2A, 9]
Jill Ann:	Yeah (giggles).[A1]
Psychologist:	Why was that, tell me about that.[1A] Did he do something that made you mad?[2B]
Jill Ann:	No, I just wanted to be silly . . . [B2] You know what?[F]
Psychologist:	What?[1A]
Jill Ann:	I always show my bottom to Daddy, and he said, and I said, look at my cute bottom, Daddy![C]
Psychologist:	What does Daddy say?[1A]
Jill Ann:	Yeah, it is cute, Jill Ann.[C] (pause) I need this.[D2]
Psychologist:	When do you show your bottom to Daddy?[1A]
Jill Ann:	Kind of like . . . I love it showing it.[C]
Psychologist:	What?[1A]
Jill Ann:	I love showing my butt.[C]
Psychologist:	You love showing your bottom to Daddy?[9] How come?[1A]
Jill Ann:	Do you like . . . ?[D1, F]
Psychologist:	Um hmm.[8] Do you want to try one?[6C]
Jill Ann:	Um kay.[D2]
Psychologist:	These are good brownies.[6C] Thank you for them.[6C] Jill Ann, tell me, how did it go at your Dad's house when you were there?[1A]
Jill Ann:	Uhhh, ish.[C] I wish my friend wasn't coming over.[C, D2]
Psychologist:	Yeah?[8] How come?[1A]
Jill Ann:	[G]
Psychologist:	Tell me something.[4] You said last time that you got in bed with your Daddy 'cause he wanted you to.[9] Does he let you sneak in there very often?[2A]
Jill Ann:	Um hmm.[A1]

Psychologist:	Uh huh.[8] How about your mom, does your mom making you sleeping in your bed?[2A]
Jill Ann:	Yeah, but . . . [A1]
Psychologist:	But what?[1A]
Jill Ann:	. . . her bed at night, too.[C]
Psychologist:	Does she?[2A]
Jill Ann:	Yeah.[A1] Not at night, she has me tell what I did today.[C]
Psychologist:	Um hmm.[8]
Jill Ann:	I got up last night . . . my mama, I went into the bathroom, and then I sneaked.[C]
Psychologist:	That was pretty good.[5] So, are you getting quarters at your Mom's house for sleeping in your bed?[2B]
Jill Ann:	Uh huh.[A1] I got $8.70.[C]
Psychologist:	Do you still like having that money?[2A]
Jill Ann:	Uh huh.[A1] And you know what?[F] I have enough at least for a Barbie.[D2] And you know what?[F]
Psychologist:	What?[6C]
Jill Ann:	I have more than enough for a Barbie.[D2]
Psychologist:	Oooh.[6C] Um, yummy.[6C] Good.[6C]
Jill Ann:	Do you like . . . brownie?[D2]
Psychologist:	I liked it better with the heart and that you made it for me.[6C]
Jill Ann:	. . . [G]
Psychologist:	Right.[8] That was fun, too, because she knew that I had a friend like you at the office that was going to . . . make it really special for me.[6C] Okay, when you sleep with your Mom, does she let you get in bed with her?[2A]
Jill Ann:	Yeah.[A1]
Psychologist:	Does she ever get mad at you about it?[2B]

Jill Ann: No.[B1] But you know what happened . . . [F]

Psychologist: What?[1A]

Jill Ann: I tipped over.[C]

Psychologist: (laughs)

Jill Ann: I tipped over . . . [C]

[Psychologist and Jill Ann both laugh]

Psychologist: Well.[8] Does your Dad give you quarters?[2A]

Jill Ann: Yeah.[A1]

Psychologist: For sleeping in your bed?[2B]

Jill Ann: Yeah.[A1]

Psychologist: But sometimes does he tell you it's okay to sleep in his bed?[2A]

Jill Ann: No.[B1]

Psychologist: I thought that you told me that he told you to come and get in bed with him?[6A, 4]

Jill Ann: Yeah, he did, but only in the morning.[A2]

Psychologist: Only in the morning time, huh?[2A, 9]

Jill Ann: In the morning it's okay.[C] He said it's okay . . . at night.[C]

Psychologist: It's not okay at night?[2A, 9]

Jill Ann: No.[B1]

Psychologist: But just in the morning?[2A,9]

Jill Ann: Um hmm.[A1]

Psychologist: How does it feel when you sleep with your mom?[1A]

Jill Ann: See, when I sleep at my mom's I am more used to it.[C]

Psychologist: Are you just more comfortable at your mom's house because it's been your house?[2B]

Jill Ann: What I'm trying to tell you is, I want to go see my dad more, so I'll get used to living there.[C]

Psychologist: Whose idea was that?[1A]

Jill Ann: Mine. . . . at my house.[C]

Psychologist: Did you tell your dad that?[2A] That you wanted to spend more time at . . . [2A]

Jill Ann: Well, they said, um, . . . said the last time with my daddy, and we talked. . . . [G] What is this?[F]

Psychologist: It's a tape recorder.[10]

Jill Ann: Oh.[8] I thought it was a camera.[D2] What is she doing?[F, D2]

Psychologist: (chuckles)

Jill Ann: . . . with a camera?[F, D2] Yeah.[D2]

Psychologist: I just thought we might want to listen to a tape of what we said sometime, so.[10] Well, you know last time we were talking about sleeping with your dad?[2A]

Jill Ann: Um hmm.[A1]

Psychologist: Really uptight about that.[9]

Jill Ann: Um hmm.[A1]

Psychologist: What, honey?[1A]

Jill Ann: My mom said it was okay that . . . [C]

Psychologist: To cry?[2A, 9]

Jill Ann: . . . [G]

Psychologist: Did you want to cry when we were talking about sleeping with your Dad?[2B]

Jill Ann: . . . [G]

Psychologist: You know what, Jill Ann?[2A] I think probably you'd feel better if you talked.[4, 6A]

Jill Ann: . . . I did . . . [G] I wish my mom would bring me some toys so we could play.[D2]

Psychologist:	Well, I thought she was going to so I didn't even think about it.[6C] Do you think she's going to?[6C]
Jill Ann:	No.[D2] Because she didn't bring anything.[D2]
Psychologist:	Well, you said that you didn't want to talk about your mom, about your dad and sleeping with your Dad.[9] Right?[2B]
Jill Ann:	Um hmm.[A1]
Psychologist:	How come, Jill Ann?[1A] Something happen there that you don't like?[2B]
Jill Ann:	. . . [G]
Psychologist:	Well, you know what?[2A]
Jill Ann:	Hmm?[F]
Psychologist:	We could draw.[10] Would you like to draw?[10] Okay, let me see if I can get . . . out of my purse.[10] So we could draw.[10] Let's see if we can . . . [10] not too heavy.[10]
Jill Ann:	Draw right here.[D2]
Psychologist:	So.[8] Was it good to get your mommy back?[2A] Yeah.[5] I bet it was.[5]
Jill Ann:	(laughs) right here.[D2]
Psychologist:	Well.[8] Fiddlesticks, let me see if I can help you here.[6C] There.[6C] That's better.[6C] You're lining them all up nicely, huh?[6C]
Jill Ann:	Why don't we go and put this in back.[D2]
Psychologist:	Well, why don't you just leave it here so we don't have to keep going back and forth, that's okay.[6C] You could put it on the floor if you don't want it up there.[6C]
Jill Ann:	I want to put it on the floor so we'll have enough room for all of this, why don't you do that.[D2]
Psychologist:	Yeah, you got too many blues, huh?[6C] Well, so Jill Ann, when you sleep at your mom's bed are you . . . [8]
Jill Ann:	Oh, my God.[D2]
Psychologist:	When you sleep in your mom's bed are you pretty comfortable?[2A]

Jill Ann:	Yeah, yeah.[A1] Do you want me to go put this back in?[F, D2]
Psychologist:	If you want to.[6C]
Jill Ann:	Okay.[8] 'Cause I don't want to . . . [D2]
Psychologist:	Okay.[8] Unh uh.[8] You know, when you talk about[8]
Jill Ann:	What is this?[F, D2]
Psychologist:	Oh, I think it's just a present that one of her little boys made for her in school.[6C] Could you draw a picture of you and your dad?[2A]
Jill Ann:	I don't know.[D3]
Psychologist:	Just try.[4]
Jill Ann:	If you want I could make a bird.[D2]
Psychologist:	Could you just try to draw a picture of you and daddy?[2A, 4]
Jill Ann:	Why?[F] You want me to draw you a house?[F, D1]
Psychologist:	You could do that.[10]
Jill Ann:	Okay.[8]
Psychologist:	Jill Ann, when I talk to you about sleeping in Daddy's bed you get really anxious and you don't want to talk about it.[9, 6A, 4] Why is that?[1A, 4]
Jill Ann:	Well, I don't know.[D3] It seems like I always feel like[G]
Psychologist:	It seems like what?[1A]
Jill Ann:	It seems like I always . . . play around, you know, because see it feels like I'm uptight or something.[C]
Psychologist:	Uh huh, when we talk about that?[2B]
Jill Ann:	Um hmm.[A1]
Psychologist:	Are you uptight when you sleep in Daddy's bed?[2B]
Jill Ann:	Yeah.[A1]
Psychologist:	There must be something that makes you uptight, huh, Sweetie?[4, 5, 6A, 2B]
Jill Ann:	Um hmm.[A1]

Psychologist:	Can you tell me what that is?[2A]
Jill Ann:	Honestly, I don't know.[D3]
Psychologist:	Really?[2A]
Jill Ann:	...[G]
Psychologist:	What does Daddy do when you sleep in his bed?[1A]
Jill Ann:	Nothing.[C] ...[G]
Psychologist:	Well, you know last time when I asked you that question, Jill Ann, you said, you started to tell me what Daddy did and then you got really scared.[9, 6A]
Jill Ann:	Why?[F]
Psychologist:	I don't know what you were going to say.[8] But it seemed to me that you got really scared and then you wanted to not talk about it any more and then you wouldn't tell me.[9, 6A]
Jill Ann:	Yeah, I know.[A2] 'Cause it's ... [G]
Psychologist:	Well, you know what Jill Ann?[2A]
Jill Ann:	Hmm.[G]
Psychologist:	I think that that's one of the reasons that you get so uptight and feel so uncomfortable.[6A, 4] So if I could know maybe I could help you and Daddy to work that out so that you weren't so uncomfortable.[6A, 4]
Jill Ann:	Umm.[G]
Psychologist:	Would you like that?[2A]
Jill Ann:	Yeah.[A1]
Psychologist:	Yeah, it would be better not to be so uptight, huh?[2A, 6A, 4] So why don't you tell me what it is that happened in Daddy's bed, so I can help you.[4]
Jill Ann:	No ... [G] I haven't used this color blue, huh?[D2, F] ... use this blue, huh, can't I?[D2, F]
Psychologist:	Uh huh.[6C]
Jill Ann:	Well, I'll just try it out.[D2]

Psychologist: You know, when you said that you sleep in Daddy's bed, and that you are uncomfortable there, that it makes you uptight, is that what you said?[2B]

Jill Ann: Why doesn't I see a blue marker?[F, D2] It doesn't say.[D2]

Psychologist: It says it's yellow, but it doesn't say that, it says "Expo," actually, it doesn't say that it's yellow but it's yellow colored, so you think it's going to be yellow but then it turns out to be orange.[6C] Oh, I know, it's because you've got the top on and you're saying it's supposed to be.[6C] You should maybe go get that other blue one, 'cause that one ends up being yellow.[6C]

Jill Ann: Yellow![D2]

Psychologist: And we don't have a blue.[6C] How's that, honey?[6C] There you go.[6C] Thank you.[6C]

Jill Ann: Yeah, you know what, see.[D2] I'll show you it writes the same.[D2] See?[F]

Psychologist: Uh hmm.[8] And the other one?[6C] What is it?[6C] It's blue![6C] Pretty crazy, huh?[6C] Let's see if we can figure out which one's which.[6C] The one that has the yellow writing is orange, okay?[6C] So Jill Ann, you tell me that when you sleep in Daddy's bed you feel kind of uncomfortable and uptight?[2B] Is that right?[2B] Can you tell me why?[2A]

Jill Ann: Why does it make that noise (referring to markers)?[D2, F]

Psychologist: Well, it just, those are squeaky guys, I don't know why they are so squeaky.[6C] Maybe it's the way you hold it.[6C] If you would turn it a little sideways maybe it wouldn't make that noise.[6C]

Jill Ann: Well, why don't I just put some of these . . . [D2] Put that one right there, and that one right there[D2]

Psychologist: Are you afraid to tell me, Jill Ann?[2B, 6A]

Jill Ann: Yeah, I think.[A2]

Psychologist: What, honey.[1A]

Jill Ann: Oh.[G]

Psychologist: What do you think will happen if you tell?[1B] Like something that's bad, or that's wrong or that you shouldn't be doing?[3B]

Jill Ann:	No.[B1]
Psychologist:	What about with Daddy?[1A] You think it's something that Daddy shouldn't do?[2B]
Jill Ann:	No.[B1] I think it's something that I, that I should be doing.[C]
Psychologist:	That you should be doing.[9] Well, if it's something that you should be doing, tell me about it.[4]
Jill Ann:	Well, where does this go.[D2, D1] The blue's not working[D2]
Psychologist:	Well, Jill Ann.[8]
Jill Ann:	Use the yellow.[D2] Find the yellow that's this color.[D2]
Psychologist:	Jill Ann?[1A]
Jill Ann:	Huh?[F]
Psychologist:	I'm wondering why if it's something that you should be doing that you're afraid to tell me.[4] Do you think I will think something bad about it?[2B]
Jill Ann:	No.[B1]
Psychologist:	What?[1A] What do you think?[1A]
Jill Ann:	See it has two doorknobs, one that . . . [D2, D1]
Psychologist:	Uh huh.[A1]
Jill Ann:	These are the two houses that . . . (Gasp)[D2] I forgot to make a doorknob on this one.[D2]
Psychologist:	No way to get inside and outside that house, huh?[6C]
Jill Ann:	Hmm.[G]
Psychologist:	Who's houses are these?[1A]
Jill Ann:	Mom's and Dad's.[C]
Psychologist:	Uh huh.[8] Which one is Mom's?[1A]
Jill Ann:	This one, because that one is Dad's, because it doesn't have a peek hole, and that's because he doesn't have . . . [C] and this one is Mom's because it has . . . [C]

Psychologist: Uh huh.[8]

Jill Ann: . . . [G]

Psychologist: Well, Jill Ann.[1A]

Jill Ann: Huh?[F] What?[F]

Psychologist: I think that we need to talk about whatever happens when you're in bed with Dad that makes you uptight.[4, 6A] 'Cause I think you're going to be uptight and you're going to feel bad inside about it as long as it's happening.[4, 6A] Is that true?[2A]

Jill Ann: No.[B1]

Psychologist: No?[2A, 9]

Jill Ann: (pause) Now I colored that.[D2, D1]

Psychologist: Does the same[8]

Jill Ann: Which one do you think the better one is?[F, D2]

Psychologist: Well, I like this one with the yellow door.[6C]

Jill Ann: No, I have to make, get this off, scoop that off, scoop this off.[D2] See I wanted to get some pink on there, because pink and purple are my favorite colors.[D2] And I like blue, and gold and silver . . . [D2]

Psychologist: Jill Ann.[1A]

Jill Ann: Hmm.[F] What?[F]

Psychologist: Why won't you tell me?[1A, 6A, 4]

Jill Ann: I just want to get done with this picture.[D1, C]

Psychologist: Yeah, I know, but you don't want to talk about it, so why do you get so scared about talking?[6A, 1A]

Jill Ann: I think, because I don't want to tell you.[C]

Psychologist: Yes, I know, but you know what?[5, 2A] It makes you uptight and unhappy, doesn't it?[2B, 4, 6A]

Jill Ann: Yeah, sometimes.[A2]

Psychologist: Yeah.[9]

Jill Ann:	But it seems like I want to keep it a secret, because.[C]
Psychologist:	What do you want to keep a secret, Jill Ann?[1A]
Jill Ann:	Oh, there's a lot of secrets.[C] I see what you did . . . make another picture.[D2]
Psychologist:	Can you draw me a picture of what happens in bed?[2A]
Jill Ann:	All right.[A1]
Psychologist:	How about that?[1A] You want to trade papers, and we'll start on a new whole story?[2A]
Jill Ann:	Yeah. (noise of paper obscures rest of child's statement)[A1]
Psychologist:	Well, we'll just put it right over here, for right now.[10] Why don't you just tear it off, 'cause I'm going to let you take it with you.[10]
Jill Ann:	No, I want to keep it with you.[D2]
Psychologist:	Oh.[8] Do you want me to hang it up in my office?[6C]
Jill Ann:	Yeah.[D2]
Psychologist:	Okay, well, let's tear it off then.[6C]
Jill Ann:	And I don't want another piece that big.[D2] And I hope you don't mind.[D2]
Psychologist:	No, it's just fine.[6C] Good, maybe you could show me in the drawing what happens and you won't have to say it so much, huh.[6A]
Jill Ann:	(whispers) Yeah.[A1]
Psychologist:	That would be easier, wouldn't it?[2B, 6A]
Jill Ann:	Here's the pillow.[C]
Psychologist:	Uh huh.[8]
Jill Ann:	Here's the other pillow.[C]
Psychologist:	Uh huh.[8]
Jill Ann:	Pillows.[C] There's the bed.[C] That's the pants, these are her legs.[C]

Psychologist: Uh huh.[8]

Jill Ann: Here's the blanket.[C] (Long pause) Okay, okay.[G]

Psychologist: Uh huh.[8]

Jill Ann: Let me make . . . Okay.[G] Now, let me wipe this off[G] . . . Okay.[G]

Psychologist: What's that?[1A]

[Child giggles.]

Jill Ann: Silly picture . . . for her, her friend's office . . . [D2]

Psychologist: Now, let me ask you something, though.[4] You didn't show me what it was the secret was.[4]

Jill Ann: The secret is, want me to draw it?[F]

Psychologist: Yeah.[8] What?[1A]

Jill Ann: Okay, I'll draw on this.[G] There.[G]

Psychologist: What's that?[1A]

Jill Ann: A heart.[C] Now I'm going to color it in.[G]

Psychologist: What's the secret, Jill Ann?[1A]

Jill Ann: I'll tell you the secret in a second.[C] This is sweet.[C] Think I'll make you a heart, too.[D2]

Psychologist: Do you have the same secret when you sleep in your mommy's bed?[2A]

Jill Ann: No.[B1] Do you want me to tell you what I have the same secret in Mamama.[C] Mamama bed.[C]

Psychologist: I want to know the secret that you have in Daddy's bed.[4]

Jill Ann: . . . [G]

Psychologist: Okay.[8]

Jill Ann: That's a deal?[F]

Psychologist: That's a deal.[8] You can tell me the secret in Daddy's bed.[9]

Jill Ann: Okay.[G] Now let me . . . [D2]

Psychologist:	Good.[5]
Jill Ann:	I have to go over this, skipped my L, that's okay.[D2]
Psychologist:	That's okay.[5]
Jill Ann:	See, there's supposed to be two L's in my name, but right there I don't want the writing, the L, but this is the kind of L's and I's that I usually write.[D2]
Psychologist:	So, let's have the secret that's in Daddy's bed.[4] You can tell me.[4]
Jill Ann:	Okay.[8] But first let me write the little . . . a little heart.[D2] Okay now, now let me write the bestest heart in the world.[D2]
Psychologist:	Good.[5]
Jill Ann:	Okay, this is my secret in Daddy's bed, let me just . . . [C]
Psychologist:	Do you need more paper?[2A] Do you want to draw the secret, or do you just want to tell me?[3A]
Jill Ann:	I just want to tell you.[C]
Psychologist:	Okay.[8]
Jill Ann:	Okay, and this is . . . [G]
Psychologist:	Right.[5]
Jill Ann:	And this is what Daddy does to me.[C]
Psychologist:	Uh huh, and what was it?[1A]
Jill Ann:	(Sound of paper obscures child's remark)[G]
Psychologist:	Jill Ann, tell me what happens in Daddy's bed, what's the secret?[4, 1A]
Jill Ann:	Um.[G]
Psychologist:	What's the secret?[1A]
Jill Ann:	Ahh.[G] We play.[C]
Psychologist:	How do you play?[1A] Can you show me how you play?[2A]
Jill Ann:	I suppose.[G] Aggle, baggle baggle.[C]

Psychologist: Uh huh.[8]

Jill Ann: Like a . . . And he'll let me cuddle.[C] And that's it.[C]

Psychologist: What else do you play, Jill Ann?[1B]

Jill Ann: That's it.[C] . . . [G]

Psychologist: Sure you can.[4]

Jill Ann: No, I can't.[D1]

Psychologist: You didn't tell me the secret, it's no secret that you play.[4] What's the secret?[1A, 4]

Jill Ann: Unnnh.[G]

Psychologist: I know that you didn't tell me.[4]

Jill Ann: All right.[G] I can't remember it.[D3] If I just could, I could tell you.[C]

Psychologist: Jill Ann I know you remember it.[4] You're just afraid to tell, aren't you?[4, 2B, 6A]

Jill Ann: I bounce on Daddy's bed.[C]

Psychologist: Uh huh.[A1] Do you bounce on Daddy?[2B, 6A]

Jill Ann: Yeah.[A1] Me and Molly.[C] Do you know what we did?[F] This is the really secret.[C]

Psychologist: What?[1A]

Jill Ann: I sit on Daddy's back, I sit on Daddy's tummy.[C]

Psychologist: Uh huh.[8]

Jill Ann: That's true.[C]

Psychologist: Can you tell me about sitting on Daddy's tummy?[2A]

Jill Ann: I rub his, I rub his tummy.[C] I rub his tummy.[C]

Psychologist: Do you rub anything else?[2B]

Jill Ann: No.[B1]

Psychologist: Hmm.[2A]

Jill Ann:	No.[B1]
Psychologist:	Are you sure?[2B, 4]
Jill Ann:	Yeah.[A1] See the . . . [G]
Psychologist:	You know, Jill Ann, I think maybe that you're not telling me the whole secret.[4]
Jill Ann:	Oh.[G]
Psychologist:	I know that you aren't.[4, 6A]
Jill Ann:	Oh . . . [G]
Psychologist:	Here, you want some more cheese?[6C]
Jill Ann:	Yeah.[D2]
Psychologist:	Oh, are you okay?[6C]
Jill Ann:	Yeah.[D2]
Psychologist:	(Intake of breath) Did that hurt?[6C]
Jill Ann:	No.[D2]
Psychologist:	Can I kiss it?[6C] Oh, did that scare you?[6C]
Jill Ann:	Um hmm.[D2]
Psychologist:	I'm sorry, I didn't know you were going to jump in there.[6C] You can cut.[6C]
Jill Ann:	. . . [G]
Psychologist:	You know, Jill Ann, I don't really think that you're telling me the whole secret.[4, 6A] 'Cause I think . . . [8]
Jill Ann:	It is.[C]
Psychologist:	Oh, well, why is that a secret?[1A]
Jill Ann:	'Cause.[D1]
Psychologist:	Do you rub anything else?[2A]
Jill Ann:	No, I don't.[B1] If I do I can't remember.[D3]

Psychologist: I think you can remember.[4] I do.[4] I think you're just trying to pretend because you don't want to think about it, is that right?[4, 2B, 6A]

Jill Ann: Yeah, but, I don't want to talk about it.[A2, D1]

Psychologist: Uh huh.[8]

Jill Ann: So.[G]

Psychologist: Does Daddy get you to rub him?[2B, 6A]

Jill Ann: No, I want to rub him.[B2]

Psychologist: You just want to rub him?[2A, 9] What else do you rub?[2B, 6A]

Jill Ann: Um.[G] When is that tape recorder going to go on?[F, D2]

Psychologist: Oh, when we turn it on, if you want.[10] Do you ever rub his penis, Jill Ann?[2B, 6A]

Jill Ann: Huh?[F]

Psychologist: You know his penis, do you know what his . . . [2A, 6A]

Jill Ann: No.[G]

Psychologist: Do you ever rub his penis?[2B, 6A]

Jill Ann: No, but I sit on it.[B2] (Giggles) He likes me to.[C]

Psychologist: He likes you to sit on his penis.[9]

Jill Ann: Um hmm.[A1]

Psychologist: Uh huh.[8] How long, has he done that a lot of times, or just once.[3A]

Jill Ann: A lot . . . on his penis, because . . . get to hold back.[C]

Psychologist: Do you know what his penis is?[2A] Oh.[8] You don't know, huh?[2A, 9]

Jill Ann: Uh uh.[B1]

Psychologist: Do you sit on his bottom, back here?[2A] Or on the front, here?[2A]

Jill Ann: On the front.[C]

Psychologist:	I see.[8] Well, that's what his penis is.[6A]
Jill Ann:	Um.[G]

Psychologist:	Has he been doing that a lot with you?[2A]
Jill Ann:	No.[B1] But I've been getting into bed with him . . . [C]

Psychologist:	Uh huh.[8] Does he do that every morning?[2A]
Jill Ann:	Uh huh.[A1]

Psychologist:	He lets you sit on his penis every morning?[2A, 9] Is that right?[2A] Does that kind of scare you a little bit?[2B, 6A]
Jill Ann:	Um um.[B1] 'Cause I'm used to it.[C]

Psychologist:	Oh.[8]
Jill Ann:	I'm used to my parents.[C]

Psychologist:	Ah, so . . . [8]
Jill Ann:	. . . [G]

Psychologist:	I can't understand you, Jill Ann.[10] What now?[1A]
Jill Ann:	. . . stay with their mom and dad and be not scared of their friends.[C]

Psychologist:	And not scared of their friends?[2A, 9]
Jill Ann:	And could be kind of scared of them.[C] . . . their mama, . . . their friends.[G]

Psychologist:	Tell me something, Jill Ann.[4]
Jill Ann:	Huh.[G]

Psychologist:	Have you been sitting on Daddy's penis a lot, or did you do that before Daddy moved out, or is it just since Daddy's had his new house?[3A]
Jill Ann:	Uhh.[G] I don't do it any more, I guess.[C]

Psychologist:	Oh, well when did you do it?[1A] Did you do it last week?[2B]
Jill Ann:	No, I did it . . . let's see.[B1] I did it only when I was, um, three.[C]

Psychologist:	But you haven't done it since Daddy's lived in his new house?[2A, 9]
Jill Ann:	No.[B1] Um, I did it since I was four and a half, and then when my, and then when I turned five I didn't do it any more, I think.[C]
Psychologist:	Oh.[8] But you seemed really uptight about it, still.[6A, 9] So sometimes, are you still doing it every once in a while now?[2B, 6A]
Jill Ann:	No.[B1]
Psychologist:	No?[2A, 9] Not since Daddy moved out?[2A, 9]
Jill Ann:	No.[B1] I, um, only for, only for when we moved into Dad's house I been sitting on his penis.[C]
Psychologist:	Since then?[2A, 9]
Jill Ann:	Um hmm.[A1]
Psychologist:	Since you moved into Dad's house?[2A, 9]
Jill Ann:	Yeah.[A1] Now I don't do it any more.[C] Now I just sit on my mama.[C]
Psychologist:	Is that . . . [8]
Jill Ann:	I can't sit on Grandma.[C] 'Cause see, um, she has a sore back.[C]
Psychologist:	Yes, she does.[9] She's got hurt places, doesn't she?[9]
Jill Ann:	Um hmm.[A1] So when, um, when it goes through it hurts.[C]
Psychologist:	Ooh, it hurts, right?[9]
Jill Ann:	Yeah, it hurts.[A2]
Psychologist:	Jill Ann, is that kind of why you were afraid to tell me, 'cause you didn't want to tell me that you were sitting on your daddy like that?[2B, 6A]
Jill Ann:	Um hmm.[A1]
Psychologist:	Um hmm.[9] Seems kind of strange, huh?[2B]
Jill Ann:	Yeah.[A1]
Psychologist:	Do you usually have any panties on when you do that, or not?[3B]

Jill Ann:	. . . [G]
Psychologist:	Well, I just kind of forgot about it.[6C]
Jill Ann:	It hurts when I put it on, and it[D2] . . . to say I put it on . . . [D2]
Psychologist:	Does it feel better to have told me?[2A]
Jill Ann:	No.[B1]
Psychologist:	It didn't help any?[2A, 9] Somehow you knew that wasn't quite the best thing for you to be doing with Daddy, huh?[2B, 6A] You were worried about that?[2B, 6A]
Jill Ann:	. . . [G]
Psychologist:	You know what, Jill Ann, I wonder if that's kind of why you're not as comfortable at Daddy's house?[6A]
Jill Ann:	Um, when is your friend gonna get back to the office?[D2, F]
Psychologist:	When is my friend going to get in my, um, she should, I don't know when she's coming this morning.[6C] It's kind of crazy, huh?[6C] You don't seem as uptight as you were.[6A]
Jill Ann:	. . . [G]
Psychologist:	You're not as uptight today as you were, how come?[2B, 6A] You been at home with Mom?[2B, 6A]
Jill Ann:	Um hmm.[A1]
Psychologist:	You know, Jill Ann, when you sit on Daddy like that, do you usually have your panties on or not?[3A] Not usually, huh?[2B]
Jill Ann:	Yes.[A1]
Psychologist:	You do, usually?[2A, 9]
Jill Ann:	. . . [G]
Psychologist:	You just gobbled it up, didn't you?[6C]
Jill Ann:	And you just gobbled it up.[D2]
Psychologist:	I know, I gobbled up my brownie, that was pretty wonderful, Jill Ann.[6C, 5]
Jill Ann:	I know, and I gobbled up my cookie.[D2]

Psychologist: Uh huh.[8]

Jill Ann: Why do they have this here?[F, D2]

Psychologist: Do you know what that does?[6C]

Jill Ann: Uh uh.[D2]

Psychologist: That pushes the chair back.[6C]

Jill Ann: Oh.[8] This way?[F]

Psychologist: Here, you can hop off and I'll show you.[6C] It goes all the way
                  back, and it's like you can lie down in it.[6C] There you go.[6C]
                  And then, you can tighten this, now I can't do it but you can tighten
                  it so it stays there, isn't that nice?[6C] Kind of comfortable, huh?[6C]
                  You want your blanket?[6C] There you go.[6C]

Jill Ann: I want to have it sit up, and lay down a little.[D2]

Psychologist: Well, tell me something.[4]

Jill Ann: Hmm.[G]

Psychologist: How are you getting along with Molly?[1A]

Jill Ann: . . . [G]

Psychologist: Yeah?[9] Better?[2A, 9] You've been with your mom this weekend.
                  You went to the HP party on Friday?[2B]

Jill Ann: Um hmm.[A1]

Psychologist: Uh huh.[9]

Jill Ann: And we went to the . . . the day before that.[C]

Psychologist: Um.[8] Did you, did you spend the whole weekend with your
                  mama?[2A] Did you see your dad some?[2A] How was that visit
                  with your dad?[1A]

Jill Ann: Good.[C]

Psychologist: What, what are you smiling about?[1A] Did Molly go with you to
                  your dad's house?[2A]

Jill Ann: Yeah.[A1]

Psychologist: Was that fun?[2A] Why did you feel like crying last time?[1A]

Jill Ann:	I don't know.[D3] I think I could go off.[C]
Psychologist:	Just felt sad inside?[9, 2A]
Jill Ann:	Um hmm.[A1]
Psychologist:	How are you feeling inside today?[1A]
Jill Ann:	Good.[C]
Psychologist:	Oh.[8] Does that feel better?[2A] Do you think that is because you spent the weekend with your mom and your mom came back from her trip, or.[2B, 6A] What do you think that, why do you feel better today?[1A]
Jill Ann:	I don't know . . . Mom's trip.[D3, C]
Psychologist:	It's nice to have your mama home, isn't it?[2A] I know.[5] Everybody likes their mom to come home.[5]
Jill Ann:	. . . [G]
Psychologist:	No.[8] My little girl doesn't like it when I have to go on a business trip, either.[5]
Jill Ann:	. . . [G]
Psychologist:	I can't, I couldn't understand, I'm sorry.[10]
Jill Ann:	Or else Daddy has to take care, or else Grandma.[C]
Psychologist:	Right.[8] Do you like your grandma?[2A]
Jill Ann:	Um hmm.[A1]
Psychologist:	Did you like playing with her?[2A]
Jill Ann:	Uh huh.[A1] Do you have press-on nails?[F, D2]
Psychologist:	I do.[6C] It's true.[6C] How could you tell?[6C]
Jill Ann:	'Cause they were long.[D2]
Psychologist:	Yeah.[6C]
Jill Ann:	I could tell because, see you know why?[D2, F]
Psychologist:	Underneath, you could tell underneath?[6C]
Jill Ann:	No.[D2]

Psychologist: Oh.[6C]

Jill Ann: I can tell because, um, . . . see that little crack.[D2] Now what I do put this right here, just go like that . . . [D2] Do you have any more grapes?[D2, F]

Psychologist: You know, I didn't bring grapes, either, but I promise you I'll bring some for you next time, okay?[6C, 5]

Jill Ann: Okay.[G]

Psychologist: Well, Jill Ann.[8]

Jill Ann: Hmm.[G]

Psychologist: I think I'm going to, our time is just about up I think I'm going to let you take the marker and the paper out into the waiting room and let you draw out there while I see your mama.[10] Is your dad coming for you?[2A]

Jill Ann: Uh huh.[A1] I think.[C]

Psychologist: So then he's going to take you to school?[2B]

Jill Ann: . . . [G] I want more cheese.[D2]

AFTERMATH

Criminal charges against Kent were filed and investigated but were dropped before the case went to trial. The prosecutor concluded that there was not enough evidence to proceed and that Jill Ann, whom he interviewed, was not a reliable or credible witness. Kent continued adamantly to deny any sexual abuse of his children. In the effort to prove his innocence, he took a polygraph and had a complete psychological evaluation at our office. This material was made available to the prosecutor by Kent's defense attorney prior to the charges being dropped.

In the meantime, Jill Ann continued to see Dr. Draper for twice-a-week sessions of therapy where the alleged abuse was regularly discussed. By court order, four months after the charges were made, the therapy sessions between Jill Ann and Dr. Draper were taped. We have tapes of several sessions. In these sessions Dr. Draper pressures Jill Ann to repeat the accusations. Jill Ann's accounts of what supposedly happened are confused and she states that she doesn't want to keep talking about the "secret" and that she is "all done with it." Dr. Draper reassures her that "I won't make you talk about your secret. You can talk about it when you feel like it. . . . " "I'm not going to talk to you any more about your secret. . . . "

Despite this, throughout this session and the others, Dr. Draper presses Jill Ann to talk about the accusations. There is nothing that can be identified as therapy in these sessions. There is only interrogation that has the goal of supporting and affirming sexual abuse by Kent. By this time, the effort to affirm abuse may also have the function of protecting Dr. Draper's interests.

In response to the continued questions and requests to describe the abuse, Jill Ann states that she only saw her Daddy's penis when he was in the shower, says that he had his pants on, and that she has no memory of his penis being put inside of her. "No, all I could see was, you know I couldn't ever see his penis, you know why? Cause all I could see is I only could see it when it was in the shower, cause you know he got up before me."

Following the criminal dismissal, the case was due to go to family court where the question of custody would be determined. But Kent decided not to fight for physical custody because he believed that Andrea was so emotionally fragile that a court battle might cause her to decompensate. He feared that the children would then be placed in foster care until the custody issue could be settled. He believed that this would be worse for the children than remaining with Andrea.

In the stipulated agreement, Kent was given joint legal custody of his daughters. Although Andrea was given physical custody, Kent was allowed supervised visits. By this time he had left his job because of the stigma of the allegations and was planning a career change. Because he moved out of state, he can only see the children four times a year. He has to be very careful in relating to Jill Ann and must accept her confused and mixed up feelings about him caused by her exposure to Dr. Draper's therapy. He has exhausted his financial resources and the family is considerably more impoverished.

Kent has filed formal complaints against Dr. Draper with the state licensing board.

Chapter 7

TRAINING CHILDREN TO PRODUCE DETAILED
FALSE ACCOUNTS

Play is an important part of children's lives and teaches them about themselves and their world. In the world's most widely read manual on child care Dr. Benjamin Spock (1985) says:

> **510. Play is serious business.** When we see children building with blocks, pretending to be airplanes, learning to skip rope, we're apt to think, in our mixed-up adult way, that these are just amusements, quite different from serious occupations such as doing lessons and holding a job. We are mixed up because most of us were taught in our childhood that play was fun but that schoolwork was a duty and a job was a grind.
> The baby passing a rattle from one hand to the other or learning to crawl downstairs, the small child pushing a block along a crack on the floor pretending it's a car, are hard at work learning about the world. They are training themselves for useful work later, just as much as the high school student studying geometry. Children love their play, not because it's easy, but because it's hard. They are striving every hour of every day to graduate to more difficult achievements and to do what the older kids and grown-ups do.
> The parents of a one-year-old boy complain that he gets bored with hollow blocks and only wants to fit pots and pans together. One reason is that he knows already that his parents play with pots and pans and not with blocks. That makes pots and pans more fun. It must be for this reason that some one year olds are fascinated with cigarettes (p. 376).

Children's play involves fantasy, pretend, and imagination. Children's capacity to tell the difference between fantasy and reality develops across time. It is not an innate ability, nor does it emerge full blown at some point. The research evidence on this issue suggests that children do not reliably distinguish between fantasy and reality until approximately age ten or eleven. This is a fact which many adults have difficulty grasping. When we become adults we can no longer know what it is like to be a child. With adult capacities we cannot go backward in development and experience not having those adult capacities.

191

As Dr. Spock observes about our mixed-up, adult way of viewing play, when we do not take into account whatever we can understand about fantasy and children's play, we are liable to make mistakes. Throughout the system dealing with accusations of sexual abuse of children, the play of children is not understood as play. Somehow, adults believe that they can invite a child to play, pretend, and fantasize, then use the child's fantasies and play as evidence about reality. Play behavior in interrogations, purported play therapy, and even naturally occurring play observed by parents or other adults, is interpreted symbolically to infer to abuse or to claim there were past real events matching the play behavior.

When adults believe play behaviors mean abuse occurred and express no cautions, qualifications, or limitations on these assumptions, there is a leap in logic that will introduce error into the adults' conclusions. The potential for mistakes in making such an uncritically, unexamined leap is compounded when a child is instructed to pretend and fantasize. In many of the interviews we have observed, the adult tells the child to pretend or imagine. The child does. The adult then concludes that the resulting pretend behavior shows that real events happened.

The interrogation continues and now the adult, believing abuse took place, talks to the child about what started out as pretend behavior but is now represented to the child as real ("Remember when you told me daddy did . . . "). In this progression, a child may be taught to believe and subjectively experience as real what started out as a response to the adult's invitation to fantasize. Anytime an adult invites a child to pretend or imagine in an interrogation, the possible impact of the adult's confusion of fantasy play with reality must be considered.

In the case from which this interview is taken, the detective used invitation to pretend as a technique when questioning children. Three children believed to have been abducted from their preschool and abused were interviewed. The child in this interview denied repeatedly all the events involving him. However, it is likely that he was able to maintain his awareness of the pretend, fantasy quality of the tale developed in this interview because his parents did not reinforce the repeated telling of the story or permit repeated interrogations of their child. After an initial period of confusion and concern the parents came to believe that nothing had happened and acted to protect their child from exposure to repeated questioning or to what is offered as therapy for child sexual abuse.

On the other hand, within days of the allegations surfacing the parents of the other two children retained a civil attorney in order to sue the preschool. There was repeated questioning of these children, including interrogations by the civil attorney and a private investigator hired by the civil attorney, as well as police officers, social workers, and prosecutors. The children were put into weekly therapy for sexual abuse and their play behavior in the sessions was offered later as support for the accusation of abuse. When civil action with possible economic benefits is initiated very early in the process, it suggests both a conviction that the abuse was real and a motivation to maintain that belief. When a civil attorney is hired, it becomes in the interest of both the parents and the attorney to establish that sexual abuse did in fact occur.

BACKGROUND

On the morning of Saturday, March 3, Evelyn Miller asked her three-year-old daughter, Chrissy, about marks on her arm and leg which the child said were mosquito bites. When she questioned the child further, Chrissy reportedly told her mother the bites were burns. A story developed about a man who took her from her preschool to his home the day before. After further intense probing, Chrissy added that the man had undressed, photographed, hugged, and kissed her. He had burned her with fire from a gun-like device. Chrissy added that a four-year-old friend of hers, Dawn O'Malley, was also there. Following these terrifying events, the man and two women took the girls back to school where they remained until picked up by their mothers.

Chrissy told this to her mother between the hours of 8:00 a.m. and 11:00 a.m. Evelyn, obviously concerned, continued questioning her and then called the family pediatrician and the police. The initial officer assigned to the case, Andrew Yoshida, arrived at the home, photographed Chrissy and questioned her. Officer Yoshida's report states he felt that the child was "drifting" and "fabricating." Although she could not name him, he did get her to describe the man who took her from school. Chrissy described an oriental, male police officer with black hair, in his forties (which approximates the appearance of Officer Yoshida) as her assailant. Despite lengthy and detailed questioning, Chrissy said nothing about sexual abuse or rape to Officer Yoshida.

Yoshida suggested to Evelyn that Chrissy be taken to the Sex Abuse Treatment Center at Children's Hospital for examination and evaluation. From 11:40 a.m. until 10:00 p.m. that night, over 10 hours, Chrissy was interviewed repeatedly by a social worker, a physician who was the resident on duty at the time, and Detective George Reilly. The social worker used the anatomical dolls to develop previously unmentioned sex abuse and rape information. Despite repeated questioning by Detective Reilly about the name of the abductor, Chrissy maintained that the man had never told her his name.

The resident physician, who had little experience doing sexual abuse examinations, found no signs of physical trauma or penetration but concluded that Chrissy may have been sexually abused based on the history given by Evelyn and the possible burns on her arms and legs. (These burns later were determined by four dermatologists to be impetigo.) However, in spite of the physician's carefully qualified and limited opinion, Detective Reilly told Mrs. Miller that the doctor said her child had been sexually abused. Together with the social worker's description of the child's behavior with the dolls, Reilly's overinterpretation of his brief conversation with the resident persuaded the Millers that authoritative experts had proven their child had been violently and brutally sexually assaulted. This absolute conviction remains unshaken in spite of massive disconfirming evidence.

Finally, in the evening of the most important day in the case for establishing what the child knew in her own words and from her own memory, Chrissy returned home after 14 grueling hours. The next day, Sunday, the Millers took Chrissy to look for the house where the incidents occurred. During the drive, the name of the Miller's realtor, Edward Conner, surfaced in the context of Chrissy saying that he had been at their house and taken them driving around looking for houses. (About six months earlier, Mr. Conner had taken the Miller family on several drives to look at homes they might buy.) Sunday, he was not mentioned in connection with the abduction. Despite driving throughout the streets of the area, Chrissy was never able to identify the house. However, Chrissy later named Conner as the person who had abducted and abused her.

The parents continued to question Chrissy. Chrissy's accusations grew and included another classmate at the preschool, Danny Anderson (age five), in addition to Dawn O'Malley. In an undated taped session between Chrissy and her mother and father, it is clear that both parents were intent on getting Chrissy to tell them what Conner did. As the interviews progressed, more detailed stories developed. The three children were reportedly kidnaped from a bathroom in their preschool by two men, transported to an unknown house where there were other adults, subjected to a variety of sexual acts, including vaginal, anal, and oral copulation (which were photographed), burned and hit, and fed corn on the cob. After these activities, the children were driven back to the preschool where they had never been missed by the teachers.

The other children were also interviewed. During an interview with Chrissy and Dawn, the two girls were seated together and made to hold hands while their mothers and two police detectives probed for information. Examination of this interview demonstrates that Dawn O'Malley neither perceived the events nor had any memory of them until she began to take lessons from Chrissy.

On March 6, Reilly conducted a 25 minute interview of Danny Anderson, the third child now said to have been abducted. Danny's mother, Carol, was present and she said later that Danny had exhibited no unusual behavior that weekend. Danny also said later that the girls' moms told him about the girls being taken from school. Danny remembered nothing and Reilly pressured him to "pretend" and tell about a "dream." Nevertheless no useful information was obtained from Danny and his mother soon became convinced that Danny never was abducted.

Over the next several months Chrissy and Dawn were interrogated repeatedly on their accusations by the Miller family's civil attorney, the police, the treating physicians, therapists, and the prosecutor's office for a total of 30 plus times for Dawn and 45 times for Chrissy. They were put into therapy for sexual abuse.

No hard evidence was ever found. The house was never located. The cars used to transport the children never surfaced. No photos were ever recovered. None of the teachers missed the three children during the time they were supposedly abducted or noticed anything unusual about their behavior during the day in question. In fact, the longest period during which either of the two girls could not be specifically accounted for by the staff was about 20 minutes, between 9:00 a.m. and 10:00 a.m. The sole evidence in the case was the children's statements accusing Conner, elicited and developed after multitudinous interrogations.

Edward Conner was an unlikely person to be the defendant in this sensational and highly-publicized case. He was a respected and successful realtor who was active in his church and community and had never been in trouble with the law before. He and his wife were in the process of adopting a five-year-old Korean child. During the day in question, his activities made it virtually impossible for him to have been involved in the events. He had been in his office in the morning, notarizing immigration papers relating to the adoption, and had then driven to the immigration office. These activities were confirmed by the notary stamp and the time and date stamp from the immigration office. Nevertheless, a year after the case began Edward Conner was indicted on 10 counts of kidnaping, rape, promoting child abuse, sexual abuse, and assault.

The following interview was made four days after the alleged events took place. In this interview, Danny Anderson is interrogated for 25 minutes by Detective Reilly. Throughout this interview, Danny repeatedly states, "I don't remember" or "I don't know" in response to Reilly's questions. Early on, Reilly responds to this by saying, "Okay, let's pretend then. Did you have a dream the other night about Friday?"

Reilly then describes the dream that Danny is supposed to remember and relates the events that he believes occurred. Danny continues responding, "I don't know," and Reilly exhorts him to "Pretend in your dream." Danny eventually begins to go along with the game. Throughout the interview he affirms some of the suggestions made by Reilly but more often states that he doesn't know or doesn't remember.

Whenever Reilly deviates from the "pretend dream" strategy, Danny denies that anything happened. For example, Reilly claims, "That's why I'm here talking to you 'cause I want to help Chrissy Miller and Dawn O'Malley and you."

Danny emphatically states, "I didn't even go in the car!"

Reilly replies, "No, I know, but we only pretended."

In the interview, Danny is taught about explicit sexual behavior. He is asked if the man or the woman made him touch his penis to Chrissy or Dawn's vagina.

Danny says "No," and Reilly says, "Okay. Did, pretend now, did the man or the woman make you do anything else that you didn't want to do?" Note the *anything else* — Reilly has not accepted Danny's denial.

Approximately two-thirds of the way into the interview, Danny seems to be going along with the game he thinks Reilly is playing with him and is laughing. He affirms that there was a big dog at the house but doesn't know what color it was. They talk about the woman who was at the house and Danny is asked repeatedly about touching Chrissy's and Dawn's vaginas. Reilly continually reminds him that what they are talking about is a dream and pretend. When Danny says about He-Man (who Danny is told to pretend is asking the questions), "He-Man's not real," Reilly reminds him that "But we're pretending though, right? We can at least pretend."

Reilly wants Danny to go for a ride to see if he can find the pretend house where the pretend events took place but Danny says, "I didn't really go," and "I've never saw them for real before." Reilly ends the interview with "Oh, we're gonna pretend now." In all, in the 25 minute interview, Reilly mentions "pretend" or "dream" 35 times.

At a deposition six months later, Danny was still insisting that he had not been abducted or abused by anyone. He also stated that the girls' mothers told him about the girls being taken from school and about the man and the car. In the interview it can be seen how he took this information to go along with Reilly in the "pretend" game but he continued to adamantly deny that he had experienced these pretend events. Needless to say, when the trial finally began over two years later, Danny was not put forth by the prosecution as a witness.

The two girls, who were younger, responded to essentially the same type of interview by developing the accusations. In addition, their mothers talked to each other, they were interviewed together, and they had been friends at the preschool. This type of cross-germination is typical of false allegations in cases involving preschool children at day care centers. In this case, the interview of the two girls together in the presence of their mothers and two detectives is an example of the social pressure for the girls to conform to the story wanted by the adults. The girls were also interviewed by several other people. In contrast, Danny was separated from the influences of group interviewing and his parents, after seeing the way he was being interviewed, moved to a different state and prevented further interviews.

Reilly's interview with Danny is presented here as an illustration of the way a child may be trained to produce false accounts by inviting the child to use fantasy and pretend in the interview. Children, subjected to this process, may eventually come to believe that the accounts are true. Danny did not reach that point primarily because his parents acted to stop the training process. Had he been questioned repeatedly, he might have started believing that what started out as a pretend game was a horrible reality.

The tape analyses for the several available interviews of the children in this case indicated that 72 percent of the interviewers' behaviors fell into the error-inducing categories.

INTERVIEW

Interviewer: Detective George Reilly

Child: Danny Anderson

Also Present: Carol Anderson (mother)

Detective: This is Detective George Reilly. I'm interviewing Danny Anderson. And Danny is sitting here with his mother Carol, and the time is now 12:05 p.m., March the 6, 1984. And today is Tuesday, yes? And we're inside a small office next to the four-year room, I guess. Danny, you see the lights come on? Everything that you, your mommy and me say is being recorded. Uh Mrs. Anderson, this is being with your knowledge and permission, is that correct?

Mother: Yes.

Detective: Okay.[8] Danny?[1]

Danny: What?[F]

Detective: Let me talk to you about what happened Friday, Friday morning when you went to . . . [4]

Danny: I don't . . . I don't remember.[D3]

Detective: Okay, let's pretend then.[4] Did you have a dream the other night about Friday?[2] You were telling your daddy about a dream, yeah?[2] Okay.[8] In your dream, what happened?[1] Can you tell me?[2]

Danny: I can't remember.[D3]

Detective: Okay, well, let me ask you this.[4] In your dream you were here at school, and you was with your friend, yeah?[2] Did you go to the bathroom and see a man inside the bathroom?[2] In your dream now.[4] Yeah?[8] Okay, can you answer?[4] This . . . I . . . see, this only records talk.[6A] When you do this when you do this the recorder doesn't pick it up.[6A] So, yes, you saw a man in the bathroom . . . [9]

Danny: Uh uh (yes).[A1]

Detective: In your dream . . . Uh uh.[9, 5] Okay, let me put this right over here.[6C] What was the man doing in the bathroom?[1]

Danny: I don't know.[D3]

Detective:	Where was he at when you seen him?[1]
Danny:	I don't know.[D3]
Detective:	Okay, but he was inside the bathroom, yeah?[9, 2] And you went to use the bathroom, and you got scared, yeah.[6A] And you walked from the bathroom and who did you see when you walked from the bathroom?[6A, 1]
Danny:	I don't know.[D3]
Detective:	In your dream now.[4] Pretend in your dream.[4] Okay?[8] Didn't you see Chrissy Miller and Dawn O?[2, 4]
Danny:	Dawn O'Malley![C]
Detective:	Right.[5] Dawn O'Malley.[5] And Chrissy Miller.[6A] You seen them, yeah?[9, 2, 6A] Tell me about the man and Chrissy Miller and Dawn O'Malley and you.[1, 4]
Danny:	They went with the man.[C]
Detective:	They went with the man.[9] Yeah?[8]
Danny:	I don't remember them going in the car![D3, C]
Detective:	But he had a car, yeah?[2] Was it a new car or a old car?[3]
Danny:	I think a old car.[C]
Detective:	Do you remember what color it was?[2]
Danny:	Yellow.[C]
Detective:	It was yellow, the same color as your hair?[9, 2] It was kinda the color your hair?[9, 2] Your hair is blonde.[8]
Danny:	(laughs) My hair isn't yellow.[B2] It's blonde.[C]
Detective:	Real blonde.[5] Was it almost the color your hair?[2]
Danny:	Yeah.[A1]
Detective:	It was.[9] And where did you sit in the car?[1, 6A] In the front seat or in the back seat?[3]
Danny:	Back seat.[C]
Detective:	In the back seat.[9] And who was in the back seat with you?[1, 6A]

Danny:	I don't know![D3]

Detective:	Both girls?[2] Was both girls in the back seat with you?[2]
Danny:	Dawn O'Malley.[C]

Detective:	Only Dawn O'Malley?[9, 2] And Chrissy Miller, she was in the front seat?[2, 6A]
Danny:	She was in front of the back of the back.[C, D2]

Detective:	Okay, and how many men was in the car?[1]
Danny:	One.[C]

Detective:	Only one man?[9]
Danny:	Yeah.[A1]

Detective:	You sure it wasn't two men?[2, 4]
Danny:	Yeah.[A1]

Detective:	It was two men inside the car.[6A, 4]
Danny:	No![B1] One![C]

Detective:	Only one man and where did the man take you?[1, 9] Is it close around here where the man took you?[2]
Danny:	I think it would have been (not clear).[C]

Detective:	Ah . . . somebody told me that you thought maybe it was one block away from here.[6A] Did you tell one of the other parents did you tell Dawn O'Malley's mother that it was one block away from here?[2, 4] Was that the truth?[2, 4] It was one block away from here?[2]
Danny:	I think . . . I forgot.[D3]

Detective:	You think you forgot?[2, 9]
Danny:	Yeah.[A1]

Detective:	That's okay[5] That's okay[5] We're just . . . we try to remember, okay?[5] Ah . . . so the man drove off and you, Dawn O'Malley and Chrissy Miller inside the car.[9] Did he take you to his house?[2] Was it a big house?[2]

Danny: Big house?[F]

Detective: Was it a big house or a small house?[3]

Danny: Big house.[C]

Detective: Do you remember what color house it was?[2]

Danny: Dark.[C]

Detective: Dark color?[9, 2] The same color his car.[6A] Dark color.[9] When you got to his house, who else was inside that house?[1]

Danny: I don't know![D3]

Detective: Okay, now try to remember back to your dream, okay?[4] Who else was inside the house?[1]

Danny: I don't . . . I can't remember![D3]

Detective: Okay, how about a lady?[1] There was a lady inside that house, right?[4, 6A] Yes?[2] Your nodding your head yes, that means yes.[9] Was this a nice lady or a bad lady?[3]

Danny: Yeah.[A1]

Detective: Did the lady talk to you?[2]

Danny: No.[B1]

Detective: Did the lady or the man give you anything to eat?[2]

Danny: Yeah.[A1]

Detective: And what did they give you?[1]

Danny: Corn.[C]

Detective: Corn, how was the corn, on a plate or what?[9, 3]

Danny: Corn, I mean the corn was on a plate.[C]

Detective: But the corn, was it corn on the cob that you eat on the cob or did you eat it from the plate?[3]

Danny: The plate.[C]

Detective: But was it corn on the cob?[4, 6A] Do you know what corn on the cob is?[2]

Danny: Uh uh (yes).[A1]

Detective: Is that the kind it was?[2]

Carol: Did you have to use a spoon?[2]

Detective: Or did you eat it from the cob?[2]

Danny: Spoon![C]

Detective: Spoon.[9] You sure?[2, 4] Okay.[8] Now, did the other two kids, the two girls, did they eat corn, too?[2] Huh?[2, 4] Did they eat corn, too?[2] Okay, after you ate corn, what happened?[1]

Danny: Um . . . [8]

Detective: What did the man . . . [8]

Danny: I don't know![D3]

Detective: Okay, now this is only pretend, right?[1, 6A] What if, right?[6A] Right?[2] Okay, what if, what if the man took Chrissy Miller's clothes off, what would you see if the man took Chrissy Miller's clothes off?[6A]

Danny: I don't know.[D3]

Detective: What if the man took Dawn O'Malley's clothes?[1, 6A]

Danny: I don't know.[D3]

Detective: And you seen . . . [8]

Danny: I don't know.[D3]

Detective: How about the man and the fire?[1]

Danny: There was no fire.[B2]

Detective: There was no fire, well, what happened to Chrissy Miller's arm?[9, 4, 1]

Danny: Oh. It got burned.[C]

Detective: That's right.[5] What with?[1] What was it?[1]

Danny: I think a lighter.[C]

Detective: Okay, what kind of lighter?[1] Did you see a lighter?[2] Was it a . . . [8]

Danny: Yeah.[A1]

Detective: What does this mean?[1] What kind of lighter is that?[1]

Danny: It means the fire is coming out.[C]

Detective: Okay.[8] Was the lighter, did it come from a pin like this?[2] Or did it come from an airplane?[2] Did it come from a truck?[2]

Danny: No.[B1]

Detective: Did it come from a gun?[2]

Danny: No.[B1]

Detective: What did the fire come from?[1]

Danny: There is no such thing as airplanes with lighters on 'em or guns with lighters on 'em.[B2]

Detective: Did you ever see a gun with lighters on 'em?[2]

Danny: No.[B1]

Detective: You never did.[9] Okay, where did the fire come from?[1]

Danny: Maybe just a plain old lighter.[C]

Detective: A plain old lighter.[9] Okay.[8] What did Chrissy Miller do when the man burned her?[1]

Danny: I don't know.[D3]

Detective: Did she cry?[2]

Danny: I don't know.[D3]

Detective: Okay, what if you saw him, would you say she was crying, if you saw?[2, 6A]

Danny: Um . . . I don't know.[D3]

Detective: Okay, now if you saw that, what did you see the man do to Chrissy Miller?[1] The man did something that you seen.[6A] What did you see the man do?[1] Something wasn't nice, yeah?[2, 6A] Wasn't nice.[6A] But it's okay to talk about it and tell me about it.[5] Because it's not gonna happen again, do you understand?[5] That's why I'm here talking to you 'cause I want to help Chrissy Miller and Dawn O'Malley and you.[5] This man . . . [8]

Danny: I didn't even go in the car![B2, C]

Detective: No, I know, but we only pretended.[6A] If it really happened, we only pretended, right?[6A]

Danny: Yeah[A1]

Detective: 'Cause we're talking about your dream[4] Okay.[8] Now, in the dream what did you see the man do to Chrissy Miller?[1] Did the man take off his clothes?[2]

Danny: Uh uh (yes).[A1]

Detective: Did the man take off Chrissy Miller's clothes?[2] Did the man do something to Chrissy Miller?[2] Okay.[8] What do you call your private part?[1] What does he call his private part?[6B]

Carol: He calls it a penis.[6A]

Detective: Do you call your private part a penis?[2] Did you see the man's penis?[2] Did you see the man's penis?[2] You did?[9, 2] Can you say yes or no?[2]

Danny: Yes.[A1]

Detective: Okay.[8] Did the man touch Chrissy Miller with his penis?[2]

Danny: No.[B1]

Detective: Now only pretend.[4] I know you weren't there, but we just pretend.[4] Okay?[8] Now, you seen the man's penis, he don't have no clothes on, Chrissy Miller has no clothes on, did you see the man touch Chrissy Miller with his penis?[2] What do you call the woman's private parts?[1] What would he call 'em?[6B]

Danny: Vagina.[C]

Detective: Vagina.[9, 5] Okay, you are smart after all.[5] Let's see, did you see the man touch Chrissy Miller's vagina with his penis?[2] You did?[9, 2] Yes or no, can you say it out loud?[3]

Danny: Yes.[A1]

Detective: Okay.[5] Did you see the man touch Dawn O'Malley's vagina with his penis?[2]

Danny: Um . . . [8]

Detective: Yes, your shaking your head, yes, does that mean yes?[9, 2] Can you say it for the tape recorder?[4]

Danny: Yes.[A1]

Detective: Okay.[5, 8] Did the man put his penis inside the two girls' vagina?[2, 6A]

Danny: . . . a vagina.[8]

Detective: But did he try?[2]

Danny: Yeah.[A1]

Detective: Okay.[8] How about the woman?[1]

Danny: I don't know.[D3]

Detective: Did the woman take her clothes off, too?[2]

Danny: Yeah.[A1]

Detective: She did, yeah?[9, 2] Who took off your clothes, a man or a woman?[6A, 3]

Danny: A woman.[C]

Detective: A woman.[9] That's what I thought.[5] And did the woman touch your penis?[2]

Danny: No.[B1]

Detective: Did the woman have you touch her vagina?[2]

Danny: No.[B1]

Detective: Did the man touch your penis?[2]

Danny: No.[B1]

Detective: Okay, who took the pictures?[1] The man or the woman?[3]

Danny: What?[F]

Detective: Remember the camera?[2, 4] Who took the pictures?[2, 4] Who took
              the pictures?[1] The man or the woman?[3]

Danny: The man.[C]

Detective: Did the man, did the man have you touch Chrissy Miller or Dawn
              O'Malley?[2]

Danny: No.[B1]

Detective: Did the man or the woman have touch your penis to Chrissy Miller
              or Dawn O'Malley's vagina?[2]

Danny: No![B1]

Detective: Only pretend now, we only pretending, okay?[5, 4, 6A] Now, if we
              were to pretend, did they make you do that?[2, 6A] Pretend.[4]
              They did?[9, 2] Can you answer yes or no for the tape?[2]

Danny: Yes.[A1]

Detective: Okay![5] Did, pretend now, did the man or the woman, did the man
              or the woman make you do anything else that you didn't want to
              do?[4, 2]

Danny: Uh uh (no).[B1]

Detective: They only made you touch the two girls with your penis on their
              vagina, that's all they made you do, and the man was taking pic-
              tures when you did that.[9, 6A] Okay.[8] Uh, Danny, can you speak
              inside this, the man was . . . [4, 8]

Danny: Yes.[A1]

Detective: Okay, now let me see how really smart you are.[4] And I think
              you're really smart.[5] Do you cameras?[2] Do you know much
              about cameras?[2] Do you know cameras take pictures?[2]

Danny: Yes.[A1]

Detective: The camera in our pretend, was it a big camera or a little camera?[3]

Danny: Big.[C]

Detective:	Big camera.[9] When the man took your picture with the camera, did pictures come out of the camera?[2]
Danny:	Uh uh (yes).[A1]
Detective:	They did?[9, 2] How many pictures do you think he took?[1] A lot of pictures or . . . [1]
Danny:	A lot.[C]
Detective:	A lot of pictures.[9] And these pictures that he took, they came out of the camera, did he lay 'em on table?[2]
Danny:	Yeah.[A1]
Detective:	Did they develop?[2]
Danny:	Yeah.[A1]
Detective:	You know what a Polaroid® camera is?[2]
Danny:	No.[B1]
Detective:	A Polaroid is a kind when you take a picture of me, the film, the picture comes out of the camera, that's the kind of picture it was?[2, 6A] Huh?[8] Was there a flash?[2] Did a bright light go off?[2] Can you answer for the camera?[4]
Danny:	Yes.[A1]
Detective:	Okay.[5] Now, who kept the pictures?[1] The man or the woman?[3]
Danny:	The man.[C]
Detective:	What was the man's name?[1]
Danny:	I, I don't know.[D3]
Detective:	What was the woman's name?[1]
Danny:	I don't know.[D3]
Detective:	How about the dog?[1, 6A] Tell me about the dog that was there.[1, 6A] You don't like dogs very much, do you?[2] Yeah?[8] How about the dog that was there— was it a big dog or a small dog?[3]
Danny:	Big.[C]

Detective: It was big.[9] What color was it?[1]

Danny: Don't know.[D3]

Detective: Was it the color of your shirt?[2] Huh?[4]

[Both parties laughing]

Danny: No dogs are blue.[B2]

Detective: Well, was it this color?[2] Right here?[2]

Danny: No.[B1]

Detective: Was it this color?[2] Black?[2] Like this?[2]

Danny: No.[B1]

Detective: Was it this color?[2] Brown?[2]

Danny: No.[B1] (Still laughing)

Detective: Okay, did it have a short tail or a long tail?[3]

Danny: Long.[C]

Detective: Did it have a collar?[2]

Danny: Yes.[A1]

Detective: What color was the collar?[1]

Danny: Blue.[C]

Detective: A blue collar.[9, 5] Okay.[8] Ah . . . did it have any clothes on?[2] The dog?[2]

Danny: No![B1]

Detective: Are you sure?[4,2]

Danny: No dogs wear clothes![B2]

Detective: No dogs wear clothes.[9] You didn't see no clothes on the dog.[9] What was the dog's name?[1] Did they tell you the dog's name?[2]

Danny: No.[B1]

Detective:	No.[8] Okay.[9] Now, come back to the woman, what did she do when took off her clothes?[1, 4, 9] Did she touch her vagina?[2]
Danny:	Yeah.[A1]
Detective:	She did.[9] Did she talk to you?[2]
Danny:	No.[B1]
Detective:	She never?[9, 2] She didn't seem like a nice woman or think she was a nice woman?[3]
Danny:	She wasn't.[C]
Detective:	She wasn't.[9] Was she a naughty lady?[2] Is that what you could say?[2] Huh?[4] Okay.[8] Did the woman talk to you?[2]
Danny:	No.[B1] (Still laughing)
Detective:	Only the man talk to you?[2]
Danny:	No.[B1]
Detective:	There, we're only pretend now.[6A, 4] Okay?[5] Let's pretend when you go back . . . [4] Did the woman talk to you?[2]
Danny:	No.[B1]
Detective:	Did the woman sit down next to you?[2]
Danny:	No.[B1]
Detective:	Did the woman have you sit down on her lap?[2]
Danny:	No.[B1]
Detective:	Only pretend now.[4] Okay?[8]
Danny:	Okay.[A1] (Still laughing)
Detective:	So the woman didn't do anything like that?[9, 2] The only thing the woman did was touch herself.[9] Did the woman touch Chrissy Miller or Dawn O'Malley?[2]
Danny:	Dawn O'Malley.[C]
Detective:	She touched Dawn O'Malley?[9,2]
Danny:	Uh huh (yes).[A1]

Detective: Where did she touch Dawn O'Malley?[1]

Danny: On her stomach.[C]

Detective: On her stomach.[9] What did she touch Dawn O'Malley on her stomach with?[1]

Danny: I don't know.[D3]

Detective: Was it her hand?[2] Her finger?[2]

Danny: Hand.[C]

Detective: How about her foot?[1]

Danny: Foot.[C]

Detective: What did she do with her foot?[1]

Danny: She touched her with her foot.[C]

Detective: Dawn O'Malley?[9, 2] Did she touch Dawn O'Malley's vagina?[2]

Danny: Uh huh, uh huh (yes).[A1]

Detective: She did?[9] Did either one, the man or the woman, make you touch Dawn O'Malley's vagina?[2]

Danny: Yes.[A1]

Detective: They did.[9] With what?[1] Your hand or your penis?[3]

Danny: My hand.[C]

Detective: Okay.[8] Did they make you touch Chrissy Miller?[2]

Danny: No.[B1]

Detective: They never.[9] You're sure now?[2, 4] This is in the dream, now, if you can remember the dream, huh.[4] Did they make you touch Chrissy Miller, too?[2] Yes or no?[3]

Danny: Yes.[A1]

Detective: And when they did this, took pictures, the man was taking pictures, you remember your dream, is that what the man was doing?[2, 4]

Danny: This isn't the same man.[BC2]

Detective:	It isn't the same man?[9, 2] It's a different man?[9, 2] So we have two men there?[2]
Danny:	No.[B1]
Detective:	Okay, tell me in the dream what it mean when you say this isn't the same man.[1] What do you mean?[1] (pause) . . . Can you explain to me?[4] Tell He-Man.[4] We'll pretend He-Man is asking you that question.[4] What would you tell He-Man?[1] Huh?[4]
Danny:	I don't know (laughing).[D3]
Detective:	'Cause He-Man would be here trying to help you, yeah.[5] 'Cause He-Man likes little boys, too.[5] He always helps little boys.[5] And little girls.[5] So if we were telling He-Man about our pretend dream, what would we tell him about this other man?[1] It would be two men?[6A, 2]
Danny:	There wasn't two men.[B2]
Detective:	How many men was there?[1]
Danny:	One.[C]
Detective:	Only one.[9] Okay.[8] What did you mean when it wasn't the same man?[1] Huh?[4]
Danny:	I, I don't know.[D3]
Detective:	Okay.[8] Now, when you and the two girls left the house, did they bring you back here?[2] Where did they park the car and let the three of you out at?[1, 6A]
Danny:	In the street.[C]
Detective:	In the street.[9] Is that the street in front of the school by the shopping center, or the street behind the school?[3, 6A]
Danny:	No.[B1] Over by my house[C]
Detective:	Over by your house?[9,2] Where do you live?[1] Close by here?[2]
Danny:	Yeah.[A1]
Detective:	Do you know where they took you to?[2] The house they took you to?[2]
Danny:	Oh, their house.[C]

Detective: Do you know where their house is?[2]

Danny: Ah . . . no.[B1]

Detective: Could you find their house?[2]

Danny: I don't know because I, I've never saw them for real before.[D3, C]

Detective: Okay[8] Do you think that you and Mommy could go with me and look real fast for their house?[2, 4] Huh?[8] And we'll pretend that we're looking for He-Man, so we tell He-Man where to go and talk to those people.[4]

Danny: He-Man's not real.[D2]

Detective: But we're pretending though, right?[4] We can at least pretend.[5]

Danny: Hey, we can bust them right out of the TV.[D2]

Detective: That's right.[5] That's right.[5] Okay?[8] So we can go for a ride and see if we can find the house?[2] You, Mommy, me and my friend who is outside.[8] Can we go and try to find the house?[2]

Danny: If He-Man's on today, I'll bust him right out of the TV.[D2]

Detective: Okay.[5] And you tell He-Man today you met a real policeman and you talked to the policeman and the policeman gave you his card, that's the policeman's badge.[4, 5] Okay?[8] And you tell him the nice policeman you met today.[4] Right?[2] Right?[2] Okay.[8] So we're . . . did anything else happen in your dream?[2] The pretend?[1]

Danny: No.[B1]

Detective: Who put on your clothes in the dream?[1] Did you put them on?[2] Or did the lady or the man put them back on?[3]

Danny: I put 'em on.[C]

Detective: How about the two girls?[1] Did they put their own clothes on?[2]

Danny: Yes.[A1]

Detective: Did the man threaten you?[2] Did he say that he's going to do anything bad to you?[2]

Danny: Uh uh (no).[B1]

Detective: He don't say nothing bad to you?[2, 9, 4] How about the girls?[1] Did he say anything bad to them?[2] Did he tell anybody he was going to put them in jail?[2] Huh?[4] Yes or no?[3]

Danny: Yes.[A1]

Detective: He did.[9] Did he say anything about hurting any of you if you told?[2]

Danny: No.[B1]

Detective: He never.[9] Who did he tell he was going to put you in jail?[1]

Danny: Chrissy . . . both of the girls.[C]

Detective: Both of the girls.[9] And he wasn't going to put you in jail, only the two girls?[2]

Danny: Um . . . yeah.[A1] But it's your job to do that.[C]

Detective: Right.[5] It's my job not his job, right?[5, 6C] And I don't put nice boys like you in jail, never.[5] Did he show you a badge?[2]

Danny: No.[B1]

Detective: Did he say he was a policeman?[2]

Danny: No.[B1]

Detective: He never.[9] Okay, do you think we could go now and try to find the place?[2, 4]

Danny: It's not the police.(Laughs)[B2]

Detective: No, the house that you went to.[8] Can we go look for it now?[2]

Danny: I didn't really go.[B2, C]

Detective: Oh, we're gonna pretend now.[4] Okay?[8]

Danny: All right.[A1]

Detective: Okay?[8] Okay.[8] I'm gonna stop the tape recorder now, the time now is 12:30 p.m., January, excuse me, it's March the 6, 1984.

(End of Interview)

AFTERMATH

In a 20-page ruling, over two and a half years after the events, Judge Robert Klein ruled that Chrissy Miller and Dawn O'Malley were incompetent to testify. In that there was no corroborating evidence, this resulted in an acquittal for Edward Conner.

In the ruling, Judge Klein stated that:

> ... what the children now know to be fact is what they have learned through the process of questioning over the span of time and under the circumstances of the investigation/therapy. ... In other words, the children lack a present memory of the events from which they can testify. ... Cross-examination could not effectively penetrate the wall of learned facts to reveal any real perception. ... (The girls) have been led and taught by the adults to produce the hoped-for responses. ... In fact, because the children now believe that such abuse occurred, they are unable to separate the facts from their learned experience and, consequently, their behavior is just the same as if they were abused. The abuse has become their reality. ... They cannot qualify as witness. ... They lack personal knowledge, because they have no memory which the court can be assured is their personal recollection of the "event" (Klein, 1986).

The outcomes of this experience for everybody involved are tragic. Mr. Conner's reputation was destroyed, and he can no longer work as a realtor. The costs of defending himself came close to bankrupting him. Emotionally, he and his wife have gone through years of anguish and stress. They say that had it not been for the support and care of their pastor and members of their church they could never have survived. But they have made it and are rebuilding their lives as best they can.

After the charges were dropped, Mr. Conner and his wife filed a malicious-prosecution lawsuit against the city. After three years of difficult and protracted litigation this was settled for $550,000. Mr. Conner feels vindicated although nothing can compensate him for the trauma of being publicly accused of heinous and deviant crimes.

The Andersons are persuaded that law enforcement and child protection systems are not to be trusted. They believe their own efforts and decisions are the only thing that saved their child from exploitation and abuse by the system. They have little trust for authority but rather a cautious, suspicious, and wary stance toward their government.

The girls and their families have also been harmed. The girls have been taught to be victims when they were not. They are likely to have a subjective certainty of having been savagely and brutally assaulted for the rest of their lives. This may affect their capacity for all interpersonal relationships, especially intimate relationships. Their self-concept may be impaired and their ability to discriminate between reality and unreality may be diminished and confused. They may never be able to return to a normal developmental track and grow into adulthood like most children. Their mothers and fathers have been subjected to intolerable stress. Believing their children were assaulted in the face of the justice system's failure to affirm their convictions cannot fail to produce bitterness, rancor, anger, and distrust. They are likely to feel alienated and isolated from their society through the rest of their lives.

When there is a false accusation of child sexual abuse nobody wins.

Chapter 8

GROUP PRESSURE TO PRODUCE
STORIES ABOUT ABUSE

Seven astronauts died when the space shuttle Challenger exploded on January 28, 1986. Extensive analysis of what went wrong reveals several instances where group pressure coerced individuals to produce false statements and encourage false hopes. NASA officials were influenced by a variety of group pressures to approve lift off. Engineers at Morton Thiokol were alarmed and wanted to cancel the launch but Thiokol administrators were told to take off their engineering hat and put on one representing management. The power of group pressure to induce conformity to error in highly trained, successful, and responsible adults is shown by the eerie full-color photos of Challenger's tragic end.

There is no better established fact in social psychology than the power and pervasiveness of group pressure to produce conformity to error by individuals. There are several points in the process of dealing with an accusation of child sexual abuse where group pressure to conform may infuse error into the decisions and outcomes. In accusations involving multiple children, the documents often include knowledge of groups actively involved in affecting what goes on. Parent groups, both formal and informal, often form soon after the accusations surface.

Sometimes, prosecutors, police officers, and mental health experts are involved in the formation of parent groups, meet with them, encourage and support them in the belief their children were abused, and orchestrate their appearance in the courtroom to maximize the effect on the jury. In a few instances parent groups have been angered by a prosecutor's reluctance to proceed in criminal court and have pressured the prosecutor's office for more vigorous pursuit of indictments and arrests.

Group pressure to conform to expectations may also be seen in the interrogation of children. Often two interviewers—high status, high power, authoritative adults—conduct the interrogations. This fact alone raises the question of group influence. Sometimes more than two persons are involved in the interrogation. We have observed in documents and tapes many situations of a single child, surrounded by from two to eight adults, being pressured to conform to adult expectations to produce statements about having been abused.

When this situation is evident, the possible effect of group pressure to agree with an account that may not be true cannot be ignored. This doesn't mean that all statements produced under this phenomenon are false. Rather, in assessing the story, the factor of group pressure and the power to produce conformity must be carefully weighed.

Three Marine guards at the Moscow embassy were said to have given detailed confessions of aiding KGB agents to breach the security of the embassy. These confessions were produced by Naval Investigative Service agents who used standard interrogation techniques known to counter-intelligence agents all over the world. No torture or physical coercion was involved. The three NIS agents used intense questioning, isolation from familiar surroundings, accusations, purported previous knowledge, and verbal harassment (Derian, 1988). It is now known that the confessions were false. If the interrogation tactics of psychological intimidation and group pressure can produce false stories from Marines specifically trained to resist such interrogation methods, when those same methods are used with three, four, five, and six year olds, the issue of group pressure and its impact on the child must be raised.

BACKGROUND

Fred and Nancy Conrad operated a day care center together. Fred was active in interacting with the children and both considered themselves to be child care professionals. They worked hard to develop a responsible and effective day care center and succeeded. The center developed a good reputation and there was a waiting list of parents wanting their children to attend there.

The allegations of sexual abuse started after Sara Brandt, the mother of three-year-old Lisa Brandt, noticed a bad odor in Lisa's underwear and in her vaginal area. Lisa was frequently scratching her genitals which appeared to be swollen and red. Sara also noticed a white substance in the lips of Lisa's vagina. When Sara put some Vaseline on her daughter's genitals, Lisa reportedly asked her to do that some more because it felt good. Lisa also started refusing to go to the bathroom by herself. About this time, Sara saw a special television program on child abuse and became suspicious that Lisa was being sexually abused at day care. She started talking to Lisa about what happened at day care and shared her suspicions with the child's grandmother who also talked to the child. Eventually the police were called and an investigation began.

During the investigation, the police talked to other children and their parents. After several weeks of this, four other children—a four-year-old girl, a five-year-old girl, a five-year-old boy, and a three-year-old boy—reportedly made statements suggesting sexual abuse. Criminal charges were then filed against Fred. Fred was accused of taking the children into the bathroom at the day care center, making them touch his penis, putting his penis into their mouths and ejaculating, rubbing his penis against their bodies and genitals and ejaculating, and taking pornographic pictures. He supposedly said that he would hurt them along with their parents if they ever told what was being done to them. As the investigation progressed, Nancy also was mentioned as being present and involved in the abuse.

Some of the interviews with the children were audiotaped. In those that we heard, several adults questioned the children. The anatomical dolls were used and the children were directed to show what had happened with the dolls. Parents were present in the interviews and often participated in the questioning. We analyzed two interviews which were provided before the trial. The proportion of error-inducing statements of the interviewers in these was 77 percent.

In the following interview, Lisa is interrogated on tape several months after the alleged events took place. There has clearly been an indeterminate number of prior interviews in the ensuing months. Lisa was three when she was at the day care center; at the time of this interview she was four.

The interview is conducted by three interviewers—two detectives and a child protection social worker, all who question her. Her mother and her grandmother are present and encourage her to talk about the abuse. The presence of five adults, all of them authority figures and all of them badgering her to tell about abuse, creates tremendous pressure on Lisa.

Whereas all of the professionals who have written about the appropriate way to interview children stress the importance of one adult interviewing the child alone, in practice this often doesn't happen. If one adult with preconceived notions is attempting to elicit statements to support these notions, the effect will be greatly magnified if five adults who all agree as to what they believe happened are interviewing the child together.

The first detective begins by telling Lisa to "Tell Grandma exactly what happened again." Lisa says, "He pinched me," and they then ask her, "What else" happened.

Lisa is resistant to talking, saying that she doesn't feel good and wants to go home. But the adults continue questioning her and urging her to describe the abuse. When Lisa produces nothing, the dolls are brought out and she is told to use the dolls to show where they touched her. Lisa keeps protesting that she doesn't know and she wants to go home.

Finally, in response to the social worker pointing out the penis on the doll and saying, "Did he touch you with that? Who did?" Lisa says, "Fred." The first detective states, "You said Fred touched you with his dick . . . " the other detective chimes in, "And you mean this dick here on this doll?" and the first detective immediately asks, "And where did he touch you with that?" The three adults have put words into Lisa's mouth and move ahead for details of the touching with the penis. Lisa doesn't know what is expected and tells the interrogators, "You gotta show me."

The interrogators continue asking questions about touching with "his dick," and the grandmother joins in by telling Lisa to pretend the girl doll is her and the boy doll is Fred and to "Show us what he did," because "We just want to make you feel better." Finally Lisa, in response to "Where did the boy doll touch you?" answers, "Across the chest." This isn't the answer that the five interrogators want and the social worker asks, "Where else?" Lisa replies, "All over."

The questioning now moves to whether Fred was sitting or standing, where these events took place, and how often it happened. Lisa says that it happened in the bathroom. They ask whether he made her kiss his dick and she says, "No." They then ask *if* he kissed her and when she doesn't answer, ask, "*Where* did he kiss you?" and "*When this happened,* did Fred take his pants off?" (Italics added).

Lisa replies, "He didn't do that" twice and the detective says, "He didn't do that—what did he do?" Lisa says, "That ow—that ouch, he did—ow he did, that ow." Recall at the very beginning of the interview, Lisa said, "He pinched me," when asked, "What happened . . . at the day care center?" (A month later, at a preliminary hearing deposition, Lisa did not make any statements about sexual conduct. She did indicate on direct exam that she did not like Fred Conrad because he had slapped her on the back. However, on cross-examination she admitted that this was not really true.)

The social worker asks if she was wearing a dress and if he pulled down her pants. Lisa says, "My dress," and the social worker responds, "Um hmmm, did you pull down your pants then, or did he pull down your pants?" This is asked even though Lisa never says that her pants were pulled down. The question therefore tells Lisa that she is expected to answer one or the other. Lisa replies, "*He* pulled down my pants." (Italics added).

They then ask her about the threats to hurt her and begin questioning her about "what happened when he put his dick—dick down here." She says, "I don't know," and they remind her that "you showed us what he did," and tell her "Why don't you show them like you showed Mama and Grandma."

Lisa starts crying in response to the badgering and the grandmother, the two detectives, and the social worker begin telling her to show them with the dolls because "that'd be easier" and "That way you won't have to do it, the dolls will be doing it."

The next series of questions have to do with Fred making her wet when he "did this to you." Lisa responds, "I don't know," to most of the questions, the interrogators continue their badgering, and Lisa says "I don't know what . . . Mommy, I don't wanna . . ." and walks away. Her grandmother calls her back.

The next questions are about Nancy's involvement and about Lisa getting picked up from day care but no information is forthcoming from Lisa and most of the talking is done by the interrogators. Lisa says, "I wanna go home" and the social worker ends the interview with, "I'm surprised we got this much out of her with all this. . . ."

INTERVIEW

Interviewers: Roger Cain, Detective; John Pratt, Detective; Judy Morse, Social Worker.

Child: Lisa Brandt

Also Present: Sara Brandt (mother), Helen Brandt (grandmother)

Roger Cain = Det. Cain; John Pratt = Det. Pratt; Judy Morse = Soc Wkr; Lisa Brandt = Lisa; Sara Brandt = Mother; Helen Brandt = Grandma.

Det. Cain:	Do you want to go sit by the table?[2] Do you want to tell Grandma what happened?[2] Okay, well, you tell Grandma exactly what happened again, okay?[4, 6A]
Lisa:	Ouch.[C]
Soc Wkr:	You were at the day care center?[2] What happened?[1]
Det. Cain:	What happened, Lisa, when you were at the day care center?[1]
Lisa:	He pinched me.[C]
Det. Cain:	He pinched you?[9, 2]
Soc Wkr:	Where did he pinch you?[1] Yeah what . . . where else?[1]
Det. Cain:	He pinched you on the arm, Lisa?[9, 2] On the left arm, too?[9, 2]
Soc Wkr:	Where else?[1] You can tell him.[4, 6A]
Det. Cain:	You can . . . can you tell me where else or anything else that happened there?[2]
Lisa:	I don't feel that good.[D1]
Det. Cain:	What was that?[1]
Lisa:	I want to go home.[D1]
Soc Wkr:	Do you want me to tell him?[2] I think it would be better though if you told him.[6A] Tell him just like you told me.[4, 6A]
Lisa:	I don't feel . . . I don't wanna.[D1]
Soc Wkr:	Huh?[1] Huh?[1]
Lisa:	I don't wanna . . . [D1]
Soc Wkr:	You don't wanna.[9] Where did Nancy touch you?[1, 6A]
Lisa:	I don't know.[D3]
Soc Wkr:	Who else touched you over there?[1, 6A]
Lisa:	I don't know.[D3]
Soc Wkr:	You can tell . . . we were gonna . . . we were gonna tell 'em so that all the worries would be all over with again.[4, 6A, 5]

[Brief indecipherable section]

Soc Wkr:	Why don't you want to tell him?[1]
Lisa:	I want to go sit in the living room.[D1]
Soc Wkr:	You want to go sit in the living room?[9, 2]
Det Pratt:	Lisa, did somebody tell you they'd hurt you if you told what happened?[2] Hum?[1]
Grandma:	If you talk about it, you'll feel better.[5, 6A] If we talk about it now, then we won't have to talk about it ever again if you don't want to.[5, 6A] Okay?[8]
Lisa:	I don't want . . . [D1]
Grandma:	I know, honey, but listen.[5, 4, 6A] Don't you see . . . can't you help him?[4, 6A] Can you tell him what happened there?[2, 6A] What they did to you?[1] What did they do?[1, 6A]
Det. Pratt:	Lisa, there's other little girls there, and we want to make sure they don't get hurt, too, but you've got to tell us so we can help them.[4, 6A] You've got to tell us what happened to you.[4] And nobody's going to hurt you if you tell us.[5, 6A] That's what the policeman is here for—to make sure nobody ever hurts you.[5, 6A]
Grandma:	Nothing's going to happen to you, honey.[5, 6A]
Det. Pratt:	Would you be able to show us on the dolls what happened to you?[2, 7] Could you show us on the dolls?[2, 7, 4] See, these are special dolls—they've got special parts.[6A, 7] Could you show us on the dolls?[2, 7, 4]
Soc Wkr:	Listen, listen—you want to show him on the dolls, or do you want to show him on Grandma?[3] Where else did they touch you?[1] Show him—show him on me.[4, 6A] Yeah . . . where else?[1] Yeah . . . where else?[1] Yeah.[8] Where else?[1] That's okay.[5] Lisa—here, look at Grandma once.[4, 6A] Lisa, what did they touch you with?[1] What did they touch you with?[1]
Lisa:	I don't know what it is.[D3]
Det. Pratt:	Get the male doll there.[6B, 7]

Grandma: You don't have to be afraid to say it.[6A, 5]

Det. Pratt: Here, Lisa, we'll pull the pants down on the male doll.[7, 6A] Can you point to the male doll what they touched you with?[2, 4, 6A] Just point.[4, 6A]

Soc Wkr: I'll go with you.[8]

Det. Pratt: Did he touch you with with a bellybutton?[2] That's a bellybutton.[6A] Did he touch you with something else?[2] Oh, he touched your bellybutton?[9, 2] What did he touch your bellybutton with?[1]

Lisa: (giggling)[E2]

Grandma: That's okay, there's nothing to be afraid of.[5, 6A]

Det. Pratt: No you're . . . you don't have to be afraid no more.[5] We're gonna[8]

Grandma: It's okay — you can do that.[5, 6A]

Lisa: I want to go home.[D1]

Det. Pratt: Hum?[1]

Soc Wkr: What is that?[1] Did he touch you with that?[2] Who did?[1] Hmm?[1]

Lisa: Fred.[C]

Grandma: Fred?[9, 2]

Det. Cain: You said Fred touched you with his dick — is that what you said, Lisa?[9, 2]

Det. Pratt: And you mean this dick here on this doll?[9, 2, 7]

Det. Cain: And where did he touch you with that?[1] On your legs?[9, 2] Between your legs, too?[9, 2]

Lisa: Know me . . . [C]

Soc Wkr: What else did he touch you with that, Lisa?[1]

Lisa: I don't . . . [D1]

Soc Wkr: Lisa, did he touch you . . . where else?[1] Did he touch you here and here with it, too?[2] Where else?[1]

Lisa: You gotta show me.[F]

Soc Wkr: I gotta show you?[9, 2] You show me, honey.[4, 6A] I forgot where you said.[8] Where else?[1]

Det. Cain: On both arms?[9, 2] On the head, too?[9, 2]

Det. Pratt: Lisa, did he make you touch his dick?[2] He did?[9, 2] Did he make you touch his dick with your hands?[2] Did he make you put it someplace?[2] Could you tell me where he made you put it?[2] Can you show me on the little girl doll what he did with it?[2, 7] Let's pretend this doll is Fred, okay?[4, 6A, 7]

Grandma: Here, this little doll's going to be you, okay?[7, 6A] Can this be you?[7, 2] And that will be Fred, okay?[6A] Can you show us what he did?[2, 7, 4] You don't have to be afraid—you won't get in no trouble.[6A, 5]

Det. Pratt: Yeah, you won't . . . nobody's going to hurt you or anything.[6A, 5] It's really important.[6A, 4]

Grandma: We just want to make you feel better.[5] Can you show us?[2]

Soc Wkr: . . . and you're not . . . for showing us, you're not going to be a naughty girl.[6A]

Grandma: That's right, you're not going to get a spanking or nothing.[6A, 5]

Det. Pratt: No, nobody's going to hurt you.[5, 6A] Did he say somebody's going to hurt you?[2]

Soc Wkr: Did he say someone's going to hurt you?[2]

Det. Pratt: If you told?[2] He did?[9, 2]

Lisa: Um hmm.[A1]

Det. Cain: Well, nobody's going to hurt you, Lisa.[5, 6A]

Det. Pratt: Nope, nobody's going to spank you or hit you or be mean to you or anything.[5, 6A]

Soc Wkr: Come up here once, hon, please.[4, 6A]

Det. Cain: Can you show us what the boy—what the Fred doll did to the little girl doll, which is you now?[2, 4, 6A, 7]

Soc Wkr: Where did the boy doll touch you?[1]

Det. Cain: Across the chest?[9, 2]

Soc Wkr: Where else?[1]

Lisa: All over.[C]

Det. Cain: All over?[9, 2]

Det. Pratt: Was Fred standing up when he made you do this?[2] Or was he laying down?[2, 3]

Lisa: Up.[C]

Det. Pratt: What?[1] Just laying down—or you were laying down?[6A, 2]

Lisa: No.[1]

Det. Pratt: You were sitting up?[9, 2]

Lisa: Yeah.[A1]

Det. Pratt: Okay.[8]

Lisa: And he was sitting down.[C]

Det. Pratt: And he was sitting down?[9, 2] Okay.[8] Where did this happen?[1] Did it happen in the bedroom, did it happen in the kitchen?[3]

Lisa: Bathroom.[C]

Det. Pratt: In the bedroom?[6A, 2] Okay.[8] Did it ever happen in the bathroom?[2]

Lisa: Hum?[F]

Det. Pratt: Did it happen in the bathroom or just the bedroom?[3]

Lisa: The bathroom.[C]

Det. Pratt: The bathroom—well, that's consistent, then.[6B] How many times did it happen, Lisa?[1]

Lisa: I don't know.[D3]

Det. Pratt:	Do you know how many times this is?[2] Yeah, that's what—does she have a concept of numbers yet?[2, 6B]
Grandma:	One, two, three, about that.[6B]
Det. Pratt:	Did it happen more than once?[2] It did, okay.[9, 8] When he made you do this, Lisa—why don't you bring the little doll up here?[2, 4, 6A, 7]
Grandma:	That's you.[6A]
Det. Pratt:	Do you want me to move the dolls around?[2, 7] Okay.[8] When he made you do these things, you said that he put his dick between your legs?[9, 2] Okay.[8] Did he ever make you go like this?[2, 6A] And put his dick in your mouth?[2, 6A] He did?[9, 2]

[Det. Pratt demonstrates with the dolls.]

Soc Wkr:	He did, yes?[9, 2]
Grandma:	Yes or no.[4, 6A] Say it.[4, 6A]
Lisa:	No.[B1]
Det. Pratt:	Did he ever make you kiss it?[2]
Lisa:	No.[B1]
Det. Pratt:	Okay.[8] Did he ever kiss you?[2]
Soc Wkr:	It's okay—did he?[5, 2]
Det. Pratt:	Did he ever tell you you were a real nice little girl?[2] Did he ever tell you he was going to give you nice things?[2] Where did he kiss you?[1] On your mouth?[2] Did he kiss you any place else?[2] When this happened, did Fred take his pants off?[2] He did?[9, 2] Did he take your pants all the way off, or just pull them down?[3]
Lisa:	He didn't do that . . . [B1]
Det. Pratt:	What?[1]
Lisa:	He didn't do that.[B1]
Det. Pratt:	He didn't do that—what did he do?[9, 1]

Lisa: That ow—that ouch, he did—ow he did.[C] That ow![C]

Det. Pratt: He did that so?[9, 2] What—what?[1]

Soc Wkr: Did he . . . did you . . . were you wearing a dress that day?[2] Did he pull up your dress?[2] Did he pull down your pants?[2]

Lisa: My dress.[C]

Soc Wkr: Um hmm, did you pull down your pants then, or did he pull down your pants?[3]

Lisa: He pulled down my pants.[C]

Soc Wkr: He pulled down your pants.[9]

Det. Pratt: When he did this, Lisa, and he said he was going to hurt you, what did he say he . . . ?[1, 6A]

Lisa: I . . . he . . . [G]

Det. Pratt: Huh?[1]

Lisa: I don't know.[D3]

Det. Pratt: Did he say he was going to hurt you?[2]

Lisa: Yeah.[A1]

Det. Pratt: Did he say he was going to hit you?[2]

Lisa: No.[B1]

Det. Pratt: Did he say he was going to spank you?[2]

Lisa: Yeah.[A1]

Det. Pratt: Did he say Grandma was going to spank you?[2] He didn't.[9] Did he say he wouldn't like you if you told anybody?[2] He didn't say that either?[9, 2] But he said he would hit you if you told?[9, 2]

Grandma: Sit still.[4, 6A]

Soc Wkr:	What happened when he . . . Lisa, can you tell them what happened when you were . . . when you . . . remember the other day when she was telling both of us here.[1, 6B] When Lisa . . . with Lisa lying down.[6A, 6B] Lisa, can you show them?[2, 4, 6A] Can you show them what happened when he put his dick . . . dick down here?[2, 4, 6A] What did he do when he did that?[1]
Lisa:	I don't know.[D3]
Soc Wkr:	Remember?[2] Remember, you showed us what he did?[2, 4]
Mother:	You showed us what he did.[4]
Lisa:	Woke up.[C]
Soc Wkr:	What did he do?[1]
Grandma:	Honey, now come on.[4] We're just trying to help, now, okay?[5, 6A] Can we try to help?[2]
Soc Wkr:	Why don't you show them like you showed Mama and Grandma?[4, 6A] What he did.[4, 6A]
Lisa:	(crying)[E1]
Grandma:	Show us with the dolls—that'd be easier.[4, 6A, 7]
Det. Pratt:	That way you won't have to do it, the dolls will be doing it.[6A, 7]
Soc Wkr:	Yeah, show it with the dolls like you showed us.[4, 6A, 7]
Det. Pratt:	Okay, yeah, you can use that doll if you want to.[5, 6A, 7]
Det. Cain:	You can use the big one, sure.[5, 6A, 7]
Det. Pratt:	Lisa, when Fred did this to you, did he make you wet?[2, 6A]
Lisa:	Yes.[A1]
Det. Pratt:	Where did he make you wet at?[1]
Lisa:	I don't know.[D3]
Soc Wkr:	Can you show me where he made you wet?[2, 4, 6A]
Lisa:	I don't know.[D3]

Soc Wkr:	Did you get kind of wet and . . . ?[2]
Grandma:	Did he get you wet when he did that?[2]
Lisa:	Yeah.[A1]
Grandma:	Where did he get you wet at?[1] You don't know?[9, 2]
Lisa:	No.[B1]
Grandma:	Well, if he got you wet, you must know where he got you wet at?[4, 2] Do you?[2]
Det. Pratt:	Did he wipe you off with a towel, Lisa?[2, 6A]
Lisa:	Yeah.[A1]
Det. Pratt:	Where did he put the towel when he wiped you off?[1] On your chest?[1, 6A]
Soc Wkr:	Did he ever put . . . look at me, honey, . . . did he ever put this here or here?[2] In your nose?[2] Did he ever put it here?[2] In there?[2]
Lisa:	No, it won't tight (?) . . . nope, got to go tight.[C]
Det. Pratt:	Lisa, when Fred got you wet on the chest, did he kind of have you in his arms?[6A, 2]
Soc Wkr:	Did he hurt you when he was doing this to you?[2]
Det. Pratt:	Did Nancy ever see Fred do this to you?[2]
Lisa:	I don't know what . . . Mommy, I don't wanna . . . [D3, D1]
Grandma:	Honey, come here.[5, 4, 6A] Come here.[4, 6A]
Soc Wkr:	Did Nancy ever do any of this to you, Lisa?[2] Did Nancy ever look up your dress or anything?[2]
Grandma:	Did Nancy—did Nancy know what was happening when Fred did that to you?[2] She didn't?[9, 2] Where was she?[1] Was she somewhere else?[2] She didn't know that, huh?[9, 2]
Soc Wkr:	Was there any other kids around when this happened?[2] Hmm?[1] There was other kids?[9, 2]

Det. Pratt:	Do you remember their names?[2] No.[9]
Grandma:	You don't remember the kids' names?[9, 2]
Det. Pratt:	Did they see Fred do this to you?[2] They did?[9, 2] Do you remember what any of the kids looked like?[2]
Grandma:	Don't you remember any of your friends that were there in the day care with you?[2, 4] Don't you remember their names?[2, 4]
Lisa:	No.[B1]
Det. Pratt:	Did Fred ever do it to anybody that you saw?[2] He did?[9, 2] Do you remember what their names were?[2]
Soc Wkr:	Did he ever get mad at Bobby when Bobby came to pick you up?[2] What did he used to say?[1] Did he holler?[2] Or . . . [8]
Grandma:	What did he say about Bobby coming to pick you up?[1] Hmm?[1]
Soc Wkr:	What did he say though—I can't remember what you told me.[1]
Lisa:	I don't know . . . [D3]
Grandma:	Did he holler at you when Bobby came?[2] What did he say?[1]
Lisa:	(Shouts) He said, "GET AWAY!"[C]
Det. Pratt:	Didn't he like Bobby?[2]
Lisa:	No.[B1]
Det. Pratt:	He didn't?[9, 2] Why not?[1]
Lisa:	'Cause . . . [C]
Det. Pratt:	Bobby's a pretty nice boy.[6A] I know Bobby.[8]
Grandma:	Well, that one day he did go pick 'em up, see, I usually picked 'em up like—picked her up like about 4:30, quarter to five, and see, he went there one day like 3:00.[6B, 6A] Which was earlier, so then he must have said something to Lisa about, you know, having to come so early.[6B, 6A]

Soc Wkr: See, when this—when she first came out with this, she had said more things about what I had told you; what he had said about, you know, ... something like, oh, slamming him (?)[6A, 6B] I mentioned to her before exactly what was said, but I don't remember either because ... her exact words.[6B, 6A] She didn't see him again.[6B, 6A] I can't remember them, so she can't remember the exact words.[6B, 6A]

Det. Pratt: Lisa, are you frightened now, are you afraid?[2] Hmm?[1] Aren't you going to answer me?[2, 4]

Det. Cain: You're not afraid of us, are you Lisa?[2, 6A]

Det. Pratt: Lisa, you did a real good job.[5] You're very brave and nobody's going to spank you or punish you for telling.[5, 6A] It's very important that you tell us this, otherwise more little girls and boys might be hurt.[4, 6A]

Soc Wkr: You wouldn't want that to happen, would you?[2, 4, 6A]

Det. Pratt: See, they might be hurt by the same person that hurt you, and we want to make sure that doesn't happen anymore.[4, 6A] We want to make sure this person doesn't hurt anybody anymore.[4, 6A]

Soc Wkr: Because you weren't the sassy person.[6A, 5] You weren't sassy.[6A, 5]

Lisa: I wanna go home ... [D1]

Soc Wkr: Wanna sit on my lap?[5, 2] I'm surprised we got this much out of her with all this ... [6B]

AFTERMATH

By the time of the trial, the defense attorney had obtained an additional audiotape—of one of the boys. The tape had both the starting time and the ending time of the interview, indicating that the interview had lasted for 45 minutes. However, the tape was only 30 minutes long.

Midway through the interview, the tape stopped and then started again. Because of the starting and ending times announced by the interrogator, it could be seen that the unrecorded portion was 15 minutes long. This tape was of interest in that the portion before the interruption was completely different from that after the interruption. At the beginning, despite techniques similar to those used in the interview of Lisa, the boy maintained that nothing happened. However, after the interruption, he agreed to the statements about abuse.

Fred Conrad was acquitted on all counts of sexual abuse. Following the trial, the jury was so incensed by what they had heard that they met for several months afterwards and led an effort to force the detectives and social workers of the child abuse unit to receive training to ensure that they never again interrogated children and investigated cases in the way they did with this case.

But Fred and Nancy have given up their dream of running a professional and competent day care center. They are struggling to recover from the tremendous emotional strain and financial cost of this ordeal. Fred wrote to us a year following the trial:

> When I first began seeking legal counsel, I encountered a number of attorneys who had apparently studied the lists of behavioral indicators of sexual abuse that seem to be so prevalent today. The attorneys also had adopted the maxim, "Children don't lie about sexual abuse."
>
> I was bewildered by such statements that seemed to come out of thin air. I knew that I had not sexually abused anyone, yet, the attorneys were telling me that children didn't lie about these things. In essence, these professionals were telling me that I was lying. . . . Finally, I found an attorney who is an independent thinker (and got) . . . your name and telephone number. . . .
>
> As a result of the still present hysteria and the ignorant and biased attitudes held by authority figures and mental health professional in my community, I felt I had no other choice but to choose another career. An accusation of child molestation is devastating to everyone involved when it is false. . . .
>
> I believe that because of your testimony, the great number of educators on my jury (4) and because of the horrendous interviewing techniques used by investigators, I was acquitted. Others who are innocent are not so lucky (personal communication, 1986).

Nancy is no longer involved in any professional activity with children. She had loved teaching. It had been her goal in life as long as she could remember. Now she is working as a secretary trying to earn enough money to get training as a paralegal. She would like to go to law school but cannot see how to manage that. She wants to be able to assist others who are accused of child sexual abuse and to do whatever she can to pursue justice for people accused.

Chapter 9

TRAINING CHILDREN IN DEVIANT SEXUALITY

When there is a report of sexual abuse there is an investigation. The investigation always includes interrogating the children who are the possible victims. Social workers, psychologists, psychiatrists, and/or law enforcement personnel are usually involved in investigations and interrogations of children. Parents or other adults question children in an indeterminate fashion, most often with no record or documentation other than after-the-fact descriptions by the adults. These interrogations during an investigation include questioning children about sexual acts. Each experience of interrogation by an adult is a learning experience for the child.

When there are multiple children involved in the allegations, the children may talk with each other about the adults questioning them or about what they see on TV or overhear from parents. This can happen in a family setting or at a school when the accusations involve a school or day care center. An investigation may begin with a social worker and/or a police officer showing up to take a child out of the classroom for questioning. When the child returns to class, other children will ask what happened. If there is publicity, children may talk to each other and to the children who are supposed to be victims.

In day care center allegations, investigators may look for all the children who have been at the facility. Lists of parents may be taken and the parents contacted and told that their children may have been abused. The parents are usually given instructions to bring their child in for questioning. As a result, hundreds of children may be interviewed. The interrogation may be done at the day care school or at a center specializing in sexual abuse evaluations. In one case, an investigator spent a month at a day care center questioning several children each day. (In this case, teachers heard the children talking to each other about the questioning and about what they had learned from the process.) In another case, about 500 children were interviewed at one specific center recommended by the police. In allegations against teachers, investigators have questioned members of a class and persons who went through the school while the accused teacher was there.

We have not seen anyone observe that when a large number of children are interrogated, chance alone means that some are likely to recall a pat or a gesture and then interpret it as abuse. Given the suggestibility of children and the learning experience of an interrogation, if 100 children are questioned, the probability is that a few may produce an account that appears to support the accusation but is, in reality, false. There is no base rate information on this issue, but probability theory suggests that as the number of children interrogated increases, the likelihood of suggested accounts learned from the interrogation process itself also increases. If such accounts are then used to corroborate and support the credibility of an initial suspicion or accusation, the investigation process has bootstrapped itself into what looks like a stronger position but is farther removed from reality.

A county attorney in a large metropolitan area, who had political aspirations, was embarrassed by a day care center accusation that ended in acquittal. He therefore formed a Mass Molestation Task Force to deal with future sexual abuse complaints involving multiple possible victims. When the next allegation surfaced in a day care center, the Task Force was alerted and assigned the investigation. Within three days of the initial report the Task Force set up four interrogation teams, each composed of a child protection worker, a policeman, and an assistant county attorney. Parents of all the children in the two facilities owned by the operator who was charged with sexual abuse were told there had been abuse and asked to bring their children to the local police station for interrogation.

The scene in the police station as described by the parents was chaotic and strange. Parents and children were sitting all over the station waiting to be called for an interrogation. Children were restless, frightened, and confused. Parents were anxious, concerned, and eager to find out about their children. Small groups of parents and children formed in halls and waiting areas and exchanged rumors, anxieties, and angers. Children were interviewed by one of the four interrogation teams in a haphazard manner. Parents were not allowed to be with their child while the interrogation was conducted. Parents were also told to take their children to one of two hospitals for medical examinations of their genitalia.

One father, who insisted on knowing what was happening to his daughter, was permitted to listen to the interrogation on an intercom. He was appalled at the way the interrogators attacked his child, pressured, and coerced her to produce a statement about having been abused. Until the trial he spoke publicly every chance he could get to describe the unconscionable emotional abuse he believed his daughter had experienced in the hands of the interrogation team.

One hundred and twenty-eight children, ages two to five, were interrogated by the four teams of the Mass Molestation Task Force. In addition to the child who was the subject of the initial report, three other children produced accounts of sexual abuse by the operator. Eight children produced accounts of seeing other children abused while maintaining they had never been abused. All other children denied any abuse. Records of the interrogations show that of the twelve children who gave accounts supporting the complaint nine were produced by one of the interrogation teams. The other three teams each reported one child saying they had observed other children being abused. A simple Chi-square analysis shows this result would occur by chance less than one time in a thousand ($p < .001$). The chances are that the one interrogation team caused the children to make statements supporting abuse by their coercive methods.

The trial lasted several weeks. The jury acquitted the operator of all charges. In the process, 128 children had been exposed to adult behaviors that frightened, confused, and, in some instances, terrorized them. They were taught about explicit, bizarre, and deviant sexual behaviors through the questions asked in the interrogation process. They were subjected to intrusive and painful medical examinations. Parents, 128 sets of them, were distressed. Some had family and marital stress generated by the investigation. Some became convinced their children had been sexually abused. Others formed a group to protest the investigation and support the operator. The emotional, financial, and relationship costs to children, families, and the community are incalculable. The long-term effects on the children are unknown but can hardly be considered positive.

In day care center allegations in which multiple children are interviewed, most children do not readily produce accounts of abuse. There may be repeated interviews of children who say nothing supporting the accusation before the investigators stop or the parents become alarmed and stop the process. Children are asked about deviant sexual behaviors across a number of interviews. Some continue to deny any abuse while others may produce an account after several sessions. Children who had no previous knowledge of specific sexual acts learn about them from the investigator. Nonabused children who go through a 45-minute interrogation using anatomical dolls, pictures, booklets, and questions about sexual acts may learn things they did not know before. A four-year-old child who has never thought about anal intercourse but is asked repeatedly if his daddy or teacher stuck his wiener or a spoon or a banana up his butt is no longer naive. The child now knows about sticking things up the butt and knows that adults are interested in this phenomenon.

Nobody has considered the effect on young children of repeated questioning about sexually deviant behaviors. Interrogations often include questioning about sadistic and masochistic behaviors in which giving or receiving pain is associated with sexuality. This is what occurs in the questions about spoons, popsicle sticks, knives, forks, and spatulas forcibly thrust into vaginas and anuses. If the children have not been abused, this questioning teaches about deviant sexual acts that may affect their understanding of human sexual behavior and their own sexuality.

The fantasies of preschool children are rich, complex, and often frightening. When adults repeatedly encourage and reinforce fantasies about destructive, horrifying, and repulsive sexual behavior, the stories may become subjectively real to the child. This is an assault upon a young child's developing ability to differentiate between fantasy and reality.

When naive children suddenly acquire knowledge of fellatio, cunnilingus, analingus, coprophilia, urophilia, frottage, exhibitionism, voyeurism, and an association between sexuality and pain or fear, some of them may try it out. Others may find adult questioning about erotic behavior reinforcing enough to begin acting out in other environments. We have documents showing young children talking to strangers about sexual deviance, masturbating frequently, grabbing adult genitalia, and experimenting with sexual acts with other children after having been interrogated. There had been no such behavior prior to the interrogation. Unfortunately, investigators then believe this new behavior means that the child was abused. But the most parsimonious explanation is the effect of the interrogation, which preceded the behavior and is closer in time. At least, the potential learning effect of the interrogation should be explored.

Another long-term unintended consequence may be that children are taught a completely genitalized view of human sexuality. The questioning is always focused on contact with genital tissue or penetration of genitals or orifices. It must be directed in this limited way because that is how the law defines sexual abuse. For a naive child, the learning experience will be that sex is limited to genitals. Mature, adult human sexuality recognizes the reality that persons, and not genitals, are what is basic to a full-orbed and complete sexuality. The genital focus of sex generated by this questioning at a young age may result in children attempting to live out the fantasies generated by the questioning when they reach adolescence or adulthood.

BACKGROUND

Tots and Fun was a summer day camp for four-year-old children. Thirty children met each day in a community center for various activities including crafts, games, outings, and swimming in an adjoining pool. Along with a head counselor, there were four additional staff members who supervised the different activities. The children moved freely from activity to activity and all of the children knew all of the counselors. The counselors were young people; the supervisor was 25 and the others were 17, 18, or 19. All of the staff were women except for a 19-year-old man, Peter Ballard, who was working at the summer camp to earn money to enter vocational school in the fall.

The allegations began when a parent of one of the children complained to the police that her daughter had told her that Peter Ballard had taken her daughter's clothes off and given her a bath. The police responded by assigning Detective Vince Marshall from the county child abuse unit to the case. Detective Marshall questioned the child in the presence of her mother and obtained a statement from the child that Peter Ballard had put her in the bathtub at camp and had kissed her on her bottom and front. (In a later tape-recorded statement to her father, the child said that she had made up the story. However, by this time the investigation was off and running. This information was not given to defense counsel until immediately before the trial began.)

Following the interview with this first child, Detective Marshall, along with a social worker from the child abuse unit, Louis Fabrini, interviewed Peter Ballard. Peter denied any sexually abusive or other inappropriate behavior. Nevertheless, he was fired immediately.

The child abuse unit then interviewed all of the 30 children, some of them several times. (We received audiotapes of interviews for 16 of these children.) As the interviews progressed, the allegations grew to include accounts of anal and vaginal penetration, cunnilingus, insertion of spoons, knives, toys, popsicle sticks, and other objects into the anus and vagina, pouring a mixture of salt and water into the vagina and anus, forcing the children to insert their fingers into each others' anuses, urinating and defecating on the children, forcing the children to eat feces, and making candy out of the children's feces. These events were all said to have occurred during a two-week period (from the date the day camp started to the day Peter was arrested) at the camp in connection with the scheduled activities. Some of the children stated that the head counselor was present during the abusive activities.

The interviews were conducted by the members of the child sexual abuse unit. Most were interviewed by Louis Fabrini, the social worker, who was sometimes accompanied by another adult male. The initial interviews often took place in the school environment and children talked to each other about what was being said to them by the investigators. Parents were also sometimes present for the interviews. The interviews show leading questions, false information given to the children, and pressure to describe abusive incidents.

Louis Fabrini routinely told children that other children had already described the incidents. He gave the names of children who he said had told him about various events. However, when we examined the transcripts of these other interviews, this was not true. Mr. Fabrini apparently used a standard procedure of saying that other children told him things which they had not. He also told some of the children that he himself had been abused as a child, which may or may not be true, but which he used to encourage the children to talk to him.

The children were asked to tell not only what had happened to them, but to talk about abuse they had observed between Peter and other children. They were told that Peter was now in jail for the terrible things he had done and by describing more of the events they would help protect other children. However, he was not telling the children the truth because at this time Peter was not in jail but was free on bail.

Children who responded to pressure by developing accounts of abuse were praised: "Okay, you've been incredibly helpful, real good, and I want to thank you so much because you're the hero here." "And you have been so helpful to us, this has been terrific because now we know who else was touched down there and we want to be able to help them and make them feel better. . . . You are a good girl." Children who persisted in denying abuse were put down. "You are afraid to tell me. Boy, even the girls told me . . . why are you such a fraidy cat?"

Several children responded to the pressure by naming the head counselor, Betty, as the counselor who was hurting the children, and other children said that she was present during the abuse. But this was ignored and no charges were brought against anyone other than Peter Ballard. Despite the preposterous nature of the allegations and the fact that the other counselors had observed nothing, stating that it would have been impossible in terms of the physical layout and daily routine for such behaviors to have taken place without their knowledge, Peter Ballard was indicted on multiple counts of child sexual abuse.

The following interview was conducted two weeks after the original report, when the child abuse investigation team began interviewing all of the 30 children. This is the first interview for this particular child, Todd Wilson. The interview is typical of those performed by Louis Fabrini, who interviewed most of the children. Also present in this interview is the police detective, Vince Marshall, and the boy's mother, who encourages him to talk to the interrogators.

Fabrini begins the interview by telling Todd that he has talked to other children at the day camp. He names the other children and states that "they were telling me that a counselor at camp was bothering them in the bathroom."

The child, Todd Wilson, denies being abused or observing any abuse. Fabrini does not accept the denial and says, "Todd, I will tell you what, first of all I know you know what I am talking about."

When Todd says, "I don't know what you are talking about," Fabrini replies, "all those kids told me the whole truth about everything that happened to them. I know about popsicle sticks, I know about spoons, I know about other stuff that is not so nice."

When Todd continues to deny the abuse, Fabrini tells him that Peter is now in jail for doing the bad things to the children and that Detective Vince has personally put Peter in jail. "And he does that because it is our job to do nothing but all we do every day is talk to little kids who grown-ups have hurt or taken advantage of. Or touched them in places where bathing suits cover."

When Todd still doesn't cooperate, his mother joins in and asks him to talk to Fabrini. But Todd continues to deny everything and says that he doesn't want to talk. Fabrini tells him, "And if you can help me you could be a little junior detective, and give us a hand. It will be very very helpful. I know about like I told you before, I know about popsicle sticks, I know about the spoons."

Todd says, "I don't want to talk no more," but his mother urges him further, saying, "Mommy wants you to talk to Lou and Lou wants you to talk to him," and Fabrini tells him, "I think your mommy and daddy would like it very much if you were to talk to me." The child is now being pressured by three adults to talk about the abuse.

Todd continues to state that he has seen nothing. Fabrini brings out the anatomical dolls, telling him that he can use the dolls to show what happened if he is afraid to talk. "Todd, do you want to know something, what happens sometimes, sometimes what I do with little kids, who are afraid to talk to me, kids who are afraid to say anything to me, I show them these strange little friends of mine. And sometimes if they can't say the words, they just point and they show me things, okay. For example, I, I bet you ain't never seen dolls like this before."

Todd continues to say that he saw nothing and attempts to leave the interview. He is getting angry about the badgering from Fabrini and says, "I don't want to talk to you."

Fabrini then accuses him of being a "fraidy cat" and when Todd says, "No," states, "Yes you are, you are afraid to tell me. Boy, even the girls told me." Shortly after this the interview ends.

The total percentage of error-inducing statements for the interviews of the 16 children in this case was 76 percent.

INTERVIEW

Interviewers:	Vince Marshall (a detective from the prosecutor's office) and Louis Fabrini (a social worker). Also present, Judy Wilson, Todd's mother
Child:	Todd Wilson

Todd Wilson = Todd; Vince Marshall = Detective; Louis Fabiano = Soc Wkr; Judy Wilson = Mom.

Detective:	Today is July 24, Vince Marshall from the Prosecutor's Office, we are going to be speaking with Todd Wilson.[10] Todd, do you want to give me your age?[2]
Todd:	No.[D1]
Detective:	No.[9]

Soc Wkr: We're talking to all the kids in your camp, do you know who I talked to already?[2, 4, 6A]

Todd: Who?[F]

Soc Wkr: Do you know Albert?[2, 4]

Todd: No.[B1]

Soc Wkr: Do you know Brent?[2, 4]

Todd: No.[B1]

Soc Wkr: Do you know Shelly?[2, 4]

Todd: No.[B1]

Soc Wkr: Do you know Diana?[2, 4]

Todd: No.[B1]

Soc Wkr: I think you are fibbing me.[4] Do you know Diana?[2, 4]

Todd: No.[B1]

Soc Wkr: Mark?[2]

Todd: No.[B1]

Soc Wkr: You know Aaron?[2, 4]

Todd: No.[B1]

Soc Wkr: Everybody knows Aaron.[4]

Todd: I don't know Aaron.[C]

Soc Wkr: Do you know Kelly?[2]

Todd: I don't know nobody.[D1]

Soc Wkr: Do you know Molly and Jessica, the little twin sisters?[2]

Todd: I don't know nobody.[D1]

Soc Wkr: I know who you know.[4] You know Shelly.[4]

Todd: I don't know nobody.[C]

Soc Wkr: Do you know Mark.[2, 4]

Todd:	No.[B1]
Soc Wkr:	Who are some of his buddies at camp?[6B]
Todd:	Andy.[6B]
Soc Wkr:	Oh, Andy.[9] Andy Martin.[9] Is he a friend of yours?[2] He is a good guy.[10] How about Sally?[1, 4] How about Michael?[1, 4]
Todd:	No.[B1]
Soc Wkr:	Laurie.[2, 4]
Mom:	Oh, come on, who did we see at the hair place.[4]
Todd:	Nobody.[D1]
Soc Wkr:	Do you know why I am talking to you?[2]
Todd:	No.[B1]
Soc Wkr:	Is that why you are not talking to me?[2] What I am doing is I am talking to the kids in Tots and Fun, I'm talking to all of them.[4, 6A] Do you know why I am talking to them?[2]
Todd:	Why?[F]
Soc Wkr:	Because, do you know a little girl named Noel?[2, 4] And Molly and Jessica and a couple other kids.[4]
Todd:	I know nobody.[D1]
Soc Wkr:	Anyway, they were telling me that a counselor at camp was bothering them in the bathroom.[6A, 4] Do you know the counselor I am talking about?[2]
Todd:	No.[B1]
Soc Wkr:	Do you remember Peter?[2, 6A]
Todd:	No.[B1]
Soc Wkr:	Yes you do.[4] Todd, I will tell you what, first of all I know you know what I am talking about.[4] Secondly, I know it is scary to talk about it.[6A, 4]
Todd:	I don't know what you are talking about.[D1]

Soc Wkr:	Because all those kids told me the whole truth about everything that happened to them.[4] I know about popsicle sticks, I know about spoons, I know about other stuff that is not so nice.[4, 6A]
Todd:	No.[B1]
Soc Wkr:	I think you know what I am talking about.[4]
Todd:	No.[B1]
Soc Wkr:	Do you know Peter?[2] Is Peter a boy or a girl?[3]
Todd:	Boy.[C]
Soc Wkr:	Was he the only boy counselor?[2]
Todd:	Yes, he is a boy.[A2]
Soc Wkr:	And he is not there any more?[2, 6A]
Todd:	No.[B1]
Soc Wkr:	Do you know why he is not there any more?[2]
Todd:	Why?[F]
Soc Wkr:	I'm asking you, do you know?[2, 4] Peter is in jail now.[6A]
Todd:	No, he's not.[B1]
Soc Wkr:	Yes, he is, do you know why he is in jail?[2]
Todd:	Why?[F]
Soc Wkr:	Because all the kids I told you before told me the truth about what happened to them.[4, 6A] And those kids also told us that Peter tried to scare them by saying if you tell anybody the police are going to get you and stuff like that.[4, 6A] I want you to understand.[10]
Todd:	The police put Peter in jail?[F]
Soc Wkr:	Yep.[10] Do you know why they did that, they did that so they can protect the kids, so that he couldn't hurt them any more.[5] How do you feel about that?[1]
Todd:	He is not in jail.[C]

Soc Wkr: I promise you, in fact you have already met the policeman who put him in jail.[5]

Todd: No.[B1]

Soc Wkr: Detective Vince, that you met over there?[2]

Todd: No.[B1]

Soc Wkr: In that office.[6A] That's the guy who put him in jail.[6A]

Todd: No.[B1]

Soc Wkr: And he does that because it is our job to do nothing but all we do every day is talk to little kids who grown-ups have hurt or taken advantage of.[4, 6A] Or touched them in places where bathing suits cover.[4, 6A]

Todd: No.[B1]

Soc Wkr: And that's um, why he is in jail right now.[6A] And we are talking to all the kids in Tots and Fun and they have been real real good so far they have been telling us the truth about all the bad stuff that he was doing.[4, 6A]

Todd: He can break out of jail.[C]

Soc Wkr: Uh?[2]

Todd: He can break out of jail.[C]

Soc Wkr: I know he said that but he can't.[6A, 5] You know what?[2] Maybe we can arrange for you to look at a jail so you could see how hard it is to break out.[5] Honest.[5]

Todd: It is hard to break out?[F]

Soc Wkr: You know, you see how big I am, I couldn't break out of jail.[6A, 5]

Todd: You couldn't?[F]

Soc Wkr: No, jail is like, did you ever go to the zoo, did you ever go to a zoo?[2]

Todd: No.[B1]

Soc Wkr: Well, a jail cell is like a bunch of steel bars that you can not break out of.[6A, 5] It has a big lock on it.[6A, 5] Jail is like where you go for a while like when you get in trouble and you get sent up to your room, that's what jail is like, but you go away a little longer.[6A] And that's why Peter is in jail.[6A] And I promise you one thing, he is never going to hurt anybody again.[5]

Todd: Can I go back now?[F, D1]

Mom: Wait, Louis still wants to talk to you.[4]

Soc Wkr: You know what we do sometimes, sometimes it's a little embarrassing if the mommies or daddies stay inside the room, so I am going to give you a chance to if you want, you could tell me something, if we want to put Mommy outside we could do that.[5, 6A] That way you won't have to be embarrassed.[6A] How do you feel about that?[1] That's what Albert did and that's what Karen did.[4] They got embarrassed so they said Mommy could you wait outside, and then they told me everything.[4, 6A] I just want you to know one thing, none of the kids that were touched or hurt did anything wrong, because he did everything wrong, he made the little kids do stuff.[4, 5, 6A] So the little kids are not going to be in any trouble and their parents know that they didn't do anything wrong either, right?[4, 5, 2]

Mom: That's right.[5] You're a good boy.[5] (Mom kisses Todd)

Todd: Yeah.[A1]

Soc Wkr: It is just that Peter made the kids do that stuff, but the kids didn't want to do it.[6A]

Todd: Mommy, I want to go back to my home.[D1]

Mom: Okay, well, I'm gonna go for a little bit, I want you to stay here and talk to Lou for a little bit.[4]

Todd: No.[D1]

Mom: I will be back.[5]

Todd: No.[D1]

Mom: Will you do that for me?[2]

Todd: No, I don't want to talk to Lou, because I'm tired.[D1]

Mom: Maybe if you sit in the chair, you can rest and talk.[5]

Todd: No.[D1]

Soc Wkr: I will let you sit in this one and you could twirl around.[5]

Todd: No.[D1] I don't want to sit, I don't want to sit there.[D1]

Soc Wkr: All right, let's make one quick deal then.[4] You don't have to talk to me now if you don't want to, but can you make me a promise.[4]

Todd: I don't want to talk to you.[D1]

Soc Wkr: Then just listen.[4] If you remember, or if you want to talk to us about anything that happened with Peter and what he did to your friends, and what some of your friends say he might have done to you, then I am going to give your mommy my number, okay, so that if you want to talk to us you can.[4] Or if you want to tell your Mom and Dad, because Mommy and Daddy know about it.[4, 6A]

Todd: I don't want to talk to you.[D1]

Soc Wkr: Do you want to talk to Vince instead?[2]

Todd: Nobody.[D1]

Soc Wkr: Okay, I am going to give Mommy my number then, and if change your mind and you remember something, please start telling Mommy or Daddy or if you just don't want to talk to them and you just want to come back and talk to Lou, then we could do that.[4, 6A] I promise you one thing, you will feel a lot better if you do talk to me about it, Because I know how it is you feel very angry about it when you think about what happened your friends and the fact that he made you do stuff that you didn't want to do.[4, 5, 6A] I know all about it.[4]

Todd: Why is Peter in jail?[F]

Soc Wkr: He's in jail because some of the kids said that he was doing bad things to them, when their pants were down and stuff like that.[4, 6A] Did you go to the trip to Radio City Music Hall?[2]

Todd: No.[B1]

Soc Wkr: No, you stayed in camp that day?[2, 9] That was one day that kids were saying that things happened.[6A, 4]

Todd:	Mom, could I go back home?[F, D1] . . . Mom, could I go in that room?[F, D1]
Mom:	Do you think we should try in that room?[6B]
Soc Wkr:	No, it's not going to make a difference.[6B]
Todd:	Mom, that's not fair, if I talk to him.[C, D1]
Soc Wkr:	Why is it not fair.[2] I know.[10]
Todd:	Because you are a stranger.[C]
Soc Wkr:	Well, that's true I'm a stranger but I know that it is not nice to talk to strangers I know but I do understand that but one hand, I am here to help little kids who might have been hurt by somebody.[6A] And if you can help me you could be a little junior detective, and give us a hand.[5, 6A] It will be very very helpful.[4] I know about like I told you before, I know about popsicle sticks, I know about the spoons[4, 6A]
Todd:	I don't know about them.[D3]
Soc Wkr:	And I know about some of the games that, like the care bear game, and it was called something else.[6A, 4] I know about the bathroom, but I really need your help because we want to make sure, do you think if somebody does something real bad, and that they should get punished?[6A, 4] Do you?[2, 4]
Todd:	I don't want to talk no more.[D1]
Mom:	Mommy wants you to talk to Lou and Lou wants you to talk to him.[4] You can help Lou with that.[4]
Soc Wkr:	Strangers could become good friends you know.[4, 6A]
Todd:	You are a stranger.[C, D1]
Soc Wkr:	But strangers could become friends, you know.[4, 6A] Everybody that is friends was once strangers.[4, 6A] I think your mommy and daddy would like it very much if you were to talk to me.[4] They want you to talk to me because if you were hurt in any we want to know so that we can help you.[4, 5]
Todd:	No.[D1]
Soc Wkr:	Yes.[4]

Todd: No.[D1]

Soc Wkr: Yes.[4] Honest.[4] I would not lie to you about that.[4] Did you see Peter hurt any little girls?[2] Did you see him hurt Monica?[2] Molly or Jessica?[2]

Todd: No, nobody.[B2]

Soc Wkr: Kelly?[2]

Todd: Nobody.[C]

Soc Wkr: Did they tell you anything about it?[2]

Mom: I'll be right back.[10] You just stay here one minute, let Mommy go to the bathroom, I'll be right back.[10] I'm coming right back.[10]

Todd: I don't want to stay here.[D1]

Mom: Well I want you to stay here with Lou for one minute, Okay.[4] I have to go to the bathroom.[10] Aren't you going to stay here until Mommy comes back?[2, 4]

Soc Wkr: Todd, do you want to know something, what happens sometimes, sometimes what I do with little kids, who are afraid to talk to me, kids who are afraid to say anything to me, I show them these strange little friends of mine.[7, 4, 6A] And sometimes if they can't say the words, they just point and they show me things, okay.[7, 4, 6A] For example, I, I bet you ain't never seen dolls like this before.[5, 7] . . . Did you say excuse me?[2, 4]

Todd: I said excuse me.[C]

Soc Wkr: Oh, that's what I thought you said.[10] Come and take a look at these little friends of mine and tell me what you see about them that looks so strange.[4, 7] Have you ever seen dolls like this before?[2, 7]

Todd: No.[B1]

Soc Wkr: Is this a boy or a girl?[3, 7]

Todd: Boy.[C]

Soc Wkr: How do you know that it is a boy?[1, 7]

Todd: Because he's got a penis.[C]

Soc Wkr: Because he's got a penis?[2, 9] And what's this one, a girl?[2, 6A, 7]

Todd: Girl.[C]

Soc Wkr: Because she's got a vagina.[6A, 7]

Todd: Vagina.[C]

Soc Wkr: Right, and what do they have back here?[1, 7] What do both of them have back here?[1, 7]

Todd: Butt.[C]

Soc Wkr: Butt, you know all the words huh?[2, 9, 5] And what are these called?[1, 7]

Todd: Chests.[C]

Soc Wkr: Chests?[2, 9] All right.[5] Now is this a big boy or a little boy?[3, 7]

Todd: Big boy.[C]

Soc Wkr: What's he have here?[1, 7]

Todd: I don't know.[D3]

Soc Wkr: What do you have here?[1, 7]

Todd: Hair.[C]

Soc Wkr: Correct.[5] Okay.[8] Did you ever see Peter's hair down there?[2]

Todd: No.[B1]

Soc Wkr: No?[9, 2] Could you understand why I wanted to ask you those questions, I mean if you didn't see anything, I understand that, but um, on the other hand don't you want to make sure that your friends feel better if they were hurt?[4, 2] You don't feel bad for them?[2, 4] Did you ever see Peter putting anything here, in the girl's vagina?[2, 6A, 7]

Todd: No.[B1]

Soc Wkr: Did you ever see Peter touch any little boys penis?[2]

Todd: No.[B1]

Soc Wkr:	No?[2, 9] Did Peter ever try to touch you and you said no, stay away from me?[6A, 2] Do you remember?[2]
Todd:	No.[B1]
Soc Wkr:	The day everybody went to New York, to Radio City, did Peter try to bother you then?[2]
Todd:	No.[B1]
Soc Wkr:	Did you ever see him hurting Monica?[2]
Todd:	No.[B1]
Soc Wkr:	Do you want to see these guys?[2, 7]
Todd:	Yes.[A1]
Soc Wkr:	This is Peter.[6A, 7] And this is one of the little girls.[6A, 7] If you don't want to say anything.[10]
Todd:	That's Betty.[C]
Soc Wkr:	Do you want it to be Betty?[2, 7]
Todd:	No.[B1]
Soc Wkr:	No, Betty is a counselor, right?[2]
Todd:	No, she's a teacher.[B2]
Soc Wkr:	That's what I mean, she's a teacher.[10] Betty is Peter's boss, right?[2]
Todd:	This is a monster.[D2]
Soc Wkr:	It's not a monster.[6C]
Todd:	Yes because it's big.[D2]
Soc Wkr:	Why don't you show me with the dollies, why don't you show me what Peter did to the little girls, if you don't want to tell me why don't you show me.[4, 7]
Todd:	He did nothing.[C] I am a person.[D2] You are a monster because you got a penis.[D2]
Soc Wkr:	He's a monster because he has a penis?[2, 6A]
Todd:	No he's not a monster because he has a penis.[B2]

Soc Wkr:	Did you ever get a chance, did you ever see any of those little girls with their pants down?[2]
Todd:	No.[B1]
Soc Wkr:	No?[9, 2] Did you ever see him touching anybody's chest?[2]
Todd:	No.[B1]
Soc Wkr:	If you did see that stuff would you tell me?[2, 4] Would you tell me the truth if you did?[2, 4]
Todd:	No.[B1]
Soc Wkr:	You would lie to me?[2, 4]
Todd:	No.[B1]
Soc Wkr:	How come you would be afraid to show me or tell me?[2, 4] Because you didn't do anything wrong.[6A, 5]
Todd:	Because Peter's in jail.[C]
Soc Wkr:	Yeah?[2] Do you know what being in jail means?[2]
Todd:	What?[F]
Soc Wkr:	Being in jail means that you can't get out.[6A] You can't do anything.[6A]
Todd:	He-man can break out of jail.[C]
Soc Wkr:	What was that?[1A]
Todd:	He-man can break out of jail.[C]
Soc Wkr:	He-man maybe and Superman maybe but not Peter.[6A, 5] I promise.[5] Peter will not break out of jail.[6A, 5] And also did he say something.[2]
Todd:	Why can't he go home?[F]
Soc Wkr:	Don't you think that Peter should be punished if he hurt some kids?[2, 4] You don't think that somebody that hurts people should be punished?[2, 4]
Todd:	Which one's the boy?[F]

Soc Wkr: You know which one is the boy.[4] Which one is the boy, you said it before.[4, 1]

Todd: This one.[C]

Soc Wkr: The one with the . . . [1]

Todd: Penis.[C]

Soc Wkr: Penis, is right.[5] Anyway, the kids were telling me that.[10]

Todd: Do you have a penis?[F]

Soc Wkr: Sure, I do, just like you do just like your daddy does.[6A] Why, you don't think that your friends are lying to me do you?[2, 4]

Todd: No.[B1]

Soc Wkr: About what happened?[1, 4]

Todd: No.[B1]

Soc Wkr: No?[2] Because what I really want to do is I really want to make sure that nobody else gets hurt.[4] Don't you?[4, 2]

Todd: Yeah.[A1]

Soc Wkr: You don't care if people get hurt?[2, 4]

Todd: I can't get out.[D2]

Soc Wkr: The door is not locked it's open.[10]

Todd: It's open?[F]

Soc Wkr: Yeah, see.[4] Come on, it's not nice to walk out on somebody when they are talking[4] Todd, come back, please.[4] Come on, please.[4]

Todd: I don't want to talk to you.[D1]

Soc Wkr: What are you so afraid of, why are you such a fraidy cat?[1, 4]

Todd: No.[B1]

Soc Wkr: Yes you are, you are afraid to tell me.[4] Boy, even the girls told me.[4] I really want your help on this, you really don't have to be scared.[4] I promise you that you don't have to be scared.[4] Did you see anything with a popsicle stick?[2]

Todd:	No.[B1]
Soc Wkr:	Back here or anything like that?[2] No, are you sure?[2, 4] How about with the girls?[1]
Todd:	No.[B1]
Soc Wkr:	Would you, if you did see that stuff, would you be afraid to tell me?[2]
Todd:	No.[B1]
Soc Wkr:	No.[9] Do you honestly, truly really didn't see anything.[2, 4] Okay.[8] Did you hear any of the other kids tell you about it?[2]
Todd:	No.[B1]
Soc Wkr:	How come you get so upset when I mention Peter?[2, 4]
Todd:	Because I don't.[C]
Soc Wkr:	Okay.[8]
Todd:	Okay.[G]
Soc Wkr:	End of statement.[10]

AFTERMATH

Two years after the original charges were made, the case came to trial. Peter Ballard was acquitted of all of the charges by a jury. He is now trying to put this experience behind him and get his life back together. His grandmother, who was retired at the time of the charges, has gone back to work to pay off the mortgage she took out to help pay for her grandson's defense. Peter's hopes to go to vocational school are over. Both he and his mother work two jobs trying to keep up with their obligations. They have thousands of dollars in legal expenses yet to pay and while they are relieved Peter did not go to prison for 100 years, they remain depressed and anxious.

Following the interviews, many of the children were placed in therapy for sexual abuse and were treated by use of a feeling-expressive, insight-oriented play therapy with puppets, dolls, play, and games, and were encouraged to talk repeatedly about the abusive events. The children were reported to be extremely anxious, distressed, and frightened of Peter. At the trial, testimony was offered to the effect that some of the children were showing suggestive sexual behaviors. Several received the diagnosis of Post-traumatic Stress Disorder (PTSD). However, in sexual abuse cases this diagnosis is often used incorrectly to infer back in time from currently observed stress symptomatology to an unobserved prior event and buttress the claim that the event was real. A requirement for the PTSD diagnosis is the stressor event be known and real.

Some of the parents who came to believe that their child had been abused are embittered and puzzled by the outcome. They had a melange of supposedly expert and authoritative professionals telling them their child had been abused, but now the jury says Peter is not guilty. Parents of children said to have been abused are caught in an dilemma. If they continue to believe the abuse was real, they can only conclude the justice system has failed them and their children. If they now doubt the abuse they can only be angry and hostile toward the professionals who led them to believe their child had been abused.

In retrospect, it seems apparent that children who have not been abused have been victimized by the system which taught them about deviant sexuality and created in them the subjective reality that they had been the victims of sadistic behaviors. While the consequences are not yet clear, it is not likely to work out for the betterment of these children's lives.

Chapter 10

A SESSION WITH A THERAPIST
AND YOUR CHILD IS GONE

Reports of suspected child sexual abuse have increased in staggering numbers in the past several years. Some commentators say there is an epidemic of sexual abuse and this increase is due to an actual increase in sexual abuse of children by adults. Others, more cautious, say we don't really know what it is but that a large part is an increase in reports that may or may not be true. Media attention has heightened public awareness of child sexual abuse and the political response has been to mandate reporting and create special treatment for child sexual abuse cases. Abuse that used to go unreported is now reported to authorities.

The proportion of reports of abuse that are not substantiated by an initial investigation has increased as well. This suggests that the increase in reports may include a larger number of false reports. There appears to be more generalized suspicion and a readiness to think there is abuse even when there is not. A California couple was playing with their child on a beach. A couple driving by thought they saw the parents sexually abusing the lad. They stopped, called in a report anonymously, and drove on. Police arrested the parents and put the child in a shelter. The anxious and frightened mother and father finally persuaded the authorities they had simply been playing normally with their son and got their child back. Their ordeal was caused by the perceptual and cognitive set of the passersby to take minimal cues and overinterpret them. Once they thought they saw abuse they did what any reasonable and responsible adult would do—report it.

Our experience is that a readiness to first suspect and then quickly believe sexual abuse has occurred is at the beginning of many cases that turn out to be false accusations. When people, professional or lay, believe that a child is being abused, they may unwittingly shape and even manufacture events to affirm that belief. When we have had tapes of interrogations available and therefore were able to check on what took place, frequently we have found that what was claimed to have occurred during an interrogation did not happen. Children did not say what the adult said they did, or the adult behaved in ways that were later denied. White (1986) reported the same experience of finding that tapes of interrogations did not contain events described by the interrogator. Herbert, Grams, and Goranson (1987) found that tapes of interrogations are essential, because without them, the reports of the interrogator contain significant distortions.

Inaccuracies by professionals are unlikely to be deliberate acts of malice. Most likely it is simply a combination of a perceptual set to see abuse and a habit of coming to premature closure on the meaning of what is seen and heard. The result is a subjective belief by the professional that a child is being abused. From that point on, everything that will support that belief is attended to, slightly shifted, possibly embellished, whereas anything that disconfirms the belief is ignored or denied.

The overdetermined response set of neighbors and a therapist/evaluator started accusations against a couple that almost destroyed their family and their lives. In a criminal trial and in a subsequent family court hearing on dependency, there was no finding of abuse but the family went through four years of anguish and terror that is just beginning to abate.

BACKGROUND

John and Sandy Thompson were a hard-working couple with one child, Maria, who was three and one-half years old at the time John was accused of sexually abusing her. John, Sandy, and Maria were a close and happy family. Their social life revolved around visits with friends and relatives and church activities. They gardened together, bowled occasionally, and sometimes went to a nearby city for a major league baseball game. Their religious convictions meant that they did not drink coffee, tea, or alcohol, or smoke, but sought to live healthful orderly lives.

John and Sandy chose to have only one child because they felt that they didn't have the time or finances to raise more than one child in the way they believed a child should be brought up. They were both devoted to Maria, played with her, and read to her every day. At the time of the allegations, John worked as foreman in a small factory and Sandy was employed part time in a print shop.

On July 22, child protection received a report that John had sexually abused Maria and the three-year-old child of a neighbor. A visiting aunt of the neighbor child felt she saw her niece showing behavioral signs of sexual abuse because the child was being overly aggressive in her play with other children. The aunt worked as a volunteer in a rape counseling center in the nearby metropolitan area. She questioned the child for several hours and then told the parents their daughter was being sexually abused. The parents immediately questioned the child and during this interrogation John's name was first mentioned along with two other adults. There was some ill feeling between the neighbors and John— they got angry when he refused to drink with them during an impromptu neighborhood block party.

The parents of the three year old called child protection. They said that John was abusing both their daughter and his own daughter, Maria. In a hasty and flawed investigation that included only brief interviews with the neighbor mother, the aunt, and the three-year-old child, a child protection worker concluded that Mr. Thompson had sexually abused Maria and the neighbor child. No records or documentation of these contacts exist other than the child protection worker's notes made after the interviews were over. There is no documentation of the lengthy interrogations of the three year old by the aunt and the parents.

The child protection worker, Dorothy Clarke, had a B.S. degree in education from a small state college. Following graduation she had been a child protection worker for two years. She had attended two workshops on child sexual abuse and sat in on three hours of in-service lectures by a local psychiatrist. She had handled about ten child sexual abuse allegations in the two years and had substantiated abuse in every one. She met with the county attorney and discussed her initial brief investigation of the accusation against John. He told her to get more evidence.

Without giving any indication that an accusation of child sexual abuse had been made and an investigation had been performed, on July 26, a police officer called, asking John to come to the law enforcement center. John thought they wanted to talk to him about an automobile accident he had witnessed a few days before. He told the officer he was taking care of his daughter while Sandy was at work and asked if he could come the next day. The officer told him, no, he should come in that night and just bring his daughter along as it would not take long. When he arrived there with Maria, county officials separated them. A police officer interrogated John and told him for the first time he was accused of sexual abuse of his daughter and the neighbor child. John was shocked, angry, frightened, and confused.

The child protection worker interrogated Maria using anatomical dolls while John was being questioned by the policeman. Sandy arrived while the interrogation was in process. The police and the social worker refused to let her see Maria or John. She was kept isolated from them. She, too, was shocked when the social worker told her John was accused of sexual abuse but said that if he did it, she was done with him. John denied that he had ever sexually abused Maria or any other child but he was arrested and jailed that night and did not see his daughter for two years.

John was freed on bond after three days and moved in with relatives because child protection told Sandy that she must keep Maria away from him. Sandy was confused about what to believe. Did John do it or not? She vigorously requested seeing an expert to try to get the facts. The county recommended a psychologist, Dr. Paula Griffin, who was a "child sexual abuse expert," one of the small approved group to whom county officials around the state referred children for evaluation. On August 3, the county social worker took Maria, accompanied by Sandy, to the office of Dr. Griffin. There was no court order nor any court process requiring this meeting. The sessions were paid for by John's medical insurance. Dr. Griffin spoke principally with Sandy and saw Maria for only a few minutes on this first session.

In the meantime, the child protection worker had interviewed Maria several times and extracted confused and conflicting statements about sexual abuse. The earlier interviews were not recorded but a later one, on July 28, was audiotaped. This recorded interview is filled with leading questions and "What else happened?" questions and it is clear from hearing it that Maria has been interviewed before.

In the interview, Maria makes statements about her Daddy peeing in her mouth, sticking his finger in her vagina and in her anus, putting his penis in her vagina, masturbating in front of her while he was dressed in Sandy's clothes (including red shoes and red underwear) and wearing perfume and red makeup. She also said that he peed in the neighbor child's mouth. As this interview progressed, Maria added that she also had peed in her father's mouth outside on top of the mower while he was cutting the grass and inside the house when he was lying down in her closet. Towards the end of this interview, in response to the "What else?" questioning, Maria added that her grandfather and a boy in her neighborhood had also done these things to her. However, no attempt was ever made to investigate these charges. Only John was investigated.

On August 9, Dr. Griffin spent an hour with Maria. This session was videotaped. The dolls were used again. This tape shows the coercive and leading nature of the interrogation by the psychologist. She keeps asking Maria to remember what she told the other lady and to tell her the same thing. In spite of this Maria says nothing that is clearly indicative of sexual abuse by John. On August 12, Dr. Griffin had another session with Maria. At the request of Sandy, this session was also recorded. Dr. Griffin said they were not set up for videotape that day but she audiotaped the session and gave the tape to Sandy at the conclusion of the session. Dr. Griffin didn't hear this tape again until the trial two years later.

In the morning before the August 12 session, the child protection worker, Dorothy Clarke, called Dr. Griffin. She said that she was concerned that Sandy was putting pressure on Maria to retract her story. She suspected Sandy was letting John see Maria in violation of the court's protective order. She asked Dr. Griffin to find out about this.

In Dr. Griffin's progress notes of her sessions with Maria there are the following entries:

Patient: Maria Thompson 8/12

I spoke this morning with Dorothy Clarke regarding my sessions thus far with Maria. She said that she is concerned about the pressure that Sandy Thompson is placing on her daughter about Sandy's very strong loyalty to her husband . . . There is some suspicion that they may have all been together last weekend, Dorothy Clarke reported. She asked me to find out from Maria about this. She also asked me to ask Maria about the trip to the dump.

I did meet with Maria for an hour later in the day. I asked Maria about last weekend and she said she didn't remember anything, and I could not get any information about that trip. . . . I asked Maria to tell me again what she had told me last time when we used the dolls and she said that Daddy had not touched her. *She also stated, however, very explicitly that her mother had said to say that her Daddy had not touched her vagina and that her daddy had not done anything to Wendy. Repeatedly, Maria stated to me that her mother told her to say these things* . . . (italics added).

Following this session, Dr. Griffin contacted Dorothy Clarke and told her that Maria had reported that her mother was telling her to say that Daddy didn't abuse her after all. They decided that Sandy was not able to protect Maria because she didn't believe that John had abused her and was pressuring Maria to retract the allegations.

In our experience, it is common for child protection workers to accuse a parent of failure to protect when the parent is uncertain, questions, or is doubtful that her spouse is actually guilty. If the parent doesn't believe the accusation the protection worker threatens to take the child away. This places a parent in an incredibly stressful dilemma. Either you disown and abandon your spouse or you may lose your child. If you remain loyal to your spouse or even say you are in conflict and you cannot decide, you may lose your child. This is exactly what happened in one case. There is no question about the mother's parenting ability nor her love and bonding with her three children. Nevertheless, because she would not agree her husband was guilty, even though he had been acquitted in a criminal trial, a judge terminated her parental rights.

We have never seen an official acknowledge that there may be some question about this use of the failure to protect provision. We have never seen anyone suggest that when the state takes a child away from parents and puts the child in foster care, denying access to family and friends, this may be seen as a total environment that is likely to encourage and elicit false accounts of abuse. On the face of it, it may be that failure to protect is the failure to protect the state's prosecution of the case rather than the child.

When the social worker decided Sandy was pressuring the child, based upon the report of Dr. Griffin, Maria was taken away from her mother on August 19 and placed in a foster home. She stayed there for a year during which Sandy was allowed supervised visitation one hour a week. Maria continued to be brought to Dr. Griffin for therapy for sexual abuse. When Maria was finally returned to Sandy, John still was not permitted to see her or talk to her. After acquittal in the criminal trial he was allowed to talk with her but was not allowed to see her for another several months until after the Family Court hearing.

During the year in the foster home, in spite of Sandy's vehement and repeated protests, Maria was taken to a different church than the one John and Sandy belonged to, taken to a different physician when Sandy observed she was covered with insect bites from head to toe, and denied any contact with her grandparents or other relatives. During the supervised visitation the supervisor did not stay an observer but dominated and controlled the time, directing Sandy on what she could and could not do with her daughter.

At a hearing on October 12, Dr. Griffin repeated the assertion that Maria told her that "Mommy said to say that Daddy didn't do it." She stated that Maria would therefore be emotionally damaged by living with her mother and added that Sandy was emotionally abusing Maria. She said that Sandy could not be trusted to protect Maria. She also said the prosecution of John would be harmed if Sandy had access to Maria. On the basis of this testimony the judge ruled that Maria must stay in foster care.

John first had a public defender who urged him to plead guilty to a reduced charge. The plea bargain would have given him probation and therapy and he could have seen his daughter. However, John refused this, saying that he was completely innocent and would not compromise his position nor his integrity. John and Sandy sold their house, borrowed from family members, and hired a private attorney.

Two years later John was acquitted of all charges in a jury trial. We were retained by defense counsel to provide expert consultation. In preparation for the trial, we studied the taped interviews and discovered that *at no point in the interview of August 12 does Maria ever say that her mommy told her to say that Daddy didn't do it.* Dr. Griffin asks Maria repeatedly (18 times) about other people talking to her and telling her what to say. Maria does not affirm or respond to any of these questions. Dr. Griffin repeatedly asks Maria if her mother told her to say that daddy didn't do it or what her mother told her. Maria does not affirm nor say that her mother told her to say that Daddy didn't do it. Asking the same question over and over and over, as Dr. Griffin does, puts great pressure on Maria to say what the psychologist believes is true and wants to hear. But, although Maria never affirms this, Dr. Griffin gave an erroneous account of this interview to the social worker and repeated it later in a hearing. Based upon this false observation, she recommended that Maria be taken away from Sandy and put in foster care. The result was that the child was taken away from her mother, placed in foster care, and kept there for a year.

During the course of the criminal trial Dr. Griffin, after being presented with the tape (which she had given to Sandy without keeping a copy for herself) admitted during cross-examination that Maria Thompson had not said that Mommy said to say that Daddy didn't do it. The following day she tried to claim during redirect examination that it was in the next session, an unrecorded session, that Maria had told her Mommy said she should say Daddy didn't do it. Sandy's testimony contradicted this claim.

It was also true that Maria had already been taken into foster care by the time of the next session.

Three taped interviews were analyzed, two by the psychologist and one by the child protection social worker. The total proportion of potential error-inducing statements for the three interviews was 69 percent.

INTERVIEW

Interviewer: Paula Griffin, Psychologist

Child: Maria Thompson

Psychologist: Record it with this while we talk, so I'm just going to set this down and put it right here, okay, and we can forget about it.[6A, 4] Now what I want to do is talk with you some more about some of the things you've told me already and your mama is telling me about the things that you and she talked about.[4, 6A] I need to check those out with you, Maria, and I know it's, I know it's real hard stuff to talk about and makes you feel all mixed up inside when you talk about these things.[4, 5, 6A] All right?[2]

Maria: It makes me mixed up.[C]

Psychologist: Does it make you mixed up when people ask you all these questions?[2, 4, 6A] I know.[5] It's real hard even for grown-ups to talk and I think it's even harder for kids to do that.[4, 6A] Who you calling up there?[1]

Maria: Be quiet.[F]

Psychologist: Oh.[8]

Maria: It's for you.[D2]

Psychologist: Oh, for me.[6C] Who is it?[6C] Who's on the phone?[6C]

Maria: Your friend.[D2]

Psychologist: My friend?[6C] Oh.[8] Hello?[6C] Yes.[6C] No, I'm really busy right now with Maria.[6C] I can't talk right now.[6C] Okay, bye.[6C] I'll call them back later.[6C] I need to check out some things with you.[4, 6A] Before I, um, do you remember the first time you came here I told you that Dorothy had already told me some of the stuff that you had told her and then I, I uh, you and I talked about . . . [2, 4, 6A] Well, should we get him up?[2]

Maria:	Yeah.[A1]
Psychologist:	You and I already talked about some of, um, you and I talked about some of the same things that you talked about with Dorothy.[4, 6A]
Maria:	Can you see the girl?[F]
Psychologist:	Okay.[8] But what I needed to check out with you was you had told me about some, some of the touching that had happened with your daddy.[4, 6A] Am I right?[2, 4] Is that what you told me about the first time?[2, 4] That your daddy, John Thompson, had touched you?[2, 6A, 4] That's what you told me, that's what I put down the first time and I want to make sure I understand, because I don't know, Maria, I wasn't there.[4, 6A] I don't know who did what and the only way we can find out is by you telling us what really happened and I do know that it's real hard to talk about.[4, 5, 6A] ... Is there somebody else who did those things that you saw Daddy do?[2] ... Are you sure?[2, 4] ... Are you scared to tell me?[2, 4] ... Are you feeling scared to tell me, Maria, about who did what?[2, 4]

[Pauses between statements but Maria doesn't answer.]

Maria:	You'll be the girl and I'll be the dad.[F]
Psychologist:	Okay.[8] You be the dad and I'll be Maria, my name is Maria.[7, 5, 6A] Hi, Dad.[7, 6A] What are we going to do today?[7, 1, 6A]
Maria:	What would you like to do?[F]
Psychologist:	Um, yeah.[10, 7, 6A] But can I have some candy?[2, 7, 6A]
Maria:	No.[B1]
Psychologist:	Why not?[2, 7, 6A]
Maria:	Because, no sugar.[C]
Psychologist:	But Tom gives me candy, he gives me gum.[7, 6A]
Maria:	No.[B1]
Psychologist:	Then how come he lets me have some gum and candy?[1, 7, 6A]
Maria:	I'm going to tell him not to.[F]
Psychologist:	Well, how come he lets me?[1, 7, 6A]

Maria: Because.[C]

Psychologist: Because why?[1, 7, 6A] . . . Maria?[1, 7, 6A]
Maria: What?[F]

Psychologist: Then how come Tom lets me have gum and candy and you won't?[1, 7, 6A]
Maria: Does Tom let you have candy?[2]

Psychologist: Um-hum.[7, 6A] And gum.[7, 6A]
Maria: And gum?[F]

Psychologist: Uh hum.[7, 6A]
Maria: That you chewing on?[F]

Psychologist: No I want gum and candy.[7, 6A]
Maria: You can't have gum and candy.[F]

Psychologist: Why not?[1, 7, 6A]
Maria: Because.[C] You can't have no gum and candy.[F]

Psychologist: Why not?[1, 7, 6A] I want it.[1, 7, 6A]
Maria: You can't have none.[F]

Psychologist: I want it.[7, 6A]
Maria: You can't have none.[F]

Psychologist: Well how come he gives it to me?[1, 7, 6A]
Maria: Because . . . [C]

Psychologist: What?[1, 7, 6A] How come you're spanking?[1, 7, 6A]
Maria: Because (inaudible) you can't have none.[C]

Psychologist: Why not?[1, 7, 6A]
Maria: Because I'm taking the candy away from you and . . . [C]

Psychologist: Why?[1, 7, 6A]
Maria: Yeah, I'm going to call somebody.[C]

Psychologist:	Who are you going to call?[1, 7, 6A]
Maria:	I won't tell you.[C]
Psychologist:	There's the telephone.[6A, 7]
Maria:	(Pause as she dials the play phone) Want to call your friend?[F]
Psychologist:	You mean Beth?[2, 6A, 7]
Maria:	Yeah.[A1]
Psychologist:	Yeah.[9, 7, 6A] Can I go over to Beth's house to play?[2, 7, 6A]
Maria:	No, first you have to call.[F]
Psychologist:	Oh.[8, 7, 6A]
Maria:	(Pause as she dials) Hello.[C]
Psychologist:	Yeah.[8] Hello?[1, 7, 6A] Can Beth play?[2, 7, 6A]
Maria:	Yeah.[A1]
Psychologist:	Okay, bye.[7, 6A]
Maria:	Bye.[C]
Psychologist:	She can play, Mom.[7, 6A]
Maria:	Okay, watch out . . . [F]
Psychologist:	Who's that?[1, 7, 6A]
Maria:	Why can't it turn?[F]
Psychologist:	Why can it turn?[10] I think it's just real wobbly.[10] . . . Okay, what should I do?[1, 7, 6A]
Maria:	Uh, pick your shoes up, put them over there . . . okay?[F]
Psychologist:	Okay.[8, 7, 6A]
Maria:	(Pause) This is Beth.[C] Hi.[C] Hi.[C]
Psychologist:	Yeah.[8, 7, 6A] Hi, Beth.[7, 6A]
Maria:	Hi.[C] I want to stay overnight.[F]

Psychologist: Oh, good.[7, 6A] That should be fun.[7, 6A]

Maria: Okay.[G] I want to call somebody.[F] I want to call my mom.[F]

Psychologist: Okay.[7, 6A]

Maria: I don't know what her number is . . . , I mean her daddy.[D3] Take your shoes off.[F] Hi.[C] Hi.[C]

Psychologist: Yeah?[10]

Maria: Take your shoes.[F]

Psychologist: Oh, Okay, thank you.[8, 7, 6A]

Maria: (Inaudible) 1,2,8,9,6,6. (Laughs)[D2]

Psychologist: Who you calling, Wendy?[1, 7, 6A]

Maria: Oh, I'm calling my mom.[C]

Psychologist: Are you going to call your dad, too?[2, 6A, 7]

Maria: Yes.[A1]

Psychologist: Should we play with your dad today?[2, 6A, 7]

Maria: He's locked up in jail but he'll come back.[C]

Psychologist: Tom is locked up in jail?[2, 7, 6A]

Maria: Uh huh.[A1]

Psychologist: How come?[1, 7, 6A]

Maria: I want him to get locked up in jail.[C]

Psychologist: You do?[2, 7, 6A] How come?[1, 7, 6A]

Maria: Because.[C]

Psychologist: Did he do something naughty that he should get locked up in jail for?[2, 7, 6A]

Maria: He put makeup on me.[C]

| Psychologist: | He put makeup on you?[9, 2, 7]...Did he?[2, 4, 7] Where did he put the makeup, Maria?[1, 7, 6A]...Show me on the little girl, show me where did he put the makeup?[4, 7]...On her cheek, on her forehead...[9, 7] |

[Pauses between statements but Maria doesn't answer.]

| Maria: | Put lipstick on.[C] |

| Psychologist: | And lipstick.[9] Did he put it on any other part of your body, on your legs or on your arms or on your tummy?[2, 4, 6A]...Or on your breast?[2, 4, 6A]...Did he?[2, 4]...Are you sure, Maria?[2, 4] |

[Pauses between statements but Maria doesn't answer.]

| Maria: | Uh hum.[A1] |

| Psychologist: | You know what your mom said the other day that I thought you said boobs but you really said a different word.[4, 6A] Do you remember what you told me?[2]...Do you remember?[2, 4] We were talking about what are the names of body parts and you told me that this part right here, what did you call that?[1, 4] |

| Maria: | A boo.[C] |

| Psychologist: | A moo?[9, 2] |

| Maria: | A boob.[C] |

| Psychologist: | You said boobs?[2, 6A]...Did you say boobs?[2, 4, 6A] Because your mom thought that you said a moo.[4, 6A] Do you remember?[2, 4] She said that that's what the word that you used to call breasts when you were really little and when you were still reaching out of your mom's breasts.[6A, 4] |

| Maria: | I know that was, that was when I was tiny baby.[C] |

| Psychologist: | When you were tiny baby that you called it a moo.[6A] But now you call it boob or a breast?[2, 6A] |

| Maria: | Breast.[C] |

| Psychologist: | Yeah.[8] Well, that's a good name for them.[5] You know the other day though that when you were talking to me and we made the movie of our talking together...[8] |

Maria: Hi, Daddy.[D2]

Psychologist: . . . did you say, did you say boob?[2, 4]
Maria: Hi, Mom.[D2]

Psychologist: Do you remember?[2, 4]
Maria: Hi.[D2] I'm going to hang up on you, Mom.[D2]

Psychologist: Maria, do you remember if you said boob or moo, or you don't
                    remember?[3, 4]
Maria: I don't remember.[D3]

Psychologist: So you think Tom should be in jail, huh, 'cause you put makeup on
                    you?[1, 9] What else did Tom do that was wrong?[1, 6A, 4]
Maria: Peed in Wendy's mouth.[C]

Psychologist: Huh?[2]
Maria: Peed in Wendy's mouth.[C]

Psychologist: You saw Tom pee in Wendy's mouth?[2, 9]
Maria: With Wendy.[C]

Psychologist: Did he pee in your mouth?[2, 4] . . . Are you sure?[2, 4] . . . Who else
                    has peed in Wendy's mouth?[1,4]
Maria: Just him.[C]

Psychologist: The other day, Maria, you told me that you saw your daddy pee in
                    Wendy's mouth, your daddy, John.[4, 6A] Did Daddy John pee in
                    Wendy's mouth, too?[2, 4] . . . Are you sure?[2, 4] . . . Did somebody
                    tell you to say that?[2, 4, 6A] . . . Did somebody tell you to say that
                    Tom peed in Wendy's mouth?[2, 4] . . . Maria?[2, 4]

[Pauses between statements but Maria doesn't answer.]

Maria: Maria.[D2]

Psychologist: Uh hm, yes.[8]

Maria: I want you to stay in the kitchen 'cause (inaudible).[F] This, this is
                    Mom and Dad.[F]

Psychologist:	Okay, so that's John and Sandy?[9, 2, 7] Okay.[8] I just want to make sure, and this is?[2, 7]
Maria:	Maria.[C]
Psychologist:	Okay.[8] Okay, Daddy.[7, 6A] Who put on the red underwear?[1, 7, 6A] Who wore the red underwear?[1, 7, 6A]
Maria:	Nobody.[C]
Psychologist:	Well, you told us, you told Dorothy . . . [4, 7, 6A]
Maria:	My mom.[C] Mom, my mom, my mom doesn't have no, no red underwear.[C]
Psychologist:	I know that, but somebody could buy red underwear, it doesn't have to be your mom.[6A, 4]
Maria:	Nope, nope, nope, no.[B1]
Psychologist:	It could be, Tom could buy it, or John could buy it, or . . . could buy it . . . [6A, 4]
Maria:	Uh uh.[B1]
Psychologist:	. . . sure they could.[4, 6A]
Maria:	Why does it blink when I talk?[D2, F]
Psychologist:	That's how we know what it's doing, except I think it doesn't pick up mine very well.[10] 'Cause it may be . . . [10]
Maria:	Hi?[D2, F] Hi.[D2]
Psychologist:	It's moving real well, and that's what's important.[10]
Maria:	Can I move it?[F, D2]
Psychologist:	Sure.[10, 5] Keep the microphone close to you, let's not move it too far back, though, because I would like it to pick up mine a little bit.[4, 10]
Maria:	Okay.[G]
Psychologist:	Yeah.[9] So it picks it up a little tiny bit.[6C] But it's your voice, Maria, that's real important for us to pick up.[6C]
Maria:	Uh huh.[A1] Hi.[D2] Hi.[D2] Want some candy?[D2, F]

Psychologist: Yeah, I do.[7, 6A]

Maria: Okay.[G]

Psychologist: Will you give me some candy, Dad?[2, 7, 6A]

Maria: Yeah.[A1] I'll give you candy and gum.[C]

Psychologist: Oh, thank you.[7, 6A]

Maria: It's in her hair.[C]

Psychologist: Huh?[2, 7, 6A]

Maria: It's in her hair.[C]

Psychologist: No, she's putting it in her mouth.[7, 6A]

Maria: The whole thing?[F]

Psychologist: One at a time.[7, 6A] She doesn't want to be a pig.[7, 6A]

Maria: See, right here's the gum right here's the candy.[C]

Psychologist: Well, she's going to eat the candy first and then when she swallow
                  that, she'll put the gum in her mouth, how's that?[1, 7, 6A]

Maria: Okay.[A1]

Psychologist: Is that how you like to do it?[7, 6A] That's how I like to do it.[7,
                  6A] . . . Maria, it's real important that we talk a little bit more about
                  those things that you told me about the first time you were here in
                  the playroom?[4, 6A]

Maria: I was back in the playroom?[F]

Psychologist: Uh huh.[8] Remember we made the movie?[2] We had the movie
                  camera and we made the movie and Mom got to see that.[6A, 4]

Maria: Okay, everybody be quiet.[D2]

Psychologist: That was the second time you came because the first time you came
                  we didn't have any time to talk, did we?[6A, 2] Mostly I just talked
                  to Mom.[10]

Maria: Hi![D1, D2]

Psychologist: Let's just talk a little bit more about this then we'll play more.[4, 5]...Have you been talking to several other people about this, Maria?[2, 4, 6A] Did your mom take you to see another doctor?[2, 6A]...Did she have you talk to the person at your church, an elder at your church?[2, 6A]...About telling the truth?[6A, 4]...Did you ever go over a Bible story about telling the truth?[2, 6A]

[Pauses between statements but Maria doesn't answer.]

Maria: When I do this why does it blink?[D2, F]

Psychologist: Why does it blink?[10] Because it's picking up your voice and that's just the way we know that it's picking up your voice.[10]

Maria: Oh.[G]

Psychologist: So this is the microphone here and that's how we know what it's doing.[10] And when you do that it's making a noise, too, so when you (thump).[10] See? It picks that up, too, uh hmm.[6C] (Pause) Maria, is it, we've talked about what's really true, right?[2, 6A, 4] And what's not really true, what's a story, or a lie, a joke, or a tease, right?[3, 6A, 4] Remember when we talked about that?[2, 4] Is it really true that...[8]...that dolly has on a blue dress?[2, 7]...Is that true, or is that false?[3, 7]

Maria: That's false.[C]

Psychologist: That's false.[9] Is it true that this girl has a strawberry on her? [2, 7]...On her jumper?[2, 7]

Maria: (assume she nods yes)[A1]

Psychologist: That's true.[9] Is it true that I am standing on my head?[2]

Maria: No.[B1]

Psychologist: Is it true that you have on, that you are sitting, uh, on your knees?[2]...Maria?[2, 4] Is that true, that you're sitting on your knees?[2]...Maria, is that true that you're sitting on your knees?[2, 4]

Maria: No.[B1]

Psychologist: Oh, I thought it was.[6A, 4] What are you sitting on?[1]

Maria: Nothing.[C]

Psychologist:	Oh, I thought you were sitting on your knees.[4, 6A] I call that sitting on your knees.[4, 6A] Is it, is it true that Tom put makeup on your face?[2]
Maria:	Hm hm (no).[B1]
Psychologist:	Maria, is that true?[2]
Maria:	No.[B1]
Psychologist:	Is it true that Tom put makeup on his own face?[2]
Maria:	Yes.[A1]
Psychologist:	Tom put makeup on his own face.[9] That's really true?[2, 4]
Maria:	Mommy and Tommy, too, I want to (inaudible).[C]
Psychologist:	Maria, is it true.[2, 4] Is it true that Tom peed in (pause) Wendy's mouth?[2]
Maria:	I want him to go to jail (inaudible) right?[C, F]
Psychologist:	You want him to go to jail and so that's why you're saying that?[2, 9] Did he really do it, though?[2, 4] Did he really pee in Wendy's mouth?[2, 4] . . . Did your daddy really pee in Wendy's mouth, too?[2, 4]
Maria:	Let's pretend you're the little girl.[F]
Psychologist:	Maria, okay, we can pretend that in a minute, honey, but we need to talk about things a little bit more.[4, 5] Is it true, Maria, that your daddy, is it really, did Daddy really really pee in your mouth?[2, 4]
Maria:	(Inaudible) Did Tom?[F, D2]
Psychologist:	No.[6A] Did Daddy John, did Daddy John Thompson pee in your mouth?[2]
Maria:	No.[B1]
Psychologist:	Did Tom Sanders pee in your mouth?[2]
Maria:	Who's that?[F]
Psychologist:	Tom, Wendy's daddy.[6A]
Maria:	No.[B1]

Psychologist:	Did Tom pee in Wendy's mouth?[2]
Maria:	Yup.[A1] Daddy's going to call somebody.[D2]
IP:	Who's he going to call?[1] Huh?[1]
Maria:	Forty.[C]
Psychologist:	Forty, who's Forty?[1]
Maria:	Um, or maybe I'm calling Ken.[D2]
Psychologist:	Who's Ken?[1]
Maria:	He's only a tiny baby.[C, D2]
Psychologist:	He's only a tiny baby.[9]
Maria:	You know what?[F, D2]
Psychologist:	What?[1]
Maria:	When we were at a picnic, you know?[F, D2]
Psychologist:	Uh huh.[9]
Maria:	You know what?[F, D2] He was there and then he pooped in his pants.[D2] It was icky.[D2]
Psychologist:	Babies do that, you know.[6C] That would be really smelly and nasty.[6C] I hear Wendy has a big sister named Anna.[6A]
Maria:	I know.[C]
Psychologist:	Does she?[2, 9] How old is Anna?[1]
Maria:	I don't know.[D3]
Psychologist:	Don't know?[2, 9]
Maria:	Um hum.[A1]
Psychologist:	Did you ever see Tom pee in Anna's mouth?[2, 4] . . . Is Anna there when, when Tom did this to Wendy?[2] . . . Where were you when this happened?[1A] Where did you see it?[1A]
Maria:	I didn't see it.[C]
Psychologist:	How do you know that Tom peed in Wendy's mouth.[1, 4]

Maria: Because.[C]

Psychologist: Because why, honey?[1] . . . Why?[1, 4]

Maria: Because I don't want to.[D1]

Psychologist: What do you mean you don't want to?[2] . . . Do you know what I'm kind of wondering?[2]

Maria: What?[F]

Psychologist: I'm kind of wondering if you feel very scared and very sad because your daddy can't come home right now and he got arrested and he's not in jail but now he still can't come home and see you and I'm wondering if you miss him a lot.[5, 6A]

Maria: I do.[C]

Psychologist: And if you're mad, and if you're mad, Maria, because that didn't happen to Tom.[6A] . . . Are you mad that Wendy still has her daddy at home?[2, 6A] . . . And so you would like him to go off to jail, too.[6A, 4]

Maria: Yup.[A1]

Psychologist: You think I'm going to make it so your dad can come home?[2, 6A] . . . Maria?[2, 4] Do you think that I'm going to make it so your daddy can come home?[2] . . . Did Mommy tell you that?[2] . . . No?[2] What did Mommy tell you?[1] . . . Maria.[4] What did Mommy tell you?[1]

[Pauses between statements but Maria doesn't answer. She plays with the phone.]

Maria: Now can I be the kid?[D2, F]

Psychologist: First we need to talk, we need to keep talking a little bit more about this, what did Mommy tell you about this?[1, 4]

Maria: (Pause, into phone) Daddy, Daddy, Dad.[C]

Psychologist: Is that Tom, Daddy Tom she's talking to?[2, 6A]

Maria: Uh hm.[A1]

Psychologist: Which daddy?[1]

Maria: Her daddy.[C]

Psychologist: Her daddy, Daddy John?[2] Maria, last time you told me that Daddy John took the red underwear and took it out to the garbage dump and took the white chair with the hole in it.[6A] Was that really true?[2, 4] Did Daddy really take the red underwear when he went to the dump, to the garbage dump?[2, 4] . . . Who had the red underwear?[1]

Maria: My mom doesn't have no red underwear.[C]

Psychologist: I know your mom doesn't.[9] But did your Daddy have some or did Tom have some or who had some?[3, 4, 6A]

Maria: Nobody.[C]

Psychologist: How come Wendy said your daddy had some?[1, 4]

Maria: (Pause) Daddy?[D2]

Psychologist: Maria, how come Wendy said that your daddy was wearing some?[1, 4] . . . Hum?[1, 4] . . . Is she mad at your daddy?[2, 4, 6A] Is Wendy mad at your daddy?[2, 4, 6A]

[Pauses between statements but Maria doesn't answer.]

Maria: Uh, no.[B1]

Psychologist: Is Wendy mad at her daddy, Tom?[2, 4] . . . Is Wendy mad at her daddy?[2, 4]

Maria: Daddy?[D2] I have to tell you something.[C]

Psychologist: Uh huh.[8]

Maria: Daddy.[D2] Daddy, I'm pushing this telephone all by myself.[D2] And then I got into big trouble.[D2] Okay?[F]

Psychologist: Uh hum.[8] Did Amy, does, uh Wendy have any other brothers or sisters besides Amy or Anna or was it just Anna and Wendy?[3]

Maria: You know what?[F, D2]

Psychologist: What?[1]

Maria: When we were sleeping, you know what?[F]

Psychologist: What?[1]

Maria: The telephone rang.[C]

Psychologist: Uh huh.[8]

Maria: And my mom . . . and it wasn't there.[C]

Psychologist: That's kind of spooky, huh, when it happens.[5]

Maria: . . . scared.[C]

Psychologist: Maria, when you saw Wendy, Tom pee in Wendy's mouth, where
                  were you?[1, 4]

Maria: At home.[C]

Psychologist: At your house, or at Wendy's house?[3]

Maria: Mine.[C]

Psychologist: At your house?[9, 2] Was Tom at your house?[1]

Maria: She went home to get her ball.[C]

Psychologist: Uh huh.[8] And then what happened?[1]

Maria: . . . started to pee in her mouth.[C]

Psychologist: And then she came back and then she told you that?[2, 4] Or did
                  you go with her, too?[2, 4]

Maria: I didn't go with her.[C]

Psychologist: Did you see Tom do this?[2]

Maria: Uh uh (negative response).[B1]

Psychologist: Did you ever see your daddy have makeup on?[2]

Maria: Um hum (negative response).[B1]

Psychologist: What are you doing there?[1, 7] . . . She's busy, talking on the phone.[7,
                  9]

Maria: Uh huh.[A1] I want the camera.[F]

Psychologist: You want the camera, okay.[9, 5] You can get the camera there.[5]

Maria: Taking a picture of all of you.[D2]

Psychologist: Okay.[8]

Maria: Get them all straightened up.[D2]

Psychologist: Get them all straightened up.[9]

Maria: And chair have them . . . oh, oh.[D2]

Psychologist: You like to see that red light go on, don't you?[6C, 5] Okay, you take their picture and then I need to ask you a couple more questions.[5, 4] We'll all smile pretty.[5, 6C]

Maria: One picture, two picture, three picture, four picture, five picture . . . [D2]

Psychologist: That's a lot of pictures.[6C]

Maria: Eight picture, eight picture.[D2]

Psychologist: Who's that one?[1] Oh, an orangutan . . . [8]

Maria: Rangtang.[D2]

Psychologist: . . . huh?[6C] It almost looks like a person, huh?[6C]

Maria: Orangutan.[D2] Is that what it says?[F, D2]

Psychologist: Um hum.[9]

Maria: Cow.[D2]

Psychologist: A hippopotamus is what that is.[6C]

Maria: See if you can see in there.[D2, F]

Psychologist: I can't see you there but I can see if you look through here.[6C] You look through there and then you can see people on the other side.[6C] . . . Well, you can see whatever is on the other side of the camera.[6C]

Maria: (Makes noise)[D2]

Psychologist: What's so scary?[1]

Maria: No.[B1]

Psychologist: Oh, I'm sorry.[6C] I see a fox now, what was there before I pushed the wrong thing?[6C] What was it?[1, 6C]

Maria: Alligator.[D2, C]

Psychologist: I don't like alligators, do you?[2, 6C] . . . Hum?[2, 6C] You do.[9] How come?[1, 6C]

Maria: 'Cause.[D2]

Psychologist: 'Cause why?[2, 6C]
Maria: (Sings) I'm going crazy.[D2]

Psychologist: You're going crazy, how come?[1]
Maria: When are we going to hear the tape?[F]

Psychologist: Oh, we can hear it in a minute.[5] Why don't you come and sit right by me because I need to ask you a couple more questions and then I have to hear the tape for a minute and you can hear just what you sound like, okay?[4, 5, 2]

Maria: Come.[G]

Psychologist: Maria, it's real real important, let's not bang, let's just forget about the little tape recording.[4]

Maria: Why?[F]

Psychologist: Why?[9, 2] I'll let you listen to it in a minute, but we need to just talk really seriously for a minute here because this is real real important stuff because I need to call Dorothy Clarke and I need to let Dorothy know what . . . [4]

Maria: (Sings into microphone)[D1, D2]

Psychologist: Maria, I'll have to turn it off if you can't keep still.[5, 4]
Maria: Why?[F]

Psychologist: Because it's real important, I'll let you fool around with the tape recorder in a minute, but right now, though, it's real real important is for you to tell me who really did what.[4] . . . It's real real important.[4] Do you remember when you told Dorothy that Daddy put his penis in your mouth?[2, 6A, 4] . . . And he had put his mouth by your vagina when you go potty.[2, 6A, 4] . . . And you told her that Daddy peed in your mouth and you told Dorothy that Daddy peed in Wendy's mouth.[2, 4, 6A] And you told me those same things, too, when you first came here.[2, 4, 6A] And now you're telling me that no, that didn't happen, and what I need to know is I don't know if you were teasing me at first or if you are scared about what you said because I know it's real real scary stuff to talk about and I know you love your daddy and it's real hard, okay we can't look at that right now, put that right down here, you can play with it in a minute.[3, 5, 4] I know it's real hard, Maria, when you love somebody and you don't want to get that person into trouble.[5, 4] Let's put that aside right now, too.[4] But what's really important, Maria, is for you to know that what, the only thing we want is for you to tell us the truth, is for you to tell us what really happened and that's all that counts, that's all that matters, that's what God wants you to do, and I really think that's what Mommy wants you to do, too.[4, 6A]

Maria: I don't know what to say.[D3]

Psychologist: You don't know what to say.[9]

[Psychologist turns tape over.]

Psychologist: You can hear both sides if you want to.[5] You said before you didn't know what to say and what I'm telling you is what's important to say.[4]

Maria: I don't know what to say.[D3]

Psychologist: Just tell me what really happened.[4] You know.[4] Your head knows and your heart knows what really happened.[4] And what is important, Maria, is just to tell me the real . . . [4]

Maria: (Makes noise)[D2, D1]

Psychologist: . . . truth and I don't know, Maria, I really don't and all I care about is making sure that's you're safe and that whoever did the naughty things . . . [4]

Maria: (Makes noise)[D2, D1]

Psychologist: . . . stops doing these naughty things and you need to know that what Mommy wants and what God wants you to do is just tell what really happened.[4, 5, 6A]

Maria: I just want to go out and see my mom.[D1]

Psychologist: Okay, you can go, we'll just see her, we'll just stop, let me just ask you this one more time:[5, 4] Who was the person that peed in your mouth and peed in Wendy's mouth?[1, 6A, 4]

Maria: Wendy.[D2]

Psychologist: Who peed in Wendy's mouth?[1]

Maria: Tom.[C]

Psychologist: Is that really, really the person that did it?[5, 4] Or are you saying that because you want him to go to jail?[2, 4, 6A]

Maria: (Pause) He really did do it.[C]

Psychologist: He really did do it?[9, 2] Why did you say your daddy did it?[1, 4] . . . Why did you say that Daddy did it?[1, 4]

Maria: I didn't want Daddy to go to jail.[C]

Psychologist: You don't, but why did, but now he went to jail because we thought your daddy did something naughty.[4, 6] You told us that Daddy did the naughty thing.[4] Why did you say Daddy did the naughty thing.[1] Did Daddy do naughty things, too?[2] Maria?[1, 4]

Maria: Uh uh.[B1]

Psychologist: No?[9] What did Mommy tell you to say?[1, 4] . . . Maria, what did Mama tell you to say?[1, 4] . . . Can you tell me?[2, 4] . . . Can you tell me?[2, 4] What did Mama tell you to say?[1, 4] Maria?[4, 2] . . . Are you going to tell me or are you scared to tell me?[3, 4]

[Maria sings as the psychologist questions her.]

Maria: I'm scared.[C]

Psychologist: How come?[1]

Maria: 'Cause.[C]

Psychologist: Are you afraid that I'll make Mommy go away or I'll get mad at Mommy?[2, 6A] Are you afraid of that?[2, 4]

Maria: I'm afraid of they'll take Mommy away.[C]

Psychologist: You're afraid, I don't think, I don't think your mommy did anything like what you said Daddy did and I don't want your mommy to go to jail.[5] I want your mommy just to keep you safe.[5] That's what I want.[5] What did Mommy say, honey?[1, 4, 5] . . . Can you tell me, what did Mommy say?[2, 4] . . . Maria, what did Mommy say?[1, 4] What did Daddy say?[1] Can you tell me what Daddy said?[2, 4] . . . Did you see Daddy when you came up here to the city last weekend?[2] Did you visit with Daddy?[2, 4] Maria?[2, 4] Did you?[2, 4]

[Pauses between statements but Maria doesn't answer.]

Psychologist: Can you tell me or are you scared?[3, 4]

Maria: I'm scared.[C]

Psychologist: Are you scared that if you tell me that you visited Daddy that I will get mad?[2, 4, 6A] Because you know what, you didn't do anything wrong.[5] The grown-ups are the people who have done naughty things, not Maria.[4, 6A] It's not your fault, honey, whatever happened is not Maria's fault because you are just a very, very, very nice little girl and it's the grown-ups who did the bad thing, not Maria.[5, 4, 6A] . . . Did you see Daddy last week-end, Maria?[2] Did you visit with Daddy?[2, 4] Just for a little while?[2, 4] Did you talk to him?[2, 4]

Maria: I talked to him on the telephone but he didn't talk back.[C]

Psychologist: He didn't talk back, huh, how did that make you feel?[9, 1] . . . How did you feel when Daddy didn't talk back?[1] . . . How did you feel?[1, 4] . . . Sad?[6A, 2] Angry or happy or what?[6A, 2] . . . Can you tell me?[2, 4] . . . Can you tell me how you felt?[2, 4] You tell me that and we'll turn off the tape.[4, 5] How did you fell when Daddy wouldn't talk back to you?[1] . . . Maria.[4] . . . Okay, let's turn off the tape.[5] You're not going to answer me.[10]

AFTERMATH

The difficulties in the interview with Dr. Griffin were compounded by her erroneous account of what actually happened in the interview. This is not an isolated case. When there are tapes, we often find that interview reports are frequently wrong about what was actually said by the child and the interrogator in the interview. In this interview, despite several questions directed towards getting her to say that her mother had told her what to say, Maria never agrees this happened. Nevertheless, Dr. Griffin contacted the social worker to tell her that Maria had reported her mother had told her to say that her Daddy didn't do it. Dr. Griffin persisted in this erroneous account of the August 12 interview until confronted with the tape in the trial two years later.

Also, Dr. Griffin told Maria, "You're afraid, I don't think, I don't think your mommy did anything like what you said Daddy did and I don't want your mommy to go to jail. I want your mommy just to keep you safe. That's what I want." But a few days later Dr. Griffin and Dorothy Clarke had arranged for Maria to be taken from her mother and placed in foster care.

When reports don't match the recorded interviews, the interrogator is not deliberately falsifying the report (although this may occasionally happen). Instead, the bias is so strong that the interrogator misperceives the child's statements at the time. In addition, the later memory of what happened is distorted. In this case, the leading and coercive interrogations by Dorothy Clarke and Paula Griffin and the erroneous report by Dr. Griffin had disastrous effects on the Thompson family.

It took another year after John's acquittal in the criminal trial before the family court ordered that the family be reunited. At the conclusion of the family court hearing, the judge made an astonishing remark. He told John and Sandy that they should not be angry even though they had been grievously harmed. He said they should just forget all this and get on with their lives.

We saw John, Sandy and Maria separately for several sessions while they did whatever was necessary to be together again. They had difficulty understanding why the acquittal did not mean immediate reunification. During one session, Maria, who was now six years old, spontaneously said to Dr. Underwager: "If you see my Daddy, tell him for me that I love him very, very, very much and I miss him and I want us all to be together again."

The family moved to a new city and John took a different job in their attempt to start over again. However, this meant that they were also transferred to the supervision of a different county's social services department until they had completed their compliance with the family court order directing reunification. Midway through that process we received a letter from this new county's child protection team asking us about our therapy. They asked us why were we not doing sexual abuse treatment for Maria and sexual abuser treatment for John and Sandy? The criminal acquittal and the family court determination of no abuse meant nothing to this county's workers. The accusation had been made, therefore it was real, and therefore we should be treating them for sexual abuse. The implicit threat was that if they were not treated for abuse, they would be seen as not complying with the court order and the child protection workers' demands. This could result in Maria being taken away again.

It took an order by the judge to forestall continued intervention in this family's life. The fear and the threat of intervention has not diminished for John and Sandy since the judge ordered them freed from any involvement of child protection. They believe that any suspicion by anybody of possible neglect or abuse of Maria would bring the powerful intervention of the child protection system immediately. They can do nothing to protect themselves or their child except do their best to stay out of any trouble that would bring them to the attention of authorities.

It was expected that the Thompsons would need extensive therapy for reunification as John had not lived with his daughter for two and a half years. However, this was accomplished more easily than anyone had expected, which is a tribute to the strength and resilience of all three members of the family. But their scars will remain forever. Sandy describes the year her daughter was taken away from her this way. "While our child called another woman Mommy, she learned to dress herself for the first time, recite the alphabet for the first time, and lost her first tooth. She also spent her first day at kindergarten, learned to ride a bike and *many* other firsts in foster care. All moments we will never ever have again. They cannot be replaced."

Chapter 11

THE TRUTH IS OBSCURED
WHEN A CHILD IS ABUSED

There are child sexual abusers who escape detection. There may also be child sexual abusers who are discovered but who avoid prosecution or conviction because leading, suggestive interviews and questioning have produced so much confusion and such bizarre and improbable accusations that by the time the case gets to a fact finder the truth cannot be sorted out.

The standard of proof in criminal cases requires that the finder of fact be certain beyond a reasonable doubt. When the record shows coercive, leading interrogations that appear to produce unbelievable and unreliable statements, a reasonable person can have sufficient doubt about the entire story to decide that there is reasonable doubt. In that case, an opinion of not guilty is required by the justice system. In noncriminal tribunals, where the standard for a guilty verdict is a preponderance of the evidence and the fact finder hears a tale that is largely implausible, the result may also be a not guilty decision. It must also be understood that a competent defense attorney is morally and ethically bound to provide the best defense possible for the accused. This means defense attorneys will make certain a fact finder hears any evidence that shows a basis for reasonable doubt.

The crucial importance of improving the way children are interrogated is not only to avoid convicting innocent people but also to produce accurate decisions when there is real abuse. The best estimate of the frequency of false negatives, that is, a decision that misses a true abuser, is that for every abuser correctly identified, a real child abuser is incorrectly classified a nonabuser (Wakefield and Underwager, 1988). It appears likely that true pedophiles abuse many, many children. If the system misses a true abuser, it may well occur that a large number of children will be abused who might not have been had the abuser been correctly identified. There is no way of knowing about this unless the missed true abuser is once again discovered and this time correctly classified.

One of the ironic tragedies of the child sexual abuse system is that we already know enough from credible scientific research to do a better job of maximizing the reliability of children's statements. We do not have to continue the coercive interrogations that produce false allegations of sexual abuse against innocent people and also obscure truth so that cases of actual abuse may not be properly handled.

BACKGROUND

In the following case, a child was sexually abused by an older man who had befriended her family. However, as a result of the repeated interviews of several children, the stories became more extreme and grew to include the man's wife and two of his neighbors. By the time the case was due for trial, the interviewing process meant that it was extremely difficult to sort out what had really happened.

All four individuals would have been tried for sexual abuse if the older man had not pled guilty in a plea bargain that included dropping the charges against the others. If he had not done this, the trial may well have resulted in either an acquittal for all or a conviction for all. In either case, justice would not have been served.

Milt and Helga Swenson were a retired couple in their late 60s. They had raised five children who now lived in other states. Milt had always loved children but had struggled with an attraction to prepubescent girls. Years earlier, he had fondled one of his own daughters. At this time, there was a family confrontation but nothing else was ever done and the behavior was not repeated.

Throughout the years, the Swensons welcomed neighborhood children who often appeared at their house for visits. Helga generally had homemade cookies available and both took time to talk or play with the children, who called them "Grandma" and "Pa Dad."

The Swensons befriended a young couple from their church, Harvey and Rose Adams, and their two children, eight-year-old Becky and six-year-old Darren. The family had moved to the small city from out of state and had no relatives nearby, and the Swensons began inviting them for dinner and holidays. Milt and Helga often babysat and the two children sometimes spent the night and played with the neighborhood children who hung around at the house.

Milt's attraction to young girls became salient with Becky, who was an attractive and affectionate child. It began with cuddling and stroking but gradually evolved into fondling and eventually he asked her to fondle his penis. The child told her mother and the police were called. The parents were furious. They felt that their friendship had been betrayed and they were determined to see Milt brought to justice. They began questioning Darren who also eventually described sexual abuse and who later made statements about another neighborhood boy, Donny, being abused at the same time as he was. The police spoke to Donny and he was also interviewed several times.

As the interviews progressed, the stories grew and became more elaborate. Helga was initially said to be in the house in another room during the abuse but was later alleged to have also sexually abused the boys. When Darren said that he had seen Donny's father at Milt's house "a thousand times," Donny's father and later his mother also fell under suspicion. Accounts of videotaped movies were given. The theory developed that this was a small sex ring where pornographic films were made.

In the following interview, Darren is interviewed by a police detective in the presence of a social worker and his parents. Harvey and Rose Adams have spoken to Darren about the abuse over the weekend and Darren is encouraged to tell the new things he has remembered to the interviewers.

It can be seen at the beginning of the interview how Darren has learned the language game of the interviewers when he says that what he forgot to tell was " . . . that Pa Dad *bad touched,* that Donny got *bad touched* with me." The term, "bad touched" to refer to sexual touching is not a term used by children on their own and its use reflects the learning that takes place in such interviews.

There are many leading questions in the interview and the interviewer continues questioning whenever he gets an answer that doesn't fit. For example, according to Darren, he and Donny were at "Pa Dad's and Grandma's house" with Milt, all three were naked, and Milt was taking movies of the two boys while "Donny sucked Pa Dad's peter." This took place downstairs while Helga was doing the dishes, also presumably downstairs. But the detective asks more leading questions that convey the message to Darren that the right story is that the movies were taken following the penis sucking and Helga was upstairs during this time. It is in this interview that Darren states that he has seen Donny's father at Milt's house "a thousand times."

For the twelve interviews that we analyzed in this case, the total percentage of interviewer behaviors that fell in the error-inducing categories was 54%.

INTERVIEW

Interviewer:	Henry Cranston
Child:	Darren Adams
Also Present:	Harvey Adams, Rose Adams, Myra Polk (social worker from child protection)

Darren Adams = Darren; Harvey Adams = Mr. Adams; Rose Adams = Mrs. Adams: Henry Cranston = Detective; Myra Polk = Soc Wkr

Detective: Today's date is July 18.[10] My name is Henry Cranston, Investigator for the County Attorney's Office.[10] I'm at the Harvey Adams residence.[10] I will be talking to Darren Adams.[10] Darren is six years old.[10] With me for the interview is Darren's mom, Rose Adams[10] Darren's dad, Harvey Adams, and Myra Polk from DHS.[10]

Okay, Darren, we talked the other day, last Friday I think it was and you told me some things that happened with you and Pa Dad, do you remember?[9, 2A]

Darren: Yeah.[A1]

Detective: Okay.[8] And then over the weekend I guess you told Mom and Dad that maybe you had remembered some things that you had forgotten to tell me.[9]

Darren: Yep.[A1]

Detective: And so that's why we're here today, right?[2B]

Darren: (no response)[G]

Detective: Okay.[8] Darren, what is it that you forgot to tell me that happened at Pa Dad's?[1A]

Darren: Umm, that Pa Dad bad touched, that Donny got bad touched with me.[C]

Detective:	Okay.[8] That's Donny?[2A, 9] Do you know Donny's last name?[2A]
Darren:	No.[B1]
Detective:	Okay, do you know where Donny lives?[2A]
Darren:	No.[B1] He lives very close to Pa Dad. Do you know that white house that you see with the red roof?[C, F]
Detective:	Uh huh.[10]
Darren:	Well, that's where he lives.[C]
Detective:	Oh, okay.[8] Are you and Donny friends?[2A]
Darren:	Yeah.[A1]
Detective:	How old is Donny?[1A]
Darren:	Beats me.[D3]
Detective:	Is he older than you or younger than you, do you know that?[3A]
Darren:	Younger.[C]
Detective:	Younger.[9] Is he smaller than you or bigger than you?[3A]
Darren:	Well, smaller.[C]
Detective:	Now, you said that Pa Dad bad touched both you and Donny?[2A, 9] Okay, can you tell me what he did when you say bad touched, Darren?[2A] What do you mean?[1A] What did Pa Dad do?[1A]
Darren:	Well, he touched our private parts.[C]
Detective:	When Pa Dad touched your private parts where were you?[1A] Were you inside or outside?[3A]
Darren:	Inside.[C]
Detective:	Whose house were you in?[1A]
Darren:	Pa Dad and Grandma's.[C]
Detective:	Okay.[8] And when Pa Dad bad touched you, how were you dressed?[1A] Did you have your clothes on or clothes off?[3A]
Darren:	Off.[C]

Detective: Pardon me?[1A]

Darren: Off.[C]

Detective: Clothes off.[9] How about Donny, did he have his clothes off?[2B]

Darren: Uh yeah.[A1]

Detective: And how about Pa Dad?[1A] How was he dressed?[1A]

Darren: Uh, without any clothes on.[C]

Detective: Without any clothes on.[9] How did Pa Dad bad touch you?[1A] Did he bad touch you with his hand?[2B]

Darren: Uh yeah.[A1]

Detective: And he bad touched you with his hand on your private parts, is that right?[2A, 9]

Darren: Right.[A1]

Detective: Okay.[8] Did Pa Dad bad touch you in any other way?[2A]

Darren: Not . . . I think . . . I don't know.[B1, D3]

Detective: Don't know.[9] Did Pa Dad bad touch Donny in any other way?[2A] Or did he just touch Donny with his hand?[2A]

Darren: With his hand.[C]

Detective: Okay.[8] Did Pa Dad have you or Donny do anything to him?[2A]

Darren: Yeah.[A1]

Detective: What did he have you do?[1A]

Darren: Bad touch him.[C]

Detective: So you would have to bad touch Pa Dad?[2A, 9]

Darren: Uh uh.[A1]

Detective: And how would you do that?[1A] Would that be with your hand?[2B]

Darren: Yeah.[A1]

Detective: Okay.[8] While this was going on, who was at home?[1B] Was it just you and Pa Dad and Donny?[2B]

Darren: No.[B1] Grandma, too.[C]

Detective: What was Grandma doing?[1A]

Darren: Umm.[G] Washing the dishes.[C]

Detective: Okay.[8] Did Pa Dad, I'm sorry, did Grandma see what you were doing?[2A]

Darren: No.[B1]

Detective: Okay.[8] Now, do you remember how long ago this was, Darren?[2A]

Darren: Uh.[G]

Detective: Does it seem like a real long, long time ago or was it just a little while ago?[3A]

Darren: A long, long time ago.[C]

Detective: Okay.[8] Can you remember back to last summer before you started school this year?[2A]

Darren: Nope.[B1]

Detective: You can't.[9] What did you do last summer?[1A] Do you know?[2A] Did you go on vacation or do anything?[2A] Play any fun games?[2A]

Darren: Um[G]

Detective: You can't remember?[2A]

Darren: I did do something for fun.[D2]

Detective: What did you do?[1A]

Darren: Today.[D2]

Detective: Oh.[6C] What did you do today?[6C]

Darren: That's fun?[F, D2]

Detective: Uh uh.[6C]

Darren: Played with trucks.[D2]

Detective: Oh.[6C] Do you like playing with trucks?[6C]

Darren: ... trucks.[D2] They're little blue things that sits under the gray things.[D2]

Detective: Oh.[6C] Okay.[6C] Where did you do that?[6C] Right here at you . . . [6C] Where did you do that?[6C]

Darren: Home.[D2] Um, Billy's house.[D2]

Detective: Oh.[6C] He's got some neat toys, huh?[6C]

Darren: Yeah.[D2] Do you know that one that's automatic that has a remote control?[D2]

Detective: Which one is that?[6C]

Darren: Um.[D2] That one that has that remote control.[D2]

Detective: Yeah, but a lot of them have remote controls.[6C]

Darren: Only one of them does.[D2]

Detective: Maybe I don't know.[6C]

Darren: And that one, well Billy has that one.[D2]

Detective: Pretty neat it sounds like to me.[6C]

Darren: But, I tried the one with the remote control but it doesn't work.[D2]

Detective: Sometimes you have to be real clever to run those remote control toys.[6C]

Darren: Uh uh.[D2]

Detective: Sometimes you can't make them work 'cause you don't know just what to do.[6C] Darren, let me ask you something else.[10] When you had to bad touch Pa Dad and Pa Dad bad touched you, how old were you?[1A] Do you know that?[2A]

Darren: Six.[C]

Detective: You were six.[9] And how old are you now?[1A]

Darren: Six.[C]

Detective: Oh.[8] So did it happen while you were six or did it happen before you were six?[3A]

Darren: When I was six.[C]

Detective: When you were six.[9] Okay.[8] And you say that happened at Pa Dad's house?[2A, 9] Grandma and Pa Dad's house?[2A, 9]

Darren: Yeah.[A1]

Detective: Okay.[8] Did ... I don't remember what Mom told me.[10] Mom said that you said a whole bunch of things and I'm not sure, did you tell Mom or Dad anything about Pa Dad taking some movies and that?[2B] Hmm?[2A] Is that a yes or a no?[3A]

Darren: Yes.[A1]

Detective: What kind of movies did Pa Dad take?[1A]

Darren: Well, he has a ... do you know those kind of cameras that you want on the birthday?[C, F] Like they put ... they record on those tapes.[C] They record the parts on the tape?[F, C]

Detective: Uh huh.[8]

Darren: Well, that's what he did it on us.[C]

Detective: Oh.[8] Where did he put the camera?[1A] Did he hold the camera in his hand?[2A]

Darren: Yeah.[A1]

Detective: Okay.[8] And while he was holding the camera in his hand, who was he taking pictures of?[1A]

Darren: Us.[C]

Detective: Us is who?[1A] You and Donny?[2B]

Darren: Yeah.[A1]

Detective: And what were you two doing?[1A]

Darren: Nothing.[C]

Detective: He just took pictures of you sitting there doing nothing?[2A, 9]

Darren: Yeah.[A1]

Detective: Well, that's kind of neat.[5] How were you dressed?[1A] Did you have your clothes on?[2B]

Darren: No.[B1]

Detective: No.[9] How come?[1A]

Darren: Because.[D1]

Detective: Because why?[1A]

Darren: Because.[D1]

Detective: Did you take your clothes off?[2A]

Darren: No . . . yeah.[A3]

Detective: How come you took your clothes off?[1A] Did somebody tell you
              to?[2B, 6A]

Darren: Yeah.[A1]

Detective: Who told you to?[1A]

Darren: I don't know.[D3]

Detective: So there was you and Donny in Pa Dad's house.[9] Were you
              upstairs or downstairs?[3A]

Darren: Down.[C]

Detective: Downstairs.[9] And you each had your clothes off?[2A, 9]

Darren: On . . . off.[C]

Detective: You had your clothes off.[9] Okay.[8] Did Donny have his clothes
              off?[2A]

Darren: No.[B1]

Detective: Donny's clothes were on?[2A, 9]

Darren: No.[B1]

Detective: Can you tell me whether Donny's clothes were on or off?[2A]

Darren: What?[F]

Detective: Were Donny's clothes on or off?[3A]

Darren: Off.[C]

Detective: Off.[9] Okay.[8] And Pa Dad was taking pictures of you and Donny,
              right?[2A, 9]

Darren: Uh huh.[A1]

Detective: And the pictures were just of you guys sitting there doing stuff, right?[2A, 9]

Darren: Yeah.[A1]

Detective: What were you doing?[1A]

Darren: Nothing.[C]

Detective: Were you playing games of some kind?[2B]

Darren: Uh, no.[B1]

Detective: No.[9] Were you sitting down or standing up?[3A] Sitting down.[9] Okay.[8] And what else did Pa Dad do?[1A]

Darren: Umm . . . I don't remember.[D3]

Detective: You don't remember.[9] I think Mom said something about you told her about something you had to do with Pa Dad.[6A] Is that right?[2B]

Darren: What is it?[F]

Detective: Or maybe it was Donny had to do something with Pa Dad.[6A] I'm not sure, can you help me?[2A, 4]

Darren: It wasn't me.[C]

Detective: It wasn't you.[9] Okay.[8] Did Donny have to do something with Pa Dad?[2A] Can you remember?[2A]

Darren: No.[B1]

Detective: Okay.[8]

Darren: Ask my mom.[F]

Detective: Ask Mom.[9] Well, Mom's right here, maybe we can ask Mom if she remembers what you told her.[10] Will that be okay?[2A] You have got to answer yes or no, Darren, so we can hear your voice.[10] You see, I can't see you on the tape recorder.[10]

Darren: Yes.[A1]

Detective: Okay.[8] Let's ask Mom.[10] Okay?[8] Darren told you something about what went on, so Mom is going to see if she can help you remember.[10]

Mother:	You mentioned something about that Donny had to do something to Pa Dad's private parts.[6A] Do you remember what you said that Donny had to do?[2B, 6A] What you saw Donny do?[1A, 6A]
Darren:	What?[F]
Mother:	One time with his . . . you said something about he had to touch Pa Dad with his private parts with something.[6A] Do you remember what that was?[2B, 6A]
Darren:	What?[F]
Mother:	Do you remember?[2A]
Darren:	No.[B1]
Mother:	Did you say that Donny did something with his mouth?[2B, 6A]
Darren:	No.[B1]
Mother:	Did Pa Dad?[2B, 6A]
Darren:	No.[B1] No.[B1]
Mother:	Are you remembering?[2A]
Darren:	What?[F] . . . [G]
Mother:	You can hang on.[10] But you also say something about that you had seen Donny have to do something to Pa Dad with his mouth.[6A]
Darren:	Oh, yeah.[A1] . . . [G]
Mother:	Oh, okay.[8]
Detective:	I didn't hear that, Darren.[10] What . . . [1A]
Darren:	He sucks his peter.[C]
Detective:	Who sucked whose peter?[1A]
Darren:	Pa Dad . . . Donny sucked Pa Dad's peter.[C]
Detective:	Donny sucked Pa Dad's peter?[9, 2A] Well, now, wait a minute, I've got a little problem.[4] I thought you said that Pa Dad was taking movies with the camera.[4]
Darren:	Yeah.[A1]

Detective: Did Pa Dad stop taking the movies while Donny sucked his peter?[2B, 6A]

Darren: Yeah.[A1]

Detective: What happened?[1A] Who took the movies?[1A]

Darren: Pa Dad.[C]

Detective: How did he do that if Donny was sucking his peter?[1A, 4]

Darren: Well . . . he sucked his peter after.[C]

Detective: After he took the movies?[2A, 9]

Darren: Yeah.[A1]

Detective: Oh.[8] So he didn't get a movie of Donny sucking Pa Dad's peter.[9]

Darren: No.[B1]

Detective: Did he put the movie camera away before Donny did that?[2B]

Darren: Yeah.[A1]

Detective: Okay.[8] Did Pa Dad ask you to suck his peter?[2B]

Darren: No.[B1]

Detective: No.[9] Okay.[8] What were you doing while Donny was sucking Pa Dad's peter?[1A] Were you there?[2A]

Darren: No.[B1]

Detective: Where were you?[1A]

Darren: Upstairs.[C]

Detective: Oh.[8] And how do you know that Donny sucked Pa Dad's peter?[1A, 4]

Darren: Because, first I saw then I went upstairs.[C]

Detective: Oh.[8] Okay.[8] When you went upstairs was Grandma upstairs?[2A] Yes or no?[4, 6A]

Darren: Yes.[A1]

Detective: Yes.[9] Okay.[8] Did you say anything to Grandma about what Donny and Pa Dad were doing?[2A]

Darren: Uh, not really.[B1] What?[F]

Detective: Did you tell Grandma what Pa Dad and Donny were doing?[2A]

Darren: What?[F]

Detective: Did you tell Grandma what was going on with Pa Dad and Donny?[2A]

Darren: No.[B1]

Detective: Okay.[8] How many times did you see Donny suck Pa Dad's peter?[1A]

Darren: Once.[C]

Detective: One time.[9] How many times can you remember that Pa Dad had you touch his private parts?[1A]

Darren: What?[F]

Detective: How many times did you touch Pa Dad's private parts?[1A]

Darren: One.[C]

Detective: One time.[9] Okay.[8] Was it all the same day that you touched Pa Dad's private parts and Donny sucked Pa Dad's peter, was that all the same day?[2A]

Darren: Yeah.[A1]

Detective: Was it?[2A, 9] Okay.[8] And was that the only time that Pa Dad had you touch his private parts?[2A]

Darren: What?[F]

Detective: Was there more than one time, Darren, that Pa Dad had you touch his private parts?[2A]

Darren: No.[B1]

Detective: No.[9] How many times do you think there were?[1A]

Darren: One.[C]

Detective:	One time.[9] Okay.[8] And Pa Dad took movies on the VCR then, huh?[2A, 9]
Darren:	Uh huh.[A1]
Detective:	And you think you were six years old when that happened?[2A, 9]
Darren:	Yep.[A1] I don't remember my age when I was that old . . . [C, D3]
Detective:	Okay.[8] Is there anything else that you can remember that you did with Grandma or Pa Dad?[2A]
Darren:	No.[B1]
Detective:	Did you and Donny ever talk about what he did with Pa Dad?[2A]
Darren:	No.[B1]
Detective:	How did Donny get down to Pa Dad's house?[1A] Did he come by himself or was somebody with him?[3A]
Darren:	Donny came down by himself.[C]
Detective:	Okay.[8] He came down by himself.[9]
Darren:	Yep.[A1]
Detective:	Have you ever seen Donny's father at Pa Dad's house?[2A]
Darren:	A thousand times.[C]
Detective:	A thousand times.[9] Donny's father was there a lot, huh?[2A, 9] Okay, Darren, you've done a good job.[5] Is there anything else that you can tell me about what's happened?[2A]
Darren:	No.[B1]
Detective:	Okay.[8] So that's everything, huh?[2A] Okay.[8] I can't think of anything else, maybe Myra can.[10] Shall we ask Myra if there is anything she can think of?[2A]
Darren:	Okay.[G]
Detective:	Okay.[8]

[Myra apparently says that she can't think of anything else.]

Detective: Myra says she can't think of anything either.[10] I think we ought to shut the tape off, what do you think?[10]

Darren: Yeah.[G]

Detective: Okay.[8] It is five minutes of two in the afternoon this will conclude the interview with Darren Adams.[10]

AFTERMATH

As the investigation and the interviews continued Helga Swenson and Donny's parents were also implicated by the children. Milt was told that the prosecutor was considering pressing criminal charges against his wife, Helga, and Donny's parents. He was told that if he pled guilty, the charges against the other three adults would not be pressed.

Milt decided to accept this plea although he continues to maintain that, although he did sexually abuse Becky, he never abused Darren and Donny. At this point, after the multiple interviews and the growing allegations, it is impossible to sort out what really did happen. Rose and Harvey are convinced that their children have had terrible things done to them and the reputations of Helga and Donny's parents are ruined. Milt was sentenced to prison with the understanding that his term would be shortened if he cooperated in therapy.

Chapter 12

INTERROGATION IN
THE PHYSICAL EXAMINATION

Physicians get neither name nor fame by pricking of wheals, or picking out thistles, or by laying of plasters to the scratch of a pin: every old woman can do this. But if they would have a name and a fame, if they will have it quickly, they must ... do some great and desperate cures. Let them fetch one to life that was dead; let them recover one to his wits that was mad; let them make one that was born blind to see; or let them give ripe wits to a fool; these are notable cures, and he that can do thus, if he doth thus first, he shall have the name and fame he desires; he may lie abed till noon.

John Bunyan: *The Jerusalem Sinner Saved; or Good News for the Vilest of Men*
Valenstein, (1986) Epigraph

The history of the practice of medicine is filled with instances where the demand to respond to grievous illness and problems has been met with attempted "great and desperate cures" that only later, after much harm done to persons, were discovered to be erroneous and folly. In psychiatry, treatments such as Wagner-Jauregg's malarial fever treatment for general paresis, for which he became the only psychiatrist ever honored with a Nobel Prize in Medicine (1927), were greeted with initial enthusiasm, glowing research studies showing phenomenal rates of cure, and rapid adoption as treatment of choice. Other examples of discredited treatments for mental illness are surgical removal of endocrine glands, prolonged narcosis (sleep therapy), carbon dioxide therapy, and aseptic meningitis induced by injecting horse blood into the spinal cord. Focal infection theory led to surgical removal of alleged sites of infection (i.e., teeth, tonsils, stomach, intestines, cervix, testes, and colon resection which produced a 30% mortality rate) from which poison supposedly spread to the mind. Insulin coma, metrazol convulsion therapies, and electroconvulsive shock were rapidly put into practice in the 1930s. All theories about them are now known to wrong and only ECT is still used even though nobody knows how it works. Psychosurgery, primarily prefrontal or transorbital lobotomy, hit a peak in 1948 with the convening of the First International Conference on Psychosurgery in Lisbon. We now know hundreds of thousands of persons were irreparably damaged by these procedures (Valenstein, 1986).

This phenomenon is not limited to psychiatry. The coronary artery bypass experience illustrates how a legitimate advance can be converted into a highly questionable procedure. Over one million people have had coronary bypass surgery. It has become the most frequent elective surgery in the United States. Recent research suggests that it has been overused, does not succeed in what most people expect it do, has a high level of negative side effects, a high mortality rate, and should be more carefully considered than is customary (Valenstein, 1986). Recent publicity about mastectomies suggests the same problem exists there.

Understanding how such things can happen includes an awareness of the pressing, immediate demands individuals or a society place upon professionals to solve problems in the absence of factual knowledge. Some individuals will see this as an opportunity to satisfy ambition while others will respond with altruistic motivations. In either case, results may be presented prematurely, successes overestimated, dangers unseen, and failures ignored.

The system dealing with child sexual abuse allegations comes out of an intent to reduce harm to children. Our society very quickly moved from ignoring child abuse to seeing it as a serious social problem (Nelson, 1984) and demanded a solution. The response developed in the absence of factual knowledge. As the history of medicine shows, it takes time for scientific research to produce knowledge. In the interval, the risks of "great and desperate cures" that turn out to be error must be faced. Although we can use reason and reflection to limit harm done until an answer is forthcoming, this did not take place in the growth of the child sexual abuse system.

In the search for better and more sure ways to tell whether abuse is real or not, the system turned to physicians for aid. The medical examination for physical signs or sequelae in sexual abuse diagnosis has been given significant importance in the judicial system. Possibly because of the lay public's elevated opinion of medicine, a physician's report is often seen by judges and juries as more factual, "hard," with less speculation than those of mental health professionals. It is now becoming evident through recent base rate studies of normal, nonabused children that many of the findings previously used to support a diagnosis of abuse are found with a high enough frequency in normals that they do not support an opinion that abuse occurred (McCann, 1988). At the same time, genitalia judged normal cannot rule out sexual abuse in that most abuse leaves no physical or medical evidence. It does not now appear that medical procedures can produce what was once anticipated, that is, greater certainty and increased ability to tell about sexual abuse.

As the system investigating cases of suspected sexual abuse evolved, a few physicians have used idiosyncratic and controversial physical methods and techniques. These methods have been proposed and adopted without any empirical data supporting their efficacy or validity. On the basis of the conclusions drawn from these unproven and untested methods, the child protection and justice systems have acted to accuse individuals, remove children from their homes and interrogate them repeatedly about abuse.

The overdetermined enthusiasm and the bias of the system to believe accusations and act precipitately is shown in the readiness to use reports and evidence from physicians whose methods are questionable and to ignore or disparage individuals who warn about the suspect nature of the procedures employed by these few physicians. Rather than proceed cautiously and reduce risks of injury or error, the system reinforces methods whose only virtue appears to be affirmation of abuse. At this level, the system as a whole bears responsibility for perpetuating and encouraging error to the detriment of individuals and the society. This is failure to limit harm until there is a better answer.

GREAT AND DESPERATE CURES

In 1987 in Cleveland County, Middlesborough, England, in about two months time, 121 children were removed from their parents and their home and "placed into care" (institutional or foster home) on the basis of something called the "reflex anal dilatation test" (Bell, 1988; Butler-Sloss, 1988; Dyer, 1988; *The London Times,* 1988; Priest, 1988). In this test, the child was assumed to have been abused if, when the anus was examined, it dilated. Two physicians in the Middlesborough general hospital in Cleveland County, England, began to check the anuses of all children brought in for whatever reason. Whenever the reflex was discovered, the child was removed from home, put into care, and subjected to repeated suggestive interviews.

At a meeting we attended in Middlesborough, December 1987, some of the parents described how they took their children to the hospital for routine checks or emergency treatment for minor injuries and while they were in the waiting room, their children were examined rectally without their knowledge. The physician would then come into the waiting room to tell them their child had been taken into custody. They were helpless because under English law, when a child is taken into care there is no recourse, no appeal.

Other physicians disagreed with the reflex and dilatation technique and the Middlesborough doctors came under mounting criticism. A Middlesborough Labor Party Member of Parliament, Mr. Stewart Bell, was informed of the events and sought an investigation. Following a public outcry and a reexamination of the issues, judges started to return some children to their parents. Eventually, most of the children were returned home and the government launched a formal inquiry into the situation which had become a national scandal. The inquiry lasted five months and Justice Butler-Sloss issued the report July 5, 1988 (Butler-Sloss, 1988). It was critical of the procedures followed and forthrightly concluded the system had made serious errors.

It is now generally acknowledged that this controversial physical procedure cannot be used to prove sexual abuse. Dr. Raine Roberts (1988) states:

> Anal dilatation is an odd and intriguing phenomenon for which there is no satisfactory explanation. It has many similarities to yawning, which occurs for a number of reasons that are ill understood . . . If it is a learned response to pain or discomfort, one must question why people with anal fissures do not learn it and why it is so variable and is extinguished so quickly. . . . Very much more work must be done to understand the normal and abnormal anus of the child. In the meantime the greatest caution must be observed in making a diagnosis of anal abuse without a clear and unprompted history from the child (pp. 446–447).

In the little town of Jordan in Scott County, Minnesota, 25 adults were accused of sexually abusing 40 children in two interlocking sex rings. Children were removed from their homes and placed into foster care where most remained for over 18 months. Some were not returned until four years after being taken away. The children were repeatedly interrogated and the stories about abuse grew into accounts of orgies, sex with animals and ritual murder and torture. Eventually, one adult pled guilty, two were acquitted, and the charges were dropped against the rest (Jones, 1985; Humphrey, 1985; Rigert, Peterson, & Marcotty, 1985).

Minnesota's attorney general, Hubert Humphrey, took over the investigation together with the Minnesota Bureau of Criminal Investigation and the Federal Bureau of Investigation. His report was sharply critical of the procedures followed in the investigation (Humphrey, 1985). Now, four years later, all of the children except those from one family have been returned home, and it is generally acknowledged that most of the adults charged did not abuse any children. If any adults really did abuse any children, it cannot be proven now because of the contaminating effects of an investigation that got completely out of control.

In addition to the multiple interrogations by the foster parents, psychologists, social workers and prosecutor, 24 of the children were examined by a family-practice physician (Breo, 1984). This physician diagnosed evidence of sexual abuse by rectal examinations. His theory was that if the children had "lax sphincters," this meant that they had been anally penetrated. His method of ascertaining this was to insert two or three fingers into the rectum. If he succeeded in this, he believed this proved that the child had been anally penetrated. William Erickson, a psychiatrist, child psychiatrist and pediatrician with a long history of experience in sexual abuse with both victims and perpetrators, states about this physician's technique:

> Dr. _____'s physical findings were the result of an entirely unorthodox and medically dangerous procedure and his conclusions from those examinations are unfounded. Dr. _____ is the first physician I have ever heard of who did rectal exams using more than one finger. If he did succeed in thrusting several fingers into the rectums of small children, he was unwise to conclude that that meant that someone had been there before him. Any penetration is very uncommon in child sex abuse because it is so exquisitely painful and results in injuries, tears and spasms rather than laxness. All but the most hardened of child sexual abusers tend to avoid anal intercourse with prepubertal children because it is painful and some strategy must be utilized to muffle the child's cries. It is impossible to accomplish without the use of lubricants or with any degree of impotence (Erickson, 1985, p. 7).

> In conclusion, I can find no basis on which to support either _____'s technique or his conclusions. Multifinger rectal examinations are potentially dangerous, risking the same sort of trauma that forcible penetration by a penis or hand causes. The practice is meaningless. Informed clinical experience and experimental studies both indicate that injury, pain or infection are the result of rectal penetration, and laxness of the rectum is unrelated to sexual experience (Erickson, 1987, p. 4).

The family practice physician had been employed by the county in a prior sexual abuse case which had had heavy local media coverage. In spite of questions raised at that time, the county continued to send children to this physician and expose them to the procedure. We have observed a number of cases around the country in which physicians' reports include a diagnosis of sexual abuse on the basis of "lax sphincter tone." There is never any research cited to show a basis for this claim but only the assertion itself.

Perhaps the most startling example of an idiosyncratic physical technique for diagnosing sexual abuse is routinely being done by a pediatrician whom we will call Dr. Anna Stearns. Dr. Stearns has developed the theory that by sticking her finger into the child's anus and/or vagina and by stroking the clitoris, she can recreate an experience and elicit memories of prior abuse. She says that one thing she can do as a physician which other child abuse investigators cannot do is actually use the child's body, by putting her finger into the child's va ina or anus and asking if this what they did to you, and do you think it went in that far, and did it bleed.

She described her technique in a recent article (Gage, 1989) this way.

> I examine the genital area closely, using a good light source. With my gloved and lubricated examining finger I touch the clitoris, the vaginal introitus (or opening), and the anus. I watch her reaction and ask if this is what the perpetrator has done. . . . Next I attempt to feel the presence of the hymen and to determine whether it obstructs my finger from entering the vaginal vault . . . At times this part of the examination proves to be uncomfortable for the child, in which case I do not persist (pp. 41–42).

Dr. Stearns claims her method produces the most accurate and precise information about an allegation of sexual abuse. Therefore she feels proud and justified and teaches her method to other physicians (Gage, 1989).

In a deposition she described her technique as follows:

> . . . Following the examination with the colposcope, I then put on the examining glove and I question the children by somewhat—I hate to use the word mimicry because I don't feel I'm being abusive—but I will touch them in sexual areas, I mean in the genital area for them to compare that sensation to what they remember feeling.

The idea is that by repeating abusive touching that a child has experienced in the past the child's memory will be refreshed and he or she can then tell the examiner more about it. The same behavior, fondling, digital penetration, and erotic stimulation, defined as abusive when another person does it, is not abusive because the pediatrician does not feel she is being abusive. Can a child make that distinction? Mathis (1981) comments that it is puzzling that although the general public believes all sexual molestation of a child is traumatic, "medical examination . . . of a child's genital area, frequently done over strenuous objection, rarely creates serious consternation to anyone except the patient" (p. 101–102).

Dr. Stearns heads an evaluation and treatment center where she evaluates approximately 200 children a year. Most of these children have been interrogated by therapists and/or child protection workers before they are brought to her. In one case, in a bitter visitation battle over a young girl, the mother brought the child in to Dr. Stearns periodically for two years in her attempt to find proof of the sexual abuse she was convinced her former husband was perpetrating on their daughter. The child was eighteen months old when first examined by Dr. Stearns who concluded she could not say abuse happened because the child could not talk. Finally, after seven examinations, with each one including the procedure of reabusing the child, when the child was three and a half, Dr. Stearns reported that she believed her examination established abuse had occurred. The case was not resolved until over a year later when the court ruled that there had been no abuse.

Dr. Stearns' procedures in the reports we have seen are all the same. She first gets a history of the alleged abuse from the individual who has referred the child, usually a child protection worker. She will interview the mother or caretaker first when the child is brought to her clinic. Following an interview with the child, she performs the physical examination. She videotapes the interviews, but generally turns the recorder off before the physical exam. Excerpts from her reports describe how she manipulates the clitoris, sometimes hurts the children when she inserts her fingers into their vaginas or anuses, and occasionally has male children rub and stimulate themselves while she watches.

These are excerpts from some of the numerous reports we have from cases in which Dr. Stearns has testified.

Six-year-old girl

I put on an examining glove and gently touched her clitoris and asked if she was ever touched or rubbed or tickled there and she said, "Yeah." I asked who did that and she said, "My mom." I asked what she did and she said, "I don't know." I asked what she touched it with and she said, "nothing, owie." I asked what she touched there with and she said, "I don't know." I then asked if anyone touched her anus and she said, "No." I asked if anyone touched her vaginal introitus and she denied this.

Four-year-old boy

I then explained to "Jeff" that I wanted to examine him to see if "Steve" had hurt him at all. He was entirely cooperative with this. As I examined him, I asked Jeff whether Steve did anything to his penis as I touched his penis. Jeff denied this. His penis, scrotum and testicles were normal. I then gently inserted my gloved index finger into his rectum and questioned him whether Steve did something there. Jeff responded, "His penis and finger in my butt." At that point I had my finger inserted way into his rectum and questioned him whether he thought it was in that far like mine. He indicated that it was. I questioned him whether there was any bleeding and he denied that. At that point Jeff said, "That hurts." I left my finger in and questioned him if it hurt like that when Steve did it. Jeff stated that it did.

Seven-year-old girl

"Bonnie" was initially cooperative, then she became very upset and seemingly fearful despite the fact that I was not hurting her and I was able to regain her confidence and questioned her more about the exam. On inspection her external genitalia appeared prepubertal without any pubic hair. I gently spread the labia and inspected the vaginal introitus. Initially I touched her clitoris with my finger and as I rubbed it, I questioned Bonnie as to whether she remembered anyone touching her there. She denied it. . . . I then gently inserted my finger into the vaginal introitus and the hymen offered no resistance to my finger to fully penetrate the vaginal vault. . . . At that point, Bonnie cried hysterically for a brief moment . . . I questioned her while my finger was far inside the vaginal vault as to whether she could tell me how far her father's finger was and whether his finger was inside like mine was.

Six-year-old boy

I then questioned "Joey" further as to whether his dad ever put his mouth on his Joey's wiener and he denied that. I asked him if he could show me exactly what his dad did to his wiener, using his own wiener. Joey then demonstrated pulling at his penis, fingering around the glans of his penis, and rubbing his scrotum — the area that he referred to as the slouffy (sic) stuff. As he demonstrated this, he stated, "It was getting hard, sort of." At that time he demonstrated it to me, Joey began to have an erection.

Four-year-old girl

I then asked her to roll over on her back again and with her legs spread apart and her relaxed, I took my gloved index finger and gently palpated the vaginal hymen. It offered no obstruction to my finger and I could barely feel it as I inserted my finger into the vaginal vault. I was able to easily insert my finger into the vault up to my first knuckle and that that point she said in an almost joking but clearly definite way that it was starting to hurt her a little bit.

Two-year-old girl

I then examined "Katie." She allowed me to remove her pants and to gently examine her genitalia. There were no abnormalities. I questioned her as I examined her and particularly questioned her whether anybody touched her there, as I touched her clitoris. I also questioned her as to whether anybody hurt her. Katie did not respond to my questions, either with a yes or no answer.

Same child, a year and a half later.

... During that part of the examination she responded to the fact that he touched her in the same manner as I did when I was touching her clitoris but that he also touched her in the area of the vaginal introitus where I was gently palpating with my gloved index finger. She seemed fearful at that time and questioned me whether I would hurt her. I reassured that I would not hurt her and that she could tell me that it was starting to hurt so that I would stop. She then informed me that it was starting to hurt and I reassured her that I would then stop. She did acknowledge, however, before I stopped, that she remembered him touching her there.

Three-year-old boy

I then touched "Willie" on the anus and asked if he remembered being touched right there and he said, "Yeah." I asked what touched there and he said, "my dad." I asked what part of his dad and he said, "With a gun." I asked if anything went inside and as I asked this I inserted my finger. Willie stated, "You're, you're a little bit hurting me." I explained that I wouldn't hurt but I asked if anything went inside like that and he said, "Yeah." I asked what went inside and he said, "Fire." I asked if Daddy's penis went inside and he said, "Yeah, you're hurting me." I then finished and told him that I wouldn't hurt him. I then touched Willie's penis and asked if anyone played or did anything naughty to him and he said, "Yeah, he put his penis in there. (A few minutes later)... I questioned Willie specifically about what he remembered happening to his anus. As I did that I actually inserted my finger first just at the anal opening and then just inside. Willie was actually a little bit frightened by my finger going inside his anus and very properly informed me that it was beginning to hurt him ...

Three-year-old girl

I asked her if anybody touches her there and she stated, "Yeah." I asked her who and she stated, "Daddy." I asked her with what and she stated,

"Hand." I asked her with anything else and she stated, "Scissors and up to the head." I asked her if he hurt her any place else and specifically palpated the clitoris and she stated, "And here" as she then pointed to her clitoris. I then gently palpated the perianal (sic) area and inserted my finger into her rectum and asked her if somebody hurt her there. Again, she stated, "Daddy."

This technique is not accepted by other physicians. The general consensus is that intracavity probing should only be done when it is essential and may need to be performed under general anesthesia (Cantwell, 1983; Durfee, Heger & Woodling, 1986; Enos, Conrath, & Byer, 1986; Mathis, 1981; Paul, 1977; Woodling, 1986; Woodling & Kossoris, 1981; Woodling & Heger, 1986). Examinations such as those performed by Dr. Stearns can be painful and traumatic and may contribute to later sexual problems (Mathis, 1981). The reports by Dr. Stearns indicate that the children frequently complain that she is hurting them. In fact, she considers the elicitation of pain to be a central part of the technique in that she inserts her finger into the anus or vagina until it hurts asking if it hurt like that when Daddy did it.

There is no empirical data for the theory that if she pokes, hurts, or manipulates the genitals of young children she will elicit memories of others who have done this first. There is no theory of memory in psychology or psychiatry to support the use of this technique. The situation of sexual abuse most likely by a relative, in a familiar location, is not the same as being manipulated by a strange woman on an examination table.

BACKGROUND

Willie and Bobby Jones were removed from home following a call to the police after a neighbor had heard gun shots in the house. When the police officer arrived, he found the house chaotic and disorganized and no food in the house. The two boys were immediately taken from home and placed in a shelter.

When the police talked to the mother, Wanda, she reported that her husband, Frank Jones, had gotten drunk and threatened her with his gun, firing several shots at her picture on the wall. She stated that although he was a loving and supportive man when sober, he became irrational and erratic after he had been drinking. Wanda was an anxious woman who was afraid that she would not be able to take care of herself without Frank. She therefore stayed with him although he was sometimes violent and abusive.

The two boys were placed in an emergency shelter and then in a foster home. The foster mother found Willie (age three) and Bobby (age five) to be fearful and insecure. Bobby missed his mother and seemed to crave attention from adults. Willie, age three, was confused and made statements that showed a confabulation of fantasy and reality. He talked frequently about guns and made many statements such as, "Mom gave Bobby an earache with her gun," "My toy is broken, my Daddy shot it with a gun."

Their foster mother, Judy Black, was a loving and nurturant individual who gave the children a great deal of attention for talking about the parents. She hugged and kissed the children in response to their statements about the terrible things that had happened to them. Sometimes she cried as she held the children on her lap and promised them that these things would never occur again. The children were placed into therapy where they were also encouraged to talk about the bad things that had happened to them with their parents. The children were also tested and Bobby was found to be of borderline intelligence.

As time went on, the stories about what had taken place at home became more and more improbable. The accusations grew to include accounts of both children being hung on hooks in the garage all night, Bobby being cooked in a kettle of hot water so the parents could eat him, and both boys being forced to watch dogs and cats being shot and skinned. There were also statements about sexual abuse that included anal and vaginal penetration and defecating on their hands. Both Wanda and Frank were implicated in the accusations and several months after the children were removed from home, criminal charges were filed against each.

By the time Willie and Bobby were evaluated by Dr. Stearns, the foster mother had been reinforcing these stories for several months and they had completed several sessions of therapy. Dr. Stearns was given the history by the child protection worker and the foster mother who had originally reported the statements. At the time of her interview, the children had been away from home for almost a year.

Bobby said little in response to the questions about physical and sexual abuse. Dr. Stearns asked many questions, but Bobby appeared confused and said nothing clearly indicating abuse. He frequently responded, "I don't know." Dr. Stearns concluded that he had not been able to describe what had happened because he had suppressed information regarding his experiences.

The interview with Willie is included here. In this instance Dr. Stearns did not turn off the video recorder during the physical examination while using her method of reabusing children. The videotape demonstrates the reality of the descriptions contained in the written reports. In the interview, Willie repeats the statements about sexual abuse in response to Dr. Stearns' leading questions. His statements are confused. For example, when asked if his Dad's penis had touched him someplace else, he answers, "With a gun. . . . with fire and it killed me." In the physical part of the examination, despite promises from Dr. Stearns that she wouldn't hurt him, he says twice that she is hurting him.

A large portion of this interview consisted of Dr. Stearns getting acquainted with Willie, hence much of the interview was rated as irrelevant, unscoreable, or ambiguous. But over half (57%) of the total interviewer behaviors fell into the error-inducing categories.

INTERVIEW

Interviewer: Dr. Anna Stearns

Child: Willie Jones

Doctor: . . . in that blue chair right there?[10]

Willie: Yeah.[G]

Doctor: Can you do that?[10] Good.[5] I'll just check things here and make sure they're okay.[10]

Willie: What's these?[F, D2]

Doctor: Well . . . [8]

Willie: A glove.[D2]

Doctor: It is a glove.[6C] You're very smart.[5] Looks like a glove doesn't it?[6C, 2A]

Willie: Yeah.[D2] Ta-da.[D2]

Doctor:	Ta-da is right.[5] What kind of a glove do you think it is?[1A]
Willie:	(garbled)[G] What's this?[F, D2]
Doctor:	(makes noise)[10]
Willie:	That's you?[F, D2]
Doctor:	Yeah, that's me.[6C]
Willie:	Right here?[F, D2]
Doctor:	That's me, and that's me, too.[6C] That's my little girl.[6C] Now what would you like to do first, Willie?[1A] We should focus— should we eat the graham cracker first . . . [6C, 2A]
Willie:	Yeah.[G]
Doctor:	. . . open it?[6C, 2A] Okay.[8] And maybe while you have a little snack you can talk to me a little bit about who you are 'cause I don't even know you. Would you like it broken in half or do you want a big one like that?[6C, 3A]
Willie:	A big one.[D2]
Doctor:	Okay.[8] This one is going to break pretty soon, I can just see there's a big crack in it right there.[6C] So, you're name is Willie and what's your last name?[1A]
Willie:	Jones.[C]
Doctor:	Willie Jones.[9] Okay.[8] And how old are you, Willie?[1A]
Willie:	Three.[C]
Doctor:	Three.[9] And I remember that you're almost going to be four pretty soon, aren't you?[2B]
Willie:	Yeah.[A1]
Doctor:	You're going to be four right around Halloween time.[9]
Willie:	(nods head) Hm hmm.[A1]
Doctor:	When it gets to be Halloween.[9] Do you remember about Halloween?[2A]
Willie:	I got a pumpkin like my other school.[D2]

Doctor: So you're making pumpkins for Halloween?[6C, 2A]

Willie: (nods head)[G]

Doctor: Uh huh.[9] Do you think you're going to have a costume— are you going to dress up like a, like a um, you going to be a ghost or a witch or a cowboy?[6C, 2A] Do you dress up like something?[6C, 2A]

Willie: Um.[G] A witch.[D2]

Doctor: Uh huh, you like to dress up like a witch.[9] What does a witch look like?[1A, 6C]

Willie: Monster.[D2]

Doctor: Monster.[9] Do they have black, do they have black hats on and black clothes?[2B, 6C] Uh huh.[8]

Willie: Yes.[D2]

Doctor: And they're scary?[2B, 6C]

Willie: (nods head)[G]

Doctor: Uh huh.[8]

Willie: When it's Halloween I will be a girl.[D2]

Doctor: Well, you could be a girl.[6C]

Willie: Yeah.[D2]

Doctor: Whose clothes would you wear if you were a girl?[1A, 6C]

Willie: I don't know.[D3, D2]

Doctor: You could dress . . . [8]

Willie: Huh![D2]

Doctor: That one is breaking, I knew that.[10] You could dress up in, um, your mom's clothes.[6C]

Willie: (shakes head)[D2]

Doctor: No.[9] Don't want to do that.[9]

Willie: No.[D2]

Doctor: No.[9] Okay.[8]

Willie: That's, that's . . . like, what, yuck.[D2] That looks yucky.[D2]

Doctor: Mom's clothes do?[6C, 2A]

Willie: (nods head)[D2]

Doctor: It wouldn't be as fun, though.[6C]

Willie: No.[D2]

Doctor: Maybe Judy will have some good ideas for you.[6C] You think she might help you figure out a costume?[6C, 2A]

Willie: (nods head)[D2]

Doctor: And then you can wear it to school?[6C, 2A]

Willie: (nods head)[D2]

Doctor: Do you go to school some days?[2A]

Willie: Maybe I will be . . . a witch![D2]

Doctor: You like that witch one, that's a scary one for you, I think.[6C] Okay.[8] Where do you sleep at Judy's house?[1A]

Willie: Hmm?[F]

Doctor: Where do you sleep at Judy's house?[1A]

Willie: (garbled)[G]

Doctor: In your room?[2B, 9]

Willie: Yeah.[A1]

Doctor: Does somebody else sleep in your room, too?[2B]

Willie: Yeah.[A1] Bobby.[C]

Doctor: Uh huh.[8] Anybody else?[2A]

Willie: Nope.[B1]

Doctor: Where does Amy sleep?[1A]

Willie: With Keith.[C]

Doctor: With Keith?[9, 2A]

Willie: In the baby room.[C]

Doctor: In the baby room?[2A, 4]

Willie: With games and toys.[C]

Doctor: Uh huh, uh huh.[8] Does she have a crib?[2A]

Willie: (nods head)[B1]

Doctor: Yeah.[9] And who is Keith?[1A] Is that, is he a baby?[2B]

Willie: Uh huh.[A1] That's my baby.[C]

Doctor: Uh huh.[8] I think Judy told me that there's two babies about ten months old, littler, littler than um, than you, hmm?[2B, 6A] That baby . . . [8]

Willie: (garbled) there isn't nobody ten.[C]

Doctor: Ten, ten months?[2B] Does, does . . . [8]

Willie: No, no Scotty is ten.[D2]

Doctor: Scotty is ten years old, yeah.[9] Does Keith walk?[2A]

Willie: Did she, did she came here before?[F]

Doctor: No, Judy was just telling me about her.[8] Where does Tommy sleep?[1A]

Willie: Upstairs.[C]

Doctor: Uh huh.[9] And where, and is the other boy Joe?[2B, 6A]

Willie: No.[B1]

Doctor: Who's the other big boy that um, that Judy has?[1A]

Willie: (Pause) John.[C]

Doctor: John.[9] That's the dad, right?[2B]

Willie: Yeah.[A1]

Doctor: Where does he sleep?[1A]

Willie: Um.[G] In the porch.[C]

Doctor: On the porch.[9] Where does Judy sleep?[1A]

Willie: In the porch, too.[C]

Doctor: Ohh, I see, uh huh.[9] Okay.[8] And isn't there another boy, is there another boy who goes to school?[2B]

Willie: I do.[C]

Doctor: Uh huh.[8] And there is another boy who goes to school there?[2B]

Willie: Know what my school's named?[F]

Doctor: What?[1A]

Willie: Happy Tots.[C]

Doctor: Happy Tots, well, that's a good place to go.[5] And do you like that?[2A]

Willie: (nods head)[A1]

Doctor: You are wonderful, you know.[5] Are you nice to your teacher?[2A]

Willie: Yes.[A1]

Doctor: Do you help?[2A]

Willie: Yeah.[A1]

Doctor: Good.[5]

Willie: I helped my teacher put pumpkins up in the sky.[C]

Doctor: Ohh, isn't that nice, uh huh?[5] How about a little drink here, do you need a little drink before we have our . . . [5]

Willie: (nods head)[G]

Doctor: Okay.[8] Now you having a good time living at Judy's house?[2A]

Willie: (nods head) My eyes are getting water.[D2]

Doctor: What made the eyes water do you think?[1A, 6C]

Willie: When I'm drinking pop.[D2]

Doctor: When you're drinking pop 'cause the bubbles were tickling you.[6C]

Willie: Yes.[D2]

Doctor: Would you like to wipe them with a Kleenex® if they have a a little bit of tears in them?[10] Are those different kind of tears than when you cry?[2A]

Willie: No.[B1]

Doctor: Is there, sometimes do you get eyes, do you get tears in yours eyes when you cry?[2A]

Willie: Yes.[A1]

Doctor: And they're the same kind of tears, aren't they?[2B]

Willie: When Bobby, when Bobby hits me, I do this (screams).[C]

Doctor: Ohh.[8]

Willie: (Makes noise) And . . . [D2]

Doctor: What other things make you cry?[1A]

Willie: And I hit the pillow and Mommy's going to get one down in the office and I can hit a brown one.[C]

Doctor: So you can hit a pillow, that's nice.[9, 5]

Willie: Yeah, when I'm mad.[A2]

Doctor: When you're mad, yeah.[9] You can hit a pillow, 'cause then that doesn't hurt anybody, does it?[2A] Nobody's (garbled).[8] Good.[5] Tell me about what makes you cry.[4] Do you get sad about things sometimes?[2B]

Willie: Where's . . . we better brush this off.[D2]

Doctor: Should we do that?[10] I'm pretty good at doing that.[10] Oh.[8]
    (Pause)
    That pretty good do you think?[10]

Willie: Yeah.[G]

Doctor: Okay, good.[5] I'm glad that you were so neat and worry about it.[5] I'll put it in the wastebasket over here.[10] There.[10] Good job.[5] You know what we need to do?[2A] We need to talk a little about — who, who washes your hair?[4, 1A]

Willie: My mom and dad.[C]

| Doctor: | John and Judy do?[2A, 9] |
| Willie: | (nods head)[A1] |

| Doctor: | Before you lived with John and Judy, do you . . . [8] |
| Willie: | In the shower.[C] |

| Doctor: | In the shower?[2A, 9] How do you like that?[1A] Do you like showers?[2A] |
| Willie: | What's this?[F, D2] |

| Doctor: | It's a bed to lay down on when you need to be laying down.[10] |
| Willie: | Be sick?[F–D2] |

| Doctor: | Hm hmm, if you get a tummy ache or when you get sick or something, yeah.[10] |
| Willie: | What's this?[F, D2] |

| Doctor: | We're going to—that's a little monster, but he doesn't work.[6C] You can take him out.[6C] I'm going to ask you a couple questions, okay?[2A, 4] |
| Willie: | Does this one?[F, D2] |

| Doctor: | Nope, neither one of them work (garbled).[6C] |
| Willie: | This one does.[D2, E2] |

| Doctor: | Does it?[6C, 2A] It's supposed to but it doesn't.[6C] It's all broken.[6C] |
| Willie: | (Playing with toy) Rargh.[E2, D2] |

| Doctor: | I'm going to ask you some questions about this.[4, 7] This is a picture of little boy.[6A, 7] Can you see that picture?[2A, 7] |
| Willie: | Yeah.[A1] |

| Doctor: | Okay.[8] Can you tell me the different names of him?[2A, 7] What are these here?[1A, 7] |
| Willie: | Eyes.[C] |

| Doctor: | And what's that there?[1A, 7] |
| Willie: | Nose.[C] |

Doctor: What's that?[1A, 7]

Willie: Mouth.[C]

Doctor: What are these here?[1A, 7]

Willie: Nipples.[C]

Doctor: Nipples, okay.[9, 7] What's that?[1A, 7]

Willie: Belly button.[C]

Doctor: What's this?[1A, 7]

Willie: Um, penises.[C]

Doctor: Penises?[2A, 9, 7] Good.[5] And what's is this back here?[1A, 7]

Willie: A bottom.[C]

Doctor: A bottom.[9] Okay.[8] Now, here, I'm going to show you a little girl here.[7, 6A] No, that's a little boy yet.[7] Here we got a little girl.[7, 6A] Okay.[8] Now this little girl's got rosy cheeks, doesn't she, because we drew those.[7] What do you call this down here on a little girl?[1A, 7]

Willie: Vagina.[C]

Doctor: Vagina.[9] Right.[5] You're learning her about all those names, aren't you?[2A, 5, 7] Learning (garbled)[8]

Willie: I'm want to try this.[F] This first.[F] Huh![D2] Mirror![D2] What's this?[F, D2] I want to try something else.[F]

Doctor: Well, I think I'd like to finish my questions first.[4] I know you'd like to play, but let's just get the questions done first.[4] Okay.[8] Can you help me first with this?[2A, 4] We still have a few crumbs here, can you push the crumbs away?[10]

Willie: Yeah.[G]

Doctor: Who has, who has vagina here like, like that?[1A, 7]

Willie: Amy.[C]

Doctor: Okay, who else has one like that?[1A, 7]

Willie: Mom.[C]

Doctor: Okay.[8] Which Mom?[1A, 7]

Willie: Judy.[C]

Doctor: Okay.[8] And who has, who has a penis like that?[1A, 7]

Willie: Me![C]

Doctor: Okay, and who else?[1A, 7]

Willie: (garbled) A girl?[F]

Doctor: Well, does, does Keith have one like that?[2B, 7]

Willie: (nods head)[A1]

Doctor: Uh huh.[9] Who else has one like that?[1A, 7]

Willie: What's that up there?[F]

Doctor: That's to test your hearing.[6C] Who has one like this?[1A, 7]

Willie: My dad.[C]

Doctor: Which dad?[1A, 7]

Willie: John.[C]

Doctor: Who else has one like that?[1A, 7]

Willie: I do not . . . [G]

Doctor: How about your dad, does your dad Frank have one like that?[2B, 7]

Willie: Uh, turn it over![F, D1, E1] Icky![D1, E1]

Doctor: Icky?[2A, 9] You don't like that?[2A] I was going to ask you a couple questions about it first (garbled) can you do that?[4, 2A] Does your daddy, does your other daddy have one like that?[2A, 7]

Willie: I'm a alligator![D1, D2, E2]

Doctor: Willie.[4]

Willie: Hmm?[F] It's kind of scary.[C]

Doctor: What's kind of scary?[1A]

Willie: When I'm talking.[C]

Doctor: Well, can we talk a little bit about what's kind of scary 'cause I didn't get to talk to anybody about that yet and I thought maybe we could talk just a little bit about one, what happens with, with, with that?[4]

Willie: What's that over there, that white thing?[F, D2]

Doctor: That white horse?[6C, 2A]

Willie: Yeah.[D2]

Doctor: That's a unicorn and I promise we can play with that in just a minute, okay, . . . [5, 6C]

Willie: Okay.[G]

Doctor: . . . but let's get just a couple more questions answered.[4] Could you tell me just a little bit about the kind of scary stuff?[4, 2A] What happens?[1A] Willie, look at me for a minute.[4] It's important that you tell me just a little bit about what happens, okay?[4, 2B]

Willie: Okay.[G]

Doctor: What was happening?[1A]

Willie: You play with this.[D2, D1]

Doctor: Hm hmm.[8] Hm hmm.[8] What was happening that was kind of scary?[1A]

Willie: What's this kind of glove?[D2, D1, F]

Doctor: It's one that's made out of a glove and let's put him back in his, in his (garbled).[6C]

Willie: Can we put our hand in there?[D2, F]

Doctor: No, it's, you can't put your hand in that any more because it's already stuffed with cotton and made into doggies.[6C] Not like a puppet.[6C] It's not like a puppet.[6C]

Willie: But Nancy does.[D2]

Doctor: Does she?[2A, 6C]

Willie: Yeah.[D2]

Doctor: Willie?[4, 2A]

Willie: Hm?[F]

Doctor: For a minute I'd just like if we could just to talk about this.[4] When I showed you this picture of a big man's peepee, uh, penis, and it asked you what it did, you said that things were kind of scary about that . . . [9, 6A]

Willie: My dad put my, his penis right back here (rubbing his behind).[C]

Doctor: Right back where?[1A] Can you show me the place where it went?[4, 2A]

Willie: (Rubbing his behind) This one.[C]

Doctor: Is that back by where you go poopee?[2B]

Willie: Yeah.[A1]

Doctor: How did that feel?[1A]

Willie: (No answer)[G]

Doctor: How did it make you feel?[1A]

Willie: It hurt.[C]

Doctor: It hurt?[2A, 9]

Willie: Yeah.[A1]

Doctor: What part hurt?[1A]

Willie: Hm?[F]

Doctor: What part hurt?[1A] Tell me.[4]

Willie: This . . . [C]

Doctor: Hm.[8]

Willie: . . . this part hurt (rubbing his behind).[C]

Doctor: Did it ever bleed?[2A]

Willie: Yes.[A1]

Doctor: Hmm, okay.[8] Can you tell me a little bit more about that?[2A, 9]

Willie: (shakes head) I can't.[D1]

Doctor: Okay.[8] Did this part here on, on Daddy, on your other daddy touch you someplace else?[2B]

Willie: Yeah.[A1]

Doctor: Where?[1A]

Willie: With a gun.[C]

Doctor: With a gun?[2A, 9]

Willie: Yes.[A1] With fire and it killed me.[C]

Doctor: (garbled, mumbling)[8]

Willie: What's that black thing up there?[F–D1]

Doctor: That's a camera.[10] Will show you that afterward.[5] We got two things, I'm going to write down that we promised Willie we'll show him the unicorn and we'll show him the camera when we're done, okay?[5, 2A] I, I promise that but we got to finish asking our questions Okay.[5, 4] Well, we're just about done asking questions.[5] Let's talk back about this thing, it's called a penis again, and we're talking about your other daddy, what's that other daddy's name?[4, 1A, 7] Who did that?[1A]

Willie: Frank Jones.[C]

Doctor: Frank Jones?[2A, 9] Okay.[8] I didn't remember his name.[8] Is that the same as your, as, no, it's not the same as your name, you're Willie Jones, right?[2B]

Willie: At summer school that's Frank.[C]

Doctor: Okay.[8]

Willie: That Frank wasn't coming to me.[C]

Doctor: He wasn't?[2A, 9] Okay.[8] What happened with, with that other, that other daddy's penis?[1A] What else happened?[1B]

Willie: He didn't anymore ows.[C]

Doctor: He didn't any more ows?[2A, 9]

Willie: No.[B1]

Doctor: Okay.[8] Did something happen to your mouth, with it?[2B, 6A]

Willie:	He put his penis in my mouth and he pottied in it.[C]
Doctor:	He pottied where?[1A]
Willie:	In my mouth.[C]
Doctor:	Can you show me about where it went, the penis?[2A, 4] Show me where it went.[4]
Willie:	(touching his mouth) In here.[C]
Doctor:	How far in there?[1A]
Willie:	Back down here (gestures at his entire body).[C]
Doctor:	Can I see down (?), show me how far it went?[3A, 4]
Willie:	(opens his mouth widely)[C]
Doctor:	And can you show me with your finger how far you remember the penis going?[2A, 4]
Willie:	(points into his mouth) Here.[C]
Doctor:	So it was kind of way, way back there, huh?[2A, 9]
Willie:	Yeah.[A1]
Doctor:	When he pottied in your mouth, what did you do with it?[1A]
Willie:	The batteries are in there?[F, D1]
Doctor:	No, the batteries . . . it's, it's just a broken wind-up toys, honey, it doesn't have batteries.[6C]
Willie:	Why?[F]
Doctor:	Broken 'cause we had him walk too much.[6C] I can show you how it's supposed to wind up but then it kind of just flips.[6C] See, you're supposed to do this.[6C]
Willie:	You can see if he walks (?).[D2]
Doctor:	(Sets toy on the desk. It hops and falls over.)[6C]
Willie:	(shouting) Yeah![D2]

Doctor: See, he tries to walk then he flips.[6C] He gets stuck.[6C] I think he's just broken.[6C] He used to be a nice toy, I think I'm going to buy another one like that, so if you come back and see me there'll be a different one.[6C] So let's just, let's just set him over there.[6C] Do you remember when he pottied, Willie, look at me for just a minute, when, when he pottied in your mouth, what did you do with the potty?[1A, 4]

Willie: Spit it in the sink what's that black thing right there?[F, C]

Doctor: That's a black thing is a microphone that, that, that plays, that's there so it can hear us talking.[10]

Willie: Want to hear it.[F]

Doctor: You can't hear it.[10] It's going to hear us.[10] It sits there and just hears us.[10] I'll show you that, too.[5]

Willie: Okay.[G]

Doctor: Okay.[8] Anything else that got hurt?[2A]
Willie: No.[B1]

Doctor: How about Mom?[1A] Did Mom, did Mom do anything that was, that was wrong to you?[2B]

Willie: (No answer)[G]

Doctor: Hmm?[1A]
Willie: We can kind of do this with. (referring to broken toy)[D2, D1]

Doctor: Kind of do that with . . . [6C]
Willie: Make it flip.[D2] See, that doesn't work.[D2]

Doctor: So, that, the other things we were talking about, was your, your, was about your, your daddy Frank, Frank Jones?[2A]

Willie: (no answer—banging toy on desk)[D1, D2]

Doctor: Willie?[4, 2A] Should we put that away?[4, 2A] I'll put this away.[4] You were (garbled) weren't you?[2B] I'll put that, I'll put this picture away because you didn't like it.[5] Should I put this one away, too?[5, 2A]

Willie: Yeah, and I don't like this one either.[F]

Doctor:	Okay.[8]
Willie:	I want to try this.[F, D1]
Doctor:	I don't think (garbled—microphone is getting pulled around) it can't, that just hears us talking, honey, that's what it does, it just hears us talking.[10] So we have to be quiet with it or it makes noise for people.[10] They can hear us when we're talking.[10]
Willie:	I want to try that camera.[F, D1]
Doctor:	We will try the camera, okay?[2A, 5] Do you remember . . . [1A]
Willie:	Hm?[F]
Doctor:	. . . anything else Mommy Wanda did?[2A]
Willie:	Nothing else.[B1]
Doctor:	Did we talk about anything?[2A]
Willie:	Yes.[A1] Nothing else they didn't do.[C] I want to try the camera.[F, D1]
Doctor:	Okay.[8] Well, maybe, maybe that's really all we have to do right now and then we'll . . . how about, how about your penis, did your penis ever get hurt?[2B] You told me that your, that your place where you go poopee got touched, but did your penis ever get hurt?[9, 2B]
Willie:	My dad didn't (?) put his penis inside of the bones here (gesturing towards his crotch).[C]
Doctor:	Inside of the bones there?[2A, 9]
Willie:	Yeah.[A1]
Doctor:	Did he ever do anything to your penis?[2B]
Willie:	Yeah.[A1]
Doctor:	What?[1A]
Willie:	He didn't put his penis inside.[C]
Doctor:	Okay.[8] Okay.[8] Well, you know what, I think we may need to (garbled) I need to show you.[10] We're going to do a check-up and I need to show you what we're going to use to check you, okay?[2A, 4]

Willie: Why need a check-up?[F]

Doctor: Well, we're going to need a very special machine to do a check-up.[10, 4]

[Interviewer off camera.]

Willie: Okay.[G]

Doctor: See this check-up machine right here?[2A]

Willie: What's that kind?[F]

Doctor: Well, it's going to, it's going to make our, our check-up that we look at big.[10] You want to look at those pictures first?[2A] That's what it does, it makes everything look very big.[F]

Willie: Hm.[G]

Doctor: Have you ever seen a machine like that?[2A]

Willie: No.[B1]

Doctor: No.[9] Okay.[8]

Willie: It'll hurt me.[E1]

Doctor: No, it doesn't hurt.[5] See, this turns on the light.[10] That's what I was going to show it to you, I was going to have you look at one of those monsters.[10] Here's another monster here, let's look at both the monsters and you can see them.[10] If we put the light on them right here, Willie, then you can come see them.[10] Come over here by my eye, see where my eye is?[2A] Can find my eye.[10]

Willie: Yep.[G] See if it works that way, okay?[F]

Doctor: Come over and stand over here, yeah.[10]

Willie: Let's see it.[F]

Doctor: Are you big enough, or do I have to, I think I may have to hold you on my knee.[10] Because you're not quite big enough to look through the light.[10] Let's put these together like that and put your eyes over there.[10] What do you see?[1A]

Willie: A monster![C]

Doctor:	Right.[5] That's a monster.[9] Okay.[8] Now look, the machine takes a picture of the monster and then it gets big, just like that.[10]
Willie:	Want to try this one.[F]
Doctor:	Want to try that one?[2A, 9] Should we put this one under there?[2A] Okay.[8]
Willie:	Put that one . . . [F]
Doctor:	And remember I told you I would show you that unicorn back there?[2A, 4] We can, we can show you the unicorn, and I'll show you what his eye looks like because unicorn, you can help take care of his eye, he has kind of a sore eye.[10] Is that pretty good?[2A]
Willie:	Yeah.[A1]
Doctor:	Okay.[8] Good.[5]
Willie:	Okay, another one.[F]
Doctor:	Let's see if it can be the unicorn now.[10] Here, have you ever seen this before?[2A]
Willie:	No, let me see that one.[F]
Doctor:	That's the unicorn's eye and he's got a little scratch on it so we need to fix it.[10] So I'll bring him over and put him on the blue chair.[10]
Willie:	Okay.[G]
Doctor:	(garbled)[10]
Willie:	What's this part?[F]
Doctor:	This part over here.[9] There, now have you seen that kind of a horsie before with a horn on his face?[2A]
Willie:	No.[B1]
Doctor:	Okay.[8] Now we need to . . . [8]
Willie:	(garbled)[G]
Doctor:	. . . yeah, we need to, to . . . [8]
Willie:	What's this?[F]

Doctor: That's just where the light comes out of.[10] It's a light bulb in there.[10] Okay.[8] Now, come over here, Willie, I'll show you again.[10]

Willie: What's . . . [F]

Doctor: We're looking at—[8]

Willie: . . . what's this thing?[F]

Doctor: We're looking at, at the bright, the bright um, marble eye, remember, it looks like a marble.[10] Does it have a scratch on it, do you think?[2A]

Willie: (no answer)[G]

Doctor: Hmm?[2A] I think maybe he does.[10]

Willie: (no answer)[G]

Doctor: Would you like to fix him, put some medicine on his eye?[2A]

Willie: Yeah.[G]

Doctor: You have to be very careful though.[10] Over here in this drawer we have some medicine.[10]

[Both off camera.]

Willie: Okay.[G] This kind of medicine.[C]

Doctor: And here is the thing that you put the medicine on with and this kind of medicine, right.[10] Okay.[8]

Willie: Okay.[G] Going to put medicine on his eye.[C]

Doctor: Okay.[8]

[Both on camera.]

Willie: I'm going to try.[C]

Doctor: I'll show you how to do it.[10] Leave it there.[10] Here, I'll show you how to do it.[10]

Willie: Okay.[8] I can.[C]

Doctor:	You're going to do it.[9]
Willie:	I can.[C]
Doctor:	You're going to do it, okay.[9] Very carefully just peel it like a doctor and take one of those sticks out.[10] Then there's a very soft, see how soft that is?[2A]
Willie:	Uh huh.[A1]
Doctor:	Cotton thing on the end.[9] If you put the cotton thing in the medicine, then you can get some medicine on it.[10] Put it in there.[10] Good.[5] Now would you like to put that medicine on, on the eye?[2A]
Willie:	Yeah.[G]
Doctor:	Good.[5]
Willie:	And rub it around?[F]
Doctor:	Hmm.[8]
Willie:	With my finger?[F]
Doctor:	Right.[5]
Willie:	I can't do it with it.[G]
Doctor:	Okay, you can do it, you can do it with either the Q-tip or your finger, doesn't matter.[10] You want to put a little more on?[2A] Or do you have enough, do you think?[2A]
Willie:	(Pause) We don't have enough.[G]
Doctor:	Then maybe when you're all done you can come and look at it.[10] See how you put that on.[10] It's all real wet looking.[10] You want to look at it again now, see if you got it right on the spot?[2A] Got to look at it up on my lap, remember?[2A]
Willie:	Will you wash this off?[F]
Doctor:	You know what we can do?[2A, 6C] We can take a Kleenex®, oops, and wipe it.[6C]
Willie:	Yeah.[G]

Doctor: You're a very good helper.[5] I think you'd like to maybe be a doctor, would you like to be a doctor someday?[2A, 5] Do you see it cover the scratch?[2A]

Willie: Yeah.[D2]

Doctor: It's nice and wet.[10] Hm hmm.[8] Good.[5] Well, that's what that machine does, it takes care of things.[10] Now, let me explain what we're going to do.[10]

Willie: Okay.[G]

Doctor: We're going to take this machine and look for a minute to look at your bottom.[4] Remember, remember where Daddy got, where you got touched by Daddy's penis?[2A]

Willie: Yeah.[A1]

Doctor: I want to see if there's any kind of an owee made from that, okay?[4, 2A] And the bottom will just look, or the light will just look.[6A, 4] It won't hurt.[6A, 4] Okay?[2A, 4]

Willie: Okay.[G]

Doctor: Now, let's do that up here on the table.[10] Want to stand up for just a minute?[10]

[Both are off camera. This next part is off camera while the child is on the examination table.]

Willie: Yeah.[G]

Doctor: Okay.[8] And then, we'll put this on.[10]

Willie: Why?[F]

Doctor: This is, it's called a doctor's, a doctor's dress or a doctor's gown and, we can put this away over here, too, and the reason for that is it covers you up while we take your pants down just for a minute, okay?[10, 2A, 4]

Willie: Okay.[8] For a few minutes?[F]

Doctor: Just for a few minutes, yep.[5] Looks to me that you got a, um, a snap, then a zipper, right?[10]

Willie: We don't take our underwear down.[D1]

Doctor: Well, in order to see the butt with the, with the machine, we do have to take your underwear down just for a minute.[10, 4]

Willie: Okay.[G]

Doctor: Do this right like that?[1A] That's it (garbled) . . . rrrrk.[8] In there.[8] And I think probably you'll have to take, oh, you have fancy socks.[5]

Willie: Yeah.[G]

Doctor: Um, who, who bought you those?[6C, 1A] Did . . . [8]

Willie: Judy.[D2]

Doctor: Did Judy buy those?[6C, 2A, 9] I thought she might.[5] Okay.[8] We'll put the machine light back on and I'm bigger than you, so I have to put it back up again.[10] Right now, you see us looking at you, right at that dress there, isn't it?[10] How about if you lie down, can you lie down on that pillow for me?[2A, 4] Willie, can you lie down on that pillow?[2A, 4] Good.[5]

Willie: Yeah.[G]

Doctor: Just lie down.[4] And I'll pull you just a little closer.[10] Good.[5] And if you'll put your legs there and your legs there.[4] And I see what I think is Snoopy underpants, is that right?[6C, 2A] With Charlie Brown.[6C]

Willie: Yeah.[D2]

Doctor: Yeah.[8] Let's just take them off of one leg.[10] You can leave them on that one so we don't lose them and we'll just put them over there like that.[10] Now.[8] Okay, now we're just going to have you draw your legs up a little bit more like that.[4] And we'll look here.[4] And I will need you to help me.[4] Will you push that button right there when I tell you to?[2A, 4] And that just flashes the light, just like it . . . [10]

Willie: Yeah, that one (garbled).[D2] Can I now?[F]

Doctor: Yeah, I think go ahead and push it.[10] Hold still though when you do it.[10]

Willie: (Pushes button)[G]

Doctor: Good.[5] Okay, one more time, I'm just going to hold it up.[10]

Willie: Okay.[G]

Doctor: I'm going to hold it up like that.[10]
Willie: Okay.[G]

Doctor: I'll try to, I'll try to open it a little bit, but you wait for me, you wait for me with that.[4]
Willie: Now can I?[F]

Doctor: Not quite.[10]
Willie: Okay.[G] (Pause) Now can I?[F]

Doctor: Uh huh.[8] Go ahead.[10]
Willie: (Pushes button)[G]

Doctor: Okay, I think I need to do that one more time.[10] Because I'm looking and I think I see a very tiny little scratch at, at about 11 o'clock.[9] (Pause) Think I just felt it with my fingernail.[9] Well, it looks pretty, pretty good . . . does that hurt when I . . . [2A]

Willie: Can I push it?[F]

Doctor: Does that I hurt when I touch that?[2A]
Willie: Yeah.[A1]

Doctor: Then I'll be very gentle.[5] Get ready to push it.[10]
Willie: (Pushes button)[G]

Doctor: Whoops, you pushed a little too soon, wait . . . [10]
Willie: (Pushes button)[G]

Doctor: . . . just a minute.[10] Oh, can you wait for me?[2A] Don't push until I tell you, you're doing a good job but just wait.[5] Don't it now push until I tell you.[10] (Pause) Okay.[8]

Willie: Now can I?[F]

Doctor: You can push now, right.[10]
Willie: (Pushes button)[G]

Doctor:	Okay, just looks like a dilated vein there.[9] Okay.[8] Now, can you show me the spot that you remembered getting hurt?[2A, 4]
Willie:	(garbled)[G]
Doctor:	Can you just point to it?[2A, 4]
Willie:	This spot right there.[C]
Doctor:	How about if you lie back so I can tell what you're pointing, point to it again, honey, and then maybe, just point to it and then I can, the part that got hurt . . . [4]
Willie:	That one.[C]
Doctor:	So was it right in that spot there?[2A, 4]
Willie:	Yeah.[A1]
Doctor:	Okay.[8] I just need to check that for a minute.[10] By doing that I'm going to have to put on gloves so my fingers don't get dirty.[10] And sometimes I have to put a little bit of . . . have you seen a glove before?[2A, 6C]
Willie:	Not plastic gloves.[D2]
Doctor:	Not rubber ones, yeah, okay.[9, 8] You can look and look at that, if you want to put it on you can.[5, 6C]
Willie:	I just don't want to.[D1]
Doctor:	You just don't want to.[9]
Willie:	This hurts.[E1] This one.[E1]
Doctor:	No, it doesn't hurt.[6A, 4]
Willie:	Oh, (garbled).[G] You can blow it up, this one.[D2]
Doctor:	We did . . . yeah, we did, we blew one up for your brother.[6C] Now, just, I'm going to ask you a question and you just see if you can, just see if you can remember.[4] Do you remember it touching right there . . . [2A, 4]
Willie:	Can we blow this one up?[F, D1]
Doctor:	. . . Willie?[2A, 4]
Willie:	Yeah?[F]

Doctor: Just for, just for a minute look at me.[4] Do you remember getting touched right there?[2A, 4]

Willie: Yeah.[A1]

Doctor: What touched there?[1A, 4]

Willie: My dad.[C]

Doctor: Your dad?[2A, 9] And what part of your dad?[1A, 4]

Willie: (No answer)[G]

Doctor: What part of your dad touched there, honey?[1A, 4]

Willie: With a gun.[C]

Doctor: Hm hmm.[8] What about, do you remember if anything went inside like that?[2A, 6A, 4]

Willie: You're, you're a little bit hurting me.[E1]

Doctor: Okay, I won't hurt you, I promise, but wanted to know if you remembered.[4] Do you remember if anything went inside like that?[2B, 4, 6A]

Willie: Yeah.[A1]

Doctor: What went inside like that?[1A, 4]

Willie: The fire.[C]

Doctor: The fire?[2A, 9] Do you remember Daddy's, did Daddy's penis go inside like that?[2B, 4, 6A]

Willie: Yeah.[A1]

Doctor: Did it go up like that?[2B, 4, 6A]

Willie: You're hurting me.[E1]

Doctor: I won't, I won't do that anymore, we want to be very gentle about it.[5] Can I wipe it off a minute?[2A]

Willie: Yeah.[A1]

Doctor: Good.[5] Good.[5] Okay.[8]

Willie: Now ... [G]

Doctor:	Now ... [10]
Willie:	... will you blow this up?[F]
Doctor:	... uh huh, but can I ask again ... did anything play or do something naughty to that thing?[2B, 4, 6A]
Willie:	Yeah.[A1]
Doctor:	What did they do to that thing?[1A, 4]
Willie:	They put his penis in there.[C]
Doctor:	In there, too, huh?[2A, 9]
Willie:	Yeah.[A1]
Doctor:	Okay.[8] Can I just check it to see if it's okay?[2A, 4]
Willie:	Yeah.[A1] It is.[C]
Doctor:	It is.[9] Okay, you're right, it is.[5] Okay.[8] Then you want to sit up for a minute?[10] Okay.[8]
Willie:	Then I'm ... [G]

AFTERMATH

After reviewing the documents and tapes of this case, we wrote an affidavit for the attorney in support of his motion that we be allowed to evaluate the children. We also wanted to carefully interview both children in an effort to sort out truth, fantasy, and learned statements about what had happened. However, we realized that after almost a year away from home, countless conversations with a foster mother who was inadvertently reinforcing statements about abuse, several interviews by the therapist, and Dr. Stearns' evaluation, the children themselves probably believed that the events they described were true. The judge granted the motion for our psychological evaluation of Bobby and Willie.

However, the stories continued to grow and the boys were deemed not competent to testify and the charges were dropped. At this point, no one can tell just what happened. The dysfunctional nature of the Jones family most likely made these children particularly susceptible to developing implausible accounts of abuse. It becomes impossible to sort out any actual neglect or abuse from the confused and improbable stories of Willie and Bobby.

Frank Jones shot a gun in front of the children and behaved erratically and sometimes violently. This was clearly frightening and confusing to the children. But by the time the children went through multiple interviews with reinforcement for statements about bizarre events, it becomes impossible to sort out truth from fantasy. The only sexual touching that we know of for certain is that performed by Dr. Stearns.

CONCLUSION

Our hopes and our fears for this book may be summed up in a verse describing the current state of the foundations of mathematics.

Little by little we subtract
Faith and fallacy from fact,
The illusory from the true
And then starve upon the residue.

(Hoffenstein, cited in Kline, p. 241)

We want this book to help uncover needed facts to find a better way to respond to the abuse and exploitation of our children. The main criticism we make of the system that has emerged in response to child sexual abuse is that it has mixed in much faith and fallacy and a dearth of fact. We believe this has caused much harm to children, to adults, and to the family and has failed to protect children adequately. We fear an unintended consequence is that nonabused children are emotionally abused by the system that tries to protect them. We fear that abused children are missed in the press of too many cases. We fear the goal of aiding families is subverted and the end result is the destruction of families. We fear the justice system is producing such a quantity of injustice it may cause unforeseen damage to individuals and our society. We fear the usual bureaucratic response of throwing more money and more people to continue a flawed system may mean that it will get worse before inertia is overcome and real change begins.

We have presented the real world of the interrogations of children when there is an accusation of child sexual abuse. We hope this will help separate the illusory from the true. The truth is that some children are subjected to powerful adult social influence that may produce inaccurate accounts of nonevents. When adults give credence to falsehood the cause of children is neither well served nor properly understood. We are convinced this truth can be grasped and people of good will and noble persuasion can work together, not always in harmony but nevertheless

341

effectively, to build a world where children are nourished and are cared for.

The deepest tragedy of our human experience is the discovery that no amount of good will, good intentions, and purity of purpose alone can guarantee good outcomes. When we have cleared our path at least to some facts, we may, indeed, starve upon the residue for a time. A period of fasting may serve to clear our minds and focus our intents upon what is basic and true. Then we can begin anew to feed ourselves and our progeny with the strong meat of facts.

REFERENCES

Aman, C., & Goodman, G. S. (1987). *Children's use of anatomically detailed dolls: An experimental study.* Paper presented at the Symposium on Interviewing Children, Washington, DC.

AMA diagnostic and treatment guidelines concerning child abuse and neglect. (1985). *Journal of the American Medical Association, 254,* 796–800.

American Psychiatric Association (1987). *Diagnostic and statistical manual of mental disorders* (3rd Edition-Revised). Washington DC: Author.

American Psychological Association (1987). *Brief of amicus curiae in support of petitioner.* Kentucky v. Sergio Stincer, No. 86-572.

Aronson, E. (1988). *The social animal.* New York: Freeman & Company.

August, R., & Forman, B. (1986, May 16). *Differences between sexually and non-sexually abused children in their behavioral responses to anatomically correct dolls.* Paper presented at the Fourth National Conference on the Sexual Victimization of Children, New Orleans, LA.

Axline, V. M. (1969). *Play therapy.* New York: Ballantine Books.

Bandura, A., & Walters, R. H. (1963). *Social learning and personality development.* New York: Holt, Rineholt & Winston.

Bell, S. (1988, July 10). Chaos in Cleveland. *The London Times,* Section C.

Besharov, D. J. (1985a). Doing something about child abuse: The need to narrow the grounds for state intervention. *Harvard Journal of Law and Public Policy, 8,* 539–589.

Besharov, D. J. (1985b, November). Paper given at the VOCAL (Victims of Child Abuse Laws) National Convention, Minneapolis, MN.

Besharov, D. J. (1985c). Right versus rights: The dilemma of child protection. *Public Welfare,* Spring, 19–27.

Besharov, D. J. (1986). Unfounded allegations—a new child abuse problem. *The Public Interest,* Spring, 18–33.

Besharov, D. J. (1988). Introduction in D. J. Besharov (Ed.), *Protecting children from abuse and neglect* (pp 3–8). Springfield, Ill: CC Thomas.

Best, R. (1983). *We've all got scars.* Indianapolis, IN: Indiana University Press

Bloch, D. (1978). *So the witch won't eat me.* New York: Grove Press.

Boat, B. W., & Everson, M. D. (undated) *The anatomical doll project: An overview.* Department of Psychiatry, University of North Carolina, Chapel Hill, NC.

Borman, M., & Joseph, G. (1986). *Report from the Attorney General's task force on child abuse within the family.* St. Paul, MN: Attorney General's Office.

Breo, D. L. (1984, October 26). MDs: Improve diagnosis of child sexual abuse. *American Medical News.*

Buros, O. K. (1972). *The seventh mental measurements yearbook* (Vol 1). Highland Park, NJ: Gryphon Press.

Butler-Sloss, E. (1988, June 6). *Report of the inquiry into child abuse in Cleveland 1987.* Presented to Parliament by the Secretary of State for Social Services by Command of Her Majesty. London, England: Her Majesty's Stationery Office.

Cantwell, H. B. (1983). Vaginal inspection as it relates to child sexual abuse in girls under thirteen. *Child Abuse & Neglect, 7,* 171–176.

Ceci, S. J., Toglia. M. P. & Ross, D. F. (1987). (Eds.). *Children's eyewitness memory.* New York: Springer-Verlag.

Ceci, S. J., Ross, D. F., & Toglia, M. P. (1987). Age differences in suggestibility: Narrowing the uncertainties. In S. J. Ceci, M. P. Toglia, & D. F. Ross (Eds.), *Children's eyewitness memory* (pp. 36–52). New York: Springer-Verlag.

Charlier, T., & Downing, S. (1988, January). Justice abused: A 1980's witch-hunt. *The Commercial Appeal.* Memphis, TN (special offprint).

Christiansen, J. R. (1987). The testimony of child witnesses: Fact, fantasy, and the influence of pretrial interviews. *Washington Law Review, 62,* 705–721.

Cohen, A. (1985). The unreliability of expert testimony on the typical characteristics of sexual abuse victims. *Georgetown Law Journal, 74,* 429–456.

Cole, C. B., & Loftus, E. F. (1987). The memory of children. In S. J. Ceci, M. P. Toglia, & D. F. Ross (Eds.), *Children's eyewitness memory* (pp. 178–208). New York: Springer-Verlag.

Cott, J. (1983). *Pipers at the gates of dawn.* New York: McGraw-Hill.

Crane, D. (1972). *Invisible colleges: Diffusion of knowledge in scientific communities.* Chicago: University of Chicago Press.

DeLipsey, J. M., & James, S. K. (1988). Videotaping the sexually abused child: The Texas experience, 1983–1987. In S. M. Sgroi (Ed.), *Vulnerable populations: Volume I* (pp. 229–264). Lexington, MA: Lexington Books.

Dent, H. R., & Stephenson, G. M. (1979). An experimental study of the effectiveness of different techniques of questioning child witnesses. *British Journal of Social and Clinical Psychology, 18,* 41–51.

Dent, H. R. (1982). The effects of interviewing strategies on the results of interviews with child witnesses. In A. T. Trankell (Ed.), *Reconstructing the past* (pp. 279–298). Deventer, The Netherlands: Kluwer.

Derian, P. (1988, January 31). Embassy scandal was fiction: Navy's inquiry blundered. *Minneapolis Star Tribune,* p. 17A.

Diaz, K. (1987, September 9). Police expert warns of Satanism: Officers are told to watch for clues. *Minneapolis Star Tribune,* p. 1B, 7B.

DiLeo, J. H. (1973). *Children's drawings as diagnostic aids.* New York: Bruner/Mazel.

Dyer, C. (1988). Cleveland inquiry: Clarity out of confusion. *British Medical Journal, 297* (6642), 157.

Dunn, D. R. F. (1981). Dissemination of the published results of an important clinical trial: An analysis of the citing literature. *Bulletin of the Medical Library Association, 69,* 301–306.

Durfee, M., Heger, A., & Woodling, B. (1986). Medical examination. In K. McFarlane

& J. Waterman (Eds.), *Sexual abuse of young children* (pp. 52–66). New York: The Guilford Press.

Eagly, A. H. (1983). Gender and social influence: A social and psychological analysis. *American Psychologist, 38,* 971–981.

Economist (1989, January 7). p. 71–74.

Ellis, A., & Abarbanel, A. (1961). *The encyclopedia of sexual behavior.* New York: Hawthorn Books, Inc.

Emery, R. E. (1982). Interparental conflict and the children of discord and divorce. *Psychological Bulletin, 92,* 310–330.

Enos, W. F., Conrath, T. B. & Byer, J. C. (1986). Forensic evaluation of the sexually abused child. *Pediatrics, 78,* 385–398.

Enright, S. (1987). *New Law Journal, 137,* 633–634.

Erickson, W. D. (1985). Unpublished report.

Erickson, W. D. (1987). Unpublished report.

Erickson, W. D., Walbek, N. H., & Seely, R. K. (1988). Behavior patterns of child molesters. *Archives of Sexual Behavior, 17,* 77–86.

Festinger, L. Riecken, H. W. & Schachter, S. (1958). When prophecy fails. In E. E. Maccoby, T. M. Newcomb, & E. L. Hartley (Eds.), *Readings in social psychology: Third edition* (pp. 156–163). New York: Holt, Rinehart & Winston.

Finkelhor, D. (1984). *Child sexual abuse: New theory and research.* New York: The Free Press.

Finkelhor, D. (1986). *A sourcebook on child sexual abuse.* Beverly Hills, CA: Sage Publications.

Furby, L., Weinrott, M.R., & Blackshaw, L. (1989). Sex offender recidivism: A review. *Psychological Bulletin, 105,* 3–30.

Gabriel, R. M. (1985). Anatomically correct dolls in the diagnosis of sexual abuse of children. *The Journal of the Melanie Klein Society, 3* (2), 41–51.

Gage, A. (1989, April). Where does it hurt. *Minnesota Monthly, 23* (4), 38–44.

Garbarino, J. & Scott, F. (1988, August 15). *Adults as recipients of information from children.* Paper presented at the 96th Annual Convention of the American Psychological Association in Atlanta, GA.

Garfield, S. L., & Bergin, A. E. (1978). *Handbook of psychotherapy and behavior change.* New York: John Wiley & Sons.

Gebhard, P., Gagnon, J., Pomeroy, W., & Christenson, C. (1965). *Sex offenders.* New York: Harper and Row.

Goodman, G. S. (1984). Children's testimony in historical perspective. *Journal of Social Issues, 40* (2), 9–31.

Goodman, G. S., Aman, C., & Hirschman, J. (1987). Child sexual and physical abuse: Children's testimony. In S. J. Ceci, M. P. Toglia, & D. F. Ross (Eds.), *Children's eyewitness memory* (pp. 1–23). New York: Springer-Verlag.

Goodman, G. S., Hepps, D., & Reed, R. S. (1986). The child victim's testimony. In A. Haralambie (Ed.), *New issues for child advocates* (pp. 167–177). Phoenix, AZ: Arizona Association of Council for Children.

Goodman, G. S., & Reed, R. S. (1986). Age differences in eyewitness testimony. *Law and Human Behavior, 10,* 317–332.

Gundersen, B. H., Melas, P. S., & Skar, J. E. (1981). Sexual behavior in preschool children: Teachers' observations. In L. L. Constantine & F. M. Martinson (Eds.), *Children and sex: New findings, new perspectives* (pp. 45–51). Boston: Little, Brown & Company.

Harris, D.B. (1963). *Children's drawings as measures of intellectual maturity: A revision and extension of the Goodenough Draw a Man Test.* New York: Harcourt, Brace and World.

Hartman, C. R., & Burgess, A. W. (1988). Information processing of trauma: Case application of a model. *Journal of Interpersonal Violence, 3,* 443–457.

Hayes, M. (1987). Child sexual abuse and the civil courts. *Civil Justice Quarterly,* 9–16.

Herbert, C. P., Grams, G. D., & Goranson, S. E. (1987). *The use of anatomically detailed dolls in an investigative interview: A preliminary study of "non-abused" children.* Department of Family Practice, University of British Columbia, Vancouver, B.C.

Hughes, H. M., & Barad, S. J. (1983). Psychological functioning of children in a battered woman's shelter: A preliminary investigation. *American Journal of Orthopsychiatry, 53,* 525–531.

Hughes, M., & Grieve, R. (1983). On asking children bizarre questions. In M. Donaldson, R. Grieve, & C. Pratt (Eds.), *Early childhood development and education* (pp. 104–114). New York: The Guilford Press.

Humphrey, H. (1985). *Report on Scott County investigations.* St. Paul, MN: Attorney General's Office.

Jaffe, P., Wolfe, D., Wilson, S., & Zak, L. (1986). Similarities in behavioral and social maladjustment among child victims and witnesses to family violence. *American Journal of Orthopsychiatry, 56,* 142–146.

Jampole, L., & Weber, M. K. (1987). An assessment of the behavior of sexually abused and non-sexually abused children with anatomically correct dolls. *Child Abuse & Neglect, 11,* 187–194.

Jensen, J. B., Realmuto, G., & Wescoe, S. (1986, October). Paper presented at the American Academy of Child Psychiatry, Washington, DC.

Johnson, M. K., & Foley, M. A. (1984). Differentiating fact from fantasy: The reliability of children's memory. *Journal of Social Issues, 40* (2), 33–50.

Jones, E. M. (1985, February). Abuse abuse: The therapeutic state terrorizes parents in Jordan, Minnesota. *Fidelity,* pp. 28–33.

Karpman, B. (1954). *The sexual offender and his offences.* New York: Julian Press, Inc.

King, M. A., & Yuille, J. C. (1987). Suggestibility and the child witness. In S. J. Ceci, M. P. Toglia, & D. F. Ross (Eds.), *Children's eyewitness memory* (pp. 24–35). New York: Springer-Verlag.

Kinsey, A., Pomeroy, W., Martin, C. & Gebhard, P. (1953). *Sexual behavior in the human female.* Philadelphia: W. B. Saunders.

Klein, R. (1986). *In re* Hawaii vs. McKellar, Criminal No. 85-0553. (Circuit Court, First Circuit Hawaii), Order Granting Defense's Motion, Jan. 15, 1986.

Kline, M. (1980). *Mathematics.* New York: Oxford University Press.

Kobasigawa, A. (1974). Utilization of retrieval cues by children in recall. *Child Development, 45,* 127–134.

Koppitz, E. M. (1968). *Psychological evaluation of children's human figure drawings.* New York: Grune and Stratton.

Landers, S. (1988). Use of "detailed dolls" questioned. *APA Monitor, 19,* 24–25.

Langevin H. (1983). *Sexual strands.* Hillsdale, NJ: Lawrence Erlbaum.

Law Week (1987, May 26). Techniques used to diagnose child sexual abuse held subject to Frye Test.

Lipton, J. P. (1977). On the psychology of eyewitness testimony. *Journal of Applied Psychology, 62,* 90–95.

Lipton, J. P., & Hershaft, A. M. (1985). On the widespread acceptance of dubious medical findings. *Journal of Health and Social Behavior, 26,* 336–351.

Loftus, E. F. (1979). *Eyewitness testimony.* Cambridge, MA: Harvard University.

Loftus, E. F., & Davies, G. M. (1984). Distortions in the memory of children. *Journal of Social Issues, 40,* 51–67.

The London Times (1988, July 10). Cleveland's cry of pain. p. B2.

Lord, C., Ross, L., & Lepper, M. (1979). Biased assimilation and attitude polarization: The effect of prior theory on subsequently considered evidence. *Journal of Personality and Social Psychology, 37,* 2098–2109.

Lusk, R., & Waterman, J. (1986). Effects of sexual abuse of children. In K. McFarlane & J. Waterman, *Sexual abuse of young children* (pp. 101–118). New York: The Guilford Press.

Mahoney, M. (1976). *Scientist as subject.* Cambridge, MA: Ballinger.

Mandler, J. M., & Johnson, N. S. (1977). Remembrance of things parsed: Story structure and recall. *Cognitive Psychology, 9,* 111–151.

Martinson, F. M. (1981). Eroticism in infancy and childhood. In L. L. Constantine & F. M. Martinson (Eds.), *Children and sex: New findings, new perspectives* (pp. 23–35). Boston: Little, Brown & Company.

Mathis, J. L. (1981). Iatrogenic sexual disturbances. *Medical Aspects of Human Sexuality, 15* (7), 96–108.

McCann, J. (1988, January). *The medical evaluation of the child sexual molest victim.* Paper presented at the Health Science Response to Child Maltreatment Conference presented by Children's Hospital and Health Center, San Diego, CA.

McIver, W., Wakefield, H., & Underwager, R. (1989). Behavior of abused and non-abused children in interviews with anatomically-correct dolls. *Issues in Child Abuse Accusations, 1* (1), 39–48.

Melton, G. B. (1987a). The clashing of symbols. *American Psychologist, 42,* 345–354.

Melton, G. B. (1987b). Bringing psychology to the legal system. *American Psychologist, 42,* 488–495.

Money, J. (1985). *Destroying angels.* Buffalo, New York: Prometheus Books.

Myers, D. V. (1978). Toward an objective evaluation procedure of the Kinetic Family Drawing (KFD): An interpretive manual. *Journal of Personality Assessment, 42,* 358–365.

National Center on Child Abuse and Neglect. (1981a). *Executive summary: National study of the incidence and severity of child abuse and neglect,* (DDHS Publication No. 81-30329). Washington, DC: U.S. Government Printing Office.

National Center on Child Abuse and Neglect. (1981b). *Study findings: National study of the incidence and severity of child abuse and neglect,* (DDHS Publication No. 81-30325). Washington, DC: U.S. Government Printing Office.

Nelson, B. J. (1984). *Making an issue out of child abuse.* Chicago: University of Chicago Press.

Ornstein, P., & Gordon, B. (1988, August 15). *Children's memory for visits to the doctor.* Paper presented at the 96th Annual Convention of the American Psychological Association in Atlanta, GA.

Paul, D. M. (1977). The medical examination in sexual offences against children. *Medical Science and the Law, 17* (4), 81–88.

Perlmutter, M., & Ricks, M. (1979). Recall in preschool children. *Journal of Experimental Child Psychology, 27,* 423–436.

Peters, D. P. (1988, August 15). *Arousal on eyewitness evidence in children.* Paper presented at the 96th Annual Convention of the American Psychological Association in Atlanta, GA.

Peters, D. P. (1987). The impact of naturally occurring stress on children's memory. In S. J. Ceci, M. P. Toglia, & D. F. Ross (Eds.), *Children's eyewitness memory* (pp. 122–141). New York: Springer-Verlag.

Porter, B. & O'Leary, D. (1980). Marital discord and childhood behavior problems. *Journal of Abnormal Psychology, 8,* 287-195.

Price, D. J. (1965). Networks of scientific papers. *Science, 149,* 510–515.

Price, D. J., & Beaver, D. (1966). Collaboration in an invisible college. *American Psychologist, 21,* 1011–1018.

Priest, J. (1988). Report of the inquiry into child abuse in Cleveland 1987. *Family Law, 18,* 286–287A.

Rape and Crisis Abuse Center (1985). *Red flag green flag people.* Fargo-Moorhead.

Raskin, D. C., & Yuille, J. C. (in press). Problems in evaluating interviews of children in sexual abuse cases. In S. J. Ceci, D. F. Ross & M. P. Toglia (Eds.), *Perspectives on children's testimony* (pp. 184–207). New York: Springer-Verlag.

Rigert, J., Peterson, D., & Marcotty, J. (1985, May 26). The Scott County case: How it grew and why it died. *Minneapolis Star Tribune.*

Roback, H. B. (1968). Human figure drawings: Their utility in the clinical psychologists' armamentarium for personality assessment. *Psychological Bulletin, 70,* 1–19.

Roberts, R. (1988). Controversy follow up. *Archives of Diseases in Childhood, 63,* 446–447.

Rosenfeld, A. A., Bailey, R., Siegel, B., & Bailey, G. (1986). Determining incestuous contact between parent and child: Frequency of children touching parents' genitals in a non-clinical population. *Journal of the American Academy of Child Psychiatry, 25,* 481–484.

Rosenfeld, A. A., Siegel, B. & Bailey, R. (1987). Familial bathing patterns: Implications for cases of alleged molestation and for pediatric practice, *Pediatrics, 79,* 224–229.

Ross, L., & Lepper, M. (1980). The perseverance of beliefs: Empirical and normative considerations. In R. Schweder (Ed.), *Fallible judgment in behavioral research: New directions for methodology of social and behavioral science.* San Francisco: Jossey-Bass.

Ross, L., Lepper, M., & Hubbard, M. (1976). Perseverance in self-perception and social perception: Biased attributional processes in the debriefing paradigm. *Journal of Personality and Social Psychology, 32,* 880–892.

Rossen, B. (1989). Personal communication.

Saywitz, K. J. (1987). Children's testimony: Age-related patterns of memory errors. In S. J. Ceci, M. P. Toglia, & D. F. Ross (Eds.), *Children's eyewitness memory* (pp. 36–52). New York: Springer-Verlag.

Scarr, S. (1985). Constructing psychology: Making facts and fables for our time. *American Psychologist, 40,* 499–512.

Sgroi, S. M. (1982). *Handbook of clinical intervention in child sexual abuse.* Lexington, MA: Lexington Books.

Sgroi, S. M. (1978). Child sexual assault: Some guidelines for intervention and assessment. In A. W. Burgess, A. N. Groth, L. L. Holmstrom, L. L., & S. M. Sgroi. *Sexual assault of children and adolescents (129-142).* Lexington, MA: D. C. Heath & Company.

Siomopoulis, V., & Goldsmith, J. (1976). Sadism revisited. *American Journal of Psychotherapy, 6,* 441–456.

Sivan, A. B., & Schor, D. P. (1987, August). *Children's labels for sexually related body parts.* Poster presented at the American Psychological Association convention, New York, NY.

Sivan, A. B., Schor, D. P., Koeppl, G. L., & Noble, L. D. (1988). Interaction of normal children with anatomical dolls. *Child Abuse & Neglect, 12,* 295–304.

Slicner, N. A., & Hanson, S.R. (1989). Guidelines for videotape interviews in child sexual abuse cases. *American Journal of Forensic Psychology, 7* (1), 61–74.

Spock, B., & Rothenberg, M. B. (1985). *Baby and child care.* New York: Pocket Books.

Tjeltveit, A. C. (1983). *Value conversion in psychotherapy: Therapist influence on client mental health values and moral values.* Unpublished doctoral thesis, Graduate School of Psychology, Fuller Theological Seminary.

Thoennes, N., & Pearson, J. (1988). A difficult dilemma: Responding to sexual abuse allegations in custody and visitation disputes. In D. J. Besharov (Ed.), *Protecting children from abuse and neglect* (pp 91–112). Springfield, Ill: CC Thomas.

Tollison, C., & Adams, H. (1979). *Sexual disorders.* New York: Gardner Press.

Turtle, J. W. & Wells, G. L. (1987). Setting the stage for psychological research on the child eyewitness. In S. J. Ceci, M. P. Toglia, & D. F. Ross (Eds.), *Children's eyewitness memory* (pp. 230–248). New York: Springer-Verlag.

Valenstein, E. S. (1986). *Great and desperate cures.* New York: Basic Books.

Wakefield, H., & Underwager, R. (1988). *Accusations of child sexual abuse.* Springfield, IL: C C Thomas.

Wallerstein, J. S., & Kelly, J. B. (1980). *Surviving the breakup: How children and parents cope with divorce.* New York: Basic Books.

Watson, M. W., & Fischer, K. W. (1980). Development of social roles in elicited and spontaneous behavior during the preschool years. *Developmental Psychology, 16,* 483–494.

White, S. (1986, August). Paper presented at the 94th Annual Convention of the American Psychological Association, Washington, DC.

White, S., Strom, G. S., & Santilli, G. (1985, June). *Interviewing young sexual abuse victims with anatomically correct dolls.* Paper presented at the 32nd Annual Meeting of the American Academy of Child Psychiatry, San Antonio, TX.

White, S., Strom, G. S., Santilli, G., & Halpin, B. M. (1986). Interviewing young sexual abuse victims with anatomically correct dolls. *Child Abuse and Neglect, 10,* 519–529.

Wolman, B. (Ed.) (1983). *Handbook of developmental psychology.* Englewood Cliffs, NJ: Prentice-Hall.

Woodling, B. A. (1986). Sexual abuse and the child. *Emergency Medical Services, 15* (3), 17–25.

Woodling, B. A,. & Kossoris, P. D. (1981). Sexual misuse: Rape, molestation, and incest. *Pediatric Clinics of North American, 28,* 481–499.

Woodling, B. A., & Heger, A. (1986). The use of the colposcope in the diagnosis of sexual abuse in the pediatric age group. *Child Abuse & Neglect, 10,* 111–114.

Yates, A., Beutler, L. E., & Crago, M. (1985). Drawings by child victims of incest. *Child Abuse & Neglect, 9,* 183–189.

Yokote, G., & Utterbach, R. A. (1974). Time lapses in information dissemination: Research laboratory or physicians office. *Bulletin of the Medical Library Association, 62,* 251–257.

Yuille, J. C. (undated). *The systematic assessment of children's testimony.* Unpublished manuscript.

AUTHOR INDEX

SUBJECT INDEX

DATE DUE

~~AB 7 99~~			
~~JE 02~~			
~~OC 15 03~~			
~~N 23 03~~			
~~NO 8 03~~			
~~NO 24 03~~			
~~MY 2 2 06~~			